Srdjan Timotić

Invisible Borders

How tax rules shape the world we trade in

to,e to

ISBN: 978-2-9702020-1-1

Published by to 'e to publishing

Neuchâtel, Switzerland

For my mother,

who taught the law to others

and taught me how to listen to it.

A Note to the Reader

This work is neither a textbook nor a novel. It is an attempt to think about VAT as it is lived, interpreted, and tested in practice, not merely as a system of rules but as a framework shaping decisions, risks, and responsibilities across borders.

The legal analysis is rigorous, and the narrative deliberate; the two are meant to work together. VAT law is abstract by design, but its effects are concrete. The book uses stories to show how the meaning of the law develops through interpretation and real-world use, and the analysis itself draws on official sources, presented in full in the bibliography.

The extended case that runs through the book is fictional but not invented. It is built by combining elements from real disputes, real tax audits, and real legal uncertainty. The facts, timelines, and technical issues reflect patterns that recur across EU VAT practice.

The book also draws on informal review from practitioners in VAT, customs, accounting, and international trade, who generously gave their time. I am particularly grateful to Alexis Hubert, Mariela Muse, Marta Bogacka, and Emmanuel Devin for reviewing parts of the manuscript. Marta's name, in particular, made its way into these pages: the inspector at the center of this book is a small tribute to her years with the Polish Tax Administration, before our paths crossed in the private sector. A very special thank you goes to my daughter Eva, whose thoughtful design of the book cover gave this work its visual identity, and a personal meaning that no acknowledgment can fully capture.

What remains, beyond the people who shaped it, is the book itself. Readers seeking certainty may not find it here, as law seldom provides it. What follows is an attempt to make the invisible visible, for the length of one transaction, in a system most people cross every day without ever seeing it.

The Invoice

The document arrived on a Tuesday morning in March, transmitted electronically from a server in Palo Alto to SilPol's accounting system in Gdańsk.

Invoice No. SI-2024-03847

From: Nano Source Corporation, 3400 Hillview Avenue, Palo Alto, CA 94304, USA

To: SilPol Fabrication sp. z o.o., ul. Gdańska 127, 80-309 Gdańsk, Poland

Description: Semiconductor lithography system with installation services included.

Amount: USD 32,000,000

Date of Issue: March 15, 2024

Thirty-two million dollars, reduced to a single line. Equipment and installation, goods and services, collapsed into one figure. A number that would cross borders, trigger obligations, and set in motion a sequence of events that no one, not the CFO who authorized it, not the engineer who would install the equipment, not the tax inspector who would later scrutinize it, fully anticipated.

The invoice was correct by the standards of U.S. accounting. It followed Generally Accepted Accounting Principles. It reflected a legitimate commercial transaction. Revenue was recognized at the time of shipment, as the textbooks prescribed. The contract was clear. The payment terms were also standard. Everything was in order.

And yet. No one knew yet that anything was wrong.

That would come later.

Somewhere between Palo Alto and Gdańsk, between the moment the container left the Port of Oakland and the moment the equipment would finally hum to life in a Polish cleanroom, the invoice would encounter a different legal universe. One where the timing of recognition mattered differently. Where the place of supply followed different rules. Where the distinction between goods and services, between shipment and installation, between legal ownership and economic control, would determine not just how much tax was owed, but to whom, and when, and why.

The invoice did not know this. Invoices never do. They are artifacts of intent, not maps of legal reality.

Michael Torres, Chief Financial Officer of Nano Source Corporation, did not think about Value Added Tax when he approved the invoice. Why would he? VAT was a European problem, something the customer would handle. Import duties, customs clearance, local compliance were their responsibility. Nano Source was a U.S. company. They shipped products. They recognized revenue. They followed the rules.

But VAT does not respect such boundaries. It doesn't care about corporate structures, national jurisdictions, and the logic of accounting standards. It operates by its own rules, which Michael would spend the next year learning slowly and painfully, through a process that felt less like education and more like excavation, digging through layers of regulation, precedent, and interpretation to discover what the law had required all along, even when no one told him.

Marta Bogacka, a tax inspector in the Polish Ministry of Finance, would see the invoice for the first time six months later, in September, when the audit file landed on her desk. By then, the equipment had been installed. The cleanroom was operational. The customer was satisfied. The money had been paid.

But something was wrong. Not fraudulent. Not criminal. Just... misaligned.

The import VAT had been paid at customs, calculated on the full invoice value, goods and installation together. SilPol Fab had claimed a deduction. The accounting was clean. The documentation was complete.

And yet, as Marta would soon discover, the right tax had not been applied, not because anyone had lied, but because the legal framework for the transaction was far more complex than anyone realized. Import VAT and domestic VAT were distinct obligations, governed by distinct rules, triggered by distinct events.

The invoice was a fiction. Not a lie, but a simplification. And VAT law does not tolerate simplification.

This is a book about that invoice, and the thousands like it that cross borders every day, revealing the invisible legal architecture governing international trade. This architecture is not based on physical structures. It consists of Directives, Regulations, and Court rulings that most people never notice.

This text is about Value Added Tax. VAT ranks as the most common consumption tax globally and one of the European Union's most important legal achievements. It generates over €1 trillion annually for the EU Member States. However, outside expert circles, it is still widely misunderstood.

VAT is designed to be neutral. Its purpose is to tax consumption without influencing business or economic decisions. In reality, however, this neutrality can only be preserved only so long as officials, judges and accountants keep reinterpreting and analyzing the rules.

It is also about the people whose lives intersect through that invoice:

- Marta Bogacka, the inspector who pieces together fragmentary documents to determine when value arose and where it was supplied, distinguishing between what the law imagines and what actually happened.
- Michael Torres, the chief financial officer (CFO) who thought he understood the rules until he saw that compliance in one country created liability in another, forcing him to navigate the gap between commercial logic and VAT logic.
- Sofia Lindberg, a Swedish VAT expert and EU policy consultant, whose career spans from the idealism of postwar tax harmonization to the

algorithmic enforcement regimes of the digital age, and who embodies the tension between neutrality as principle and neutrality as machinery.

- Elise Moreau, a French legal scholar who witnessed VAT's birth in the 1950s, who taught generations of students to believe in its promise of fairness, and who watches as that promise becomes conditional, contextual, fragile.
- Jakub Kowalczyk, a Polish engineer installing the equipment, whose hands-on work reveals the gap between legal categories and physical reality, between what contracts say and what machines require.

Through their interconnected experiences, this book traces how a single transaction becomes a legal problem, how that problem exposes fundamental tensions in the architecture of global trade, and how the invisible borders constructed by VAT law are being redrawn in the age of digitalization, algorithmic governance, and automated compliance.

The story begins in Paris in the mid-1950s, when a French civil servant named Maurice Lauré imagined a tax that would be neutral, transparent, efficient. A tax that would fall on consumption but be collected incrementally throughout the production chain. A tax that would replace the cascading turnover taxes that were strangling postwar recovery.

He could not have known that his invention would become the nervous system of the European Union, the invisible constitution that would bind Member States more effectively than any treaty. He could not have foreseen that VAT would spread to over 170 countries, generating more revenue than any other tax except income tax. He could not have imagined that by the twenty-first century, VAT would be administered by algorithms, enforced through real-time reporting systems, and applied to platform transactions, data monetization, influencer marketing, that did not exist when the system was designed.

But he understood something important. He understood that taxation is not only a way for governments to collect money. It is also a way of organizing how economic activity is viewed and understood. Through taxation, states classify human actions, decide what has value, and set the rules within which trade and business take place.

VAT's genius lies in its invisibility. Consumers pay it without thinking. Businesses collect it without bearing its burden. Governments receive a steady stream of revenue without the political cost of direct taxation. The system works because most people never see it.

But being invisible has a downside. Concealed systems are difficult to assess, and their problems and weaknesses remain hidden. Rules operating in the background can confuse anyone who is not a specialist, and when neutrality relies on technical details rather than clear principles, the system becomes prone to misuse and misinterpretation.

This book makes the invisible visible.

It shows that VAT law functions beyond a static list of rules. It is something that must be interpreted all the time. Every transaction involves decisions. Every audit demands reconstructing the true sequence of events. Every court decision requires choosing among conflicting objectives, weighing the interests of taxpayers, regulators, and the public, often without the possibility of fully satisfying all of them.

It reveals how the promise of neutrality, that VAT will not distort economic decisions, requires ever more complex rules to achieve, and how each new rule creates new opportunities for arbitrage, new sources of confusion, new gaps between what the law intends and what it accomplishes.

It traces the transformation of VAT enforcement in the digital age, as real-time reporting systems turn taxation into continuous surveillance, as algorithmic risk assessment inverts the burden of proof, as the human judgment that has always animated VAT law risks being displaced by code.

It also asks an important question about the future of global trade.

When borders are no longer based on geography and exist instead through software and data flows, what will happen to the architecture of legal systems that regulate and control trade?

The invoice is still there, archived in databases on both sides of the Atlantic. A single line in a ledger. A number in a system.

But behind that number is a very complex system. Its legal principles were developed over many years. Its institutions were shaped through difficult negotiations during times of crisis. Its methods of interpretation were built step by step through individual decisions of the Court of Justice of the European Union.

Behind that number are people, tax inspectors and auditors, finance directors and engineers, judges and legal advisers, policymakers and consultants. All of them work within a system that is at the same time simple and complicated, stable and fragile, essential and mostly unseen.

Behind that number is a question that this book attempts to answer. How did a tax that was designed to be neutral, transparent, and efficient become the hidden framework of global commerce? And what happens when that framework, built for a world of factories and warehouses and paper invoices, must govern a world of platforms and algorithms and instantaneous data flows?

The story that follows focuses on a single transaction and the audit that triggered a legal dispute, but it also speaks to every transaction and every moment when legal categories collide with economic reality, forcing someone to decide which version of events will prevail.

It is a story about law, but also about interpretation. It is about trade and business, but also about power. It is also about taxation, about sovereignty, and the invisible borders that are difficult to define.

It is a story about the architecture of the invisible.

And it begins with an invoice.

PART I - THE ARCHITECTURE OF THE INVISIBLE

How VAT became the global grammar of trade

1.1 THE TAX THAT BUILT EUROPE

Paris, 1957.

The room was filled with smoke and heated discussions.

Seated at a long table in the French Ministry of Finance, Maurice Lauré drummed his pen against his notebook and looked out of the window. At the same time, colleagues debated a revolutionary tax concept. The Seine was visible, but no one except Lauré paid attention to it. They were absorbed in discussing a new tax system, abstract, almost philosophical, while Lauré was lost in his thoughts.

In 1954, France would become the first country in the world to introduce the 'taxe sur la valeur ajoutée' - the value-added tax. But in that January meeting three years later, the idea was still tender, embryonic, untested. It was more philosophy than policy. Just over ten years after the war, France was still rebuilding. The government was focused on restoring the economy and fortifying its position in Europe. Meeting those goals required vast financial resources, yet traditional turnover taxes were full of inefficiencies. Cascading 'tax-on-tax' effects, at each stage of production, distorted prices and discouraged domestic manufacturing.

"Turnover taxes," Lauré said, tired of repeating himself, "are taxes on motion. The faster goods move, the more they are taxed. Currently, we are punishing the very activity we claim to promote."

The Ministry of Finance needed a solution that could generate substantial revenue without stifling the industrial revival France desperately needed. In this context, Maurice Lauré, a senior civil servant in the tax division, began a couple of years earlier developing his radical idea. His plan was a tax collected incrementally throughout the production chain that would ultimately fall only on the final consumer. Each business would pay tax only on the value it added, receiving credit for taxes already paid on inputs.

The idea was simple in logic but revolutionary in effect. If implemented, it would stop the tax-on-tax that raised final prices, boost the competitiveness of French firms, and create a system that verified taxes at each stage and was difficult to evade. The tax would be included in the final price that consumers pay, but revenue would still be collected steadily at every step of production and sale.

"Ah, so you mean the consumer ends up paying the tax anyway, even though every business along the way barely contributes?" - a junior official from Alsace sarcastically asked.

Lauré smiled. "Not quite 'barely.' Each business pays tax only on the value it adds, deducting what it already paid on inputs. This ensures the final consumer pays a charge proportional to the final price, while making it much harder to evade than if we taxed only the last sale."

Officials in Bonn, Rome, and Brussels took notice. The idea spread quietly. A tax that would not distort prices, could be refunded across borders, and might eventually make customs barriers obsolete.

Lauré could not have known that the system he sketched that winter would become the backbone of the European Union and influence tax systems far beyond.

Brussels, 1967.

Ten years later, at a similar table in the European Commission headquarters, the mood was noticeably heavier, more bureaucratic, and with a sense of idealism. A group of civil servants from six countries gathered around a long table, jackets off and looking tired. The agenda was straightforward yet unachievable. It was all about figuring out how to impose taxes without borders.

"Gentlemen," began a German delegate, "we are not discussing just a tax. We are discussing the mechanism by which Europe will think."

VAT had become more than an administrative instrument. It was a grammar of trade. The 1967 First and Second VAT Directives aimed to harmonize the different national systems, replacing cascading turnover taxes with a framework that let goods move as if the continent were one internal market.

The debates sound dry today. Articles 2, 10, and 11 were technical rules only civil servants cared for. Yet they concealed a far-reaching ambition. A uniform VAT became Europe's unseen constitution, a promise that no border would stand between a manufacturer in Milan and a customer in Munich.

When the European Commission settled into the Berlaymont in 1967, the building's new corridors reflected both fresh construction and the ambition of a growing institution in Brussels. Secretaries hurried past with binders stamped CEE – Taxation and Customs Union. In an office overlooking the Rue de la Loi, a thin man in rimless glasses, Pierre Pescatore, lawyer and professor wrote a memorandum to the Commission's Legal Service. He had come from Luxembourg, a country so small it depended on the clarity of other nations' rules.

"Integration," he wrote, "will not be achieved by flags or anthems but by a single logic of commerce."

That logic took shape in VAT.

In the years after the Treaties of Rome, the Community's economists recognized that tariffs could be dismantled only if something else kept national treasuries afloat. VAT, levied everywhere in the same way, promised to do that. It was a peace treaty written in the language of invoices.

The First Directive of 1967 sketched the principles. Tax on consumption, deduction of inputs, neutrality in trade. The Second Directive detailed how to compute it. But the true transformation began a decade later, when the European Court of Justice started to speak.

Luxembourg, 1981.

The Grand Courtroom of the European Court of Justice was made of dark wood and looked very serious. Daylight diffused light over the tables and the stacks of files waiting for decisions.

Advocate General Jean-Pierre Warner rose to deliver his opinion in *Coöperatieve Aardappelenbewaarplaats BA* (Case 154/80), the potato storage case.

Warner stressed principle, not potatoes. VAT, he argued, must follow economic reality. A cooperative that stores its members' potatoes for a fee performs a taxable service, and without a fee and without a payment directly linked to that service, there is no VAT. The Court agreed.

The new tax had reached its first important legal milestone. In later cases such as *Bockemühl, Tolsma, Halifax,* and *Budimex*, the Court reshaped the meaning of a "supply," shifting VAT law away from formal contracts and invoices toward examining whether there was real consideration, genuine economic activity, and a transaction that reflected commercial reality rather than legal form.

From that day, the ECJ became Europe's fiscal conscience.

By the early 1980s, VAT was common everywhere. From Lisbon to Copenhagen, it appeared on bills and grocery receipts. Economists called it the best tax. It was easy to check, clear, and fair across countries. Old customs posts were disappearing. Even though customs controls were still in place, trucks passed through with their papers stamped and everything in good order.

But the dream carried its own paradox.

A tax that was supposed to be neutral had become a tool of sovereignty. Each Member State insisted on its own tax rate, its special exemptions, and the way of administering the system. While Brussels pushed for harmonization, national ministries saw it as interference. The literature from that era reads like an endless family argument. Efficiency vs. autonomy, neutrality vs. identity.

In the cafés around Place du Luxembourg, civil servants argued about Article 95 of the Treaty of Rome as if it were a religious debate. After a couple of drinks, they began to wonder if a tax could be European if it was levied by individual Member States. They debated whether neutrality, i.e., that businesses should not bear VAT as a cost, was a real moral principle or just an accounting trick.

By the 1990s, some scholars were calling VAT Europe's "invisible constitution." Legal experts such as Ben Terra and Peter Wattel argued that VAT, more than any treaty, pushed Member States to think and act collectively. Terra noted, "Every deduction a trader claims is a statement of mutual trust."

The Sixth Directive, first introduced in 1977 and revised in 2006 as Directive 2006/112/EC, pulled many years of experimentation into a single framework. Articles 63 to 66 defined the "tax point," which is the moment when VAT becomes chargeable. The tax point proved problematic for auditors and large companies because it determines when VAT becomes payable and must be declared.

Article 44 set out the place-of-supply rule for business services.

Together, these provisions raised fundamental questions about how the place of supply is determined, and how the law fixes the time of supply.

Economists observed that VAT was highly effective while remaining largely invisible. It generated more than 20% of Member States' revenue and rarely provoked public demonstrations. It was too abstract for protest, too widespread for praise.

In 1993, the transitional system for intra-Community trade was implemented, whereby supplies between VAT-registered businesses were zero-rated in the Member State of dispatch and taxed in the Member State of arrival. It was intended as a temporary measure. However, three decades later, the system still exists. A temporary fix that became permanent.

Fraudsters took advantage of loopholes with carousel schemes, claiming VAT on goods that never moved. Experts talked about "missing traders." For every idealist in Brussels, there was a criminal group actively working around the rules. The system brought structure but also confusion side by side.

Another crucial decision came in 2006 with the *Halifax* judgment (Case C-255/02) in which the Court introduced the abuse of rights doctrine. The Court held that even transactions that are lawful can be disregarded if their sole purpose is to obtain a tax advantage that conflicts with the Directive's objectives. This decision sparked extensive debate. Some praised it for its clarity, while others worried about the subjectivity of intent. Tax authorities could redefine the "purpose" even when the written law is clear, whenever they didn't like a particular structure. Has this decision sacrificed legal certainty for the sake of combating abuse?

"It … assumes that it is possible to determine 'the purpose of the law'. … In many situations … it is not always possible to divine a clear intention. … The law is just the law… you do what it says …"

From a policy perspective, the doctrine indicated that the system had reached a more sophisticated stage. VAT came to be seen as a set of moral principles guiding its application. It demanded sincerity.

At the beginning of the 21st century, every item, invoice, and digital service in the EU included VAT.

Customs controls were no longer needed. The only borders left were digital ones.

VAT accomplished what neither treaties nor armies could. It normalized interdependence. The simple process of claiming tax deductions on purchases in one Member State assumed that another Member State had correctly reported corresponding tax on sales. Europe had transformed into a network of shared accounting responsibilities.

At the same time, success also brought new tensions. Multinational companies from Silicon Valley or Seoul began entering the European market with structures unimaginable in 1957. They provided equipment bundled with installation services, cloud subscriptions, and online marketplaces. Transactions where time, place, and value were not clear.

The European Court of Justice was formally renamed to the Court of Justice of the European Union (CJEU).

Inspectors encountered challenges that Maurice Lauré would have struggled to illustrate back in the days, even after a few glasses of an inspiring French wine.

The Present Day

One morning in Warsaw, decades after Lauré's cigarette smoke had faded, a tax inspector named Marta Bogacka opened a file stamped 'US Semiconductor Group – Installation Projects 2025'. Of average height and reserved in manner, she moved with a calm, careful assurance that reflected a personality of someone who knew her work thoroughly.

Her blond hair was usually loose and easy to manage. When she concentrated, she would push a loose hair behind her ear without realizing it. It was a small, unconscious ritual that would indicate she was focusing.

There was something immediately composed about Marta, but not distant. Her presence suggested attentiveness rather than control, a readiness to listen before deciding. She absorbed details almost instinctively, and once absorbed, they stayed with her. Colleagues noticed that she rarely forgot a fact, a tone, or an inconsistency, especially when it touched on questions of responsibility or fairness. Beneath her calm exterior ran an intense inner focus, a seriousness that surfaced most clearly when a case involved hidden motives or truths buried beneath formal structure.

Professionally, Marta was decisive. She did not hesitate once her reasoning was complete, and when she spoke, her conclusions had the force of something already tested. She was known for taking responsibility in complex cases and for presenting arguments that others were often hesitant to make. There was an intellectual courage in the way she worked, a willingness to stand alone in an interpretation if she believed it preserved the integrity of the system.

Still, her authority was flexible. Marta had an intuitive sense for the human dimension of law. Lived reality behind contracts, the intentions behind compliance strategies, the emotional weight carried by administrative decisions. She understood that legal frameworks depend on delicate trust, and that once compromised, such trust is difficult to repair.

This made her cautious with judgment, but relentless with analysis. She would take a file home and let it marinate until she felt ready, returning to it from unexpected angles and often finding clarity where others reached only fatigue.

There was also a private side to her, carefully guarded. Marta kept much of her thinking to herself, working through contradictions internally before sharing them. For her, silence created meaning rather than emptiness. Those who knew her well understood that her silence was active, dense with thought, and that when she finally spoke, the conversation would change direction.

In balancing resolve with receptivity, Marta embodied the modern European tax authority at its best. Analytical but also humane. Principled without being inflexible. She believed that law must ultimately answer to reality, not merely to form. Despite her strong self-discipline, Marta never saw the law as a fixed or unchangeable system. She knew that ideas, like cases, were shaped as much in conversation as in files and that some of the best ideas came from outside offices and books.

Outside the office, though, Marta's world was broader. She still remembered the weekend in Stockholm when she had met Sofia Lindberg, a Swedish VAT expert with a sharp mind and an irrepressibly warm laugh. They had shared a panel at a tax technology conference. After the event, Sofia suggested taking a break from the technical discussions and walked with Marta through the boutiques of Gamla Stan. Between trying on scarves and eating cardamom buns, they had debated fixed establishments, digital reporting, and the future of neutrality as if discussing clothes and books. It had been one of those rare professional encounters that turned into something almost like friendship, a mutual respect that lingered in emails exchanged once or twice a year.

Now, as Marta scrolled through invoices and emails, she thought for a moment about Sofia's comment during that Stockholm afternoon: 'VAT is just geography in disguise. You map people, not rules.' The words returned to her often, especially on cases like this one.

She did not know it, but every paragraph of the Directive, each opinion from every Advocate General, every ruling of the Court of Justice stood behind her. The architecture built in Paris and Brussels now lived in her fingertips as she worked.

Europe's tax had come full circle, moving from theory to practical application, from written law to her daily work.

A year later, Marta saw Sofia Lindberg again, this time at a VAT digitalization conference in Amsterdam. They recognized each other instantly across the registration hall, two women who had shared both cardamom buns and the study of law. Over coffee on the second day, Sofia asked, with that knowing Scandinavian calm, whether Marta had followed the recent Court developments. She was already fully aware of the direction Marta's audit was taking.

They spoke in the way only VAT people speak. Half in doctrine, half in metaphor. Sofia said softly,

"Your case shows it again, VAT is geography. You lay out the movement of goods, the place and timing of services, and the presence of people, decisions, and associated risks. Everything else is secondary."

Marta was contemplative, finding it true well before its full meaning became clear. Their conversation drifted from fixed establishments to algorithmic audits, from neutrality to the politics beneath it all, weaving threads that echoed the very themes now shaping Marta's professional life.

1.2 THE CROSS-BORDER SALE

The boardroom lamps at Nano Source Corp. in Silicon Valley illuminated the expansive meeting table. Michael Torres sat at the head of the table, his shoulders slightly bent forward. He wasn't tired. He was lost in thought. To anyone watching, he had an easy, confident look with his unbuttoned blazer over a T-shirt, a subtle smartwatch, and a calm self-assurance. He seemed at home in boardrooms alike. But inside, he was filled with doubt. The amount on the invoice represented significance beyond its monetary value. It marked a new market and a moral responsibility he could not ignore.

He reviewed the invoice for the $32 million semiconductor lithography system scheduled for delivery to Poland. The figures reflected more than revenue. They reflected the company's entry into a new jurisdiction and its first engagement with a customer across that border. The authorization was his, and whatever followed would also be his responsibility.

He imagined the tax inspectors, auditors, lawyers, and the tribunal in Warsaw. They all seemed like parts of his conscience, ready to question his actions. His hands shook slightly, a natural tremor he tried to calm with a sip of whiskey, a routine... But he always trusted systems. His team was paid to make sure the numbers obeyed the laws, and laws followed logic, and logic followed reason. But now, as he crossed real and imagined borders, he felt himself losing focus.

In a small office in Warsaw, Jakub Kowalczyk looked at a clipboard. He was checking the layout of the Polish cleanroom where the same machine would soon be installed. Jakub's tall and thin figure often made him seem a little unsure of himself. His face had small scratches from working late at night with metal and wires. He trusted machines for their ability to perform tasks precisely. People, on the other hand, were harder for him to understand.

Jakub had recently joined the Polish Nano Source subsidiary. And despite years in Poland's semiconductor sector, he had to relearn how this new organization worked. How reporting lines worked, how decisions were escalated, and which approvals were required at each stage. For much of his career, Jakub had helped translate technical concepts into operational plans in Poland's semiconductor sector. He had guided the introduction of the first advanced lithography systems, framing complex technology so that cautious, risk-averse managers could understand and accept it. He had spent long meetings with SilPol's executives, describing what the system could realistically do and turning technical details into arguments the board was willing to approve.

Now, Jakub's thoughts were scattered and confused, like an engine starting up. He wondered, 'When the machine arrives, will they judge it by how well it works or just by the signature on the delivery note?' He didn't know the answer, but this question affected everything he did in the coming weeks. The $32 million invoice had been sent from California before he even had the right setup for the project. He felt like he was part of a process he didn't fully understand, involving accounting rules, legal requirements, and decisions made far away from the workshop.

Michael did not yet know Jakub. And Jakub, in the Nano Source Warsaw subsidiary, did not yet know Michael. But the future of the two men was closely connected, even though they did not know each other yet. Both were involved in a situation shaped by laws and business rules, even though many details were still unclear. The machine itself was large and carefully engineered, impressive but distant, unaffected by the worry and pressure felt by the people responsible for it.

In the interval between the date of the invoice and the subsequent installation, Michael reached a troubling realization. The tax authorities in Poland, formal and bureaucratic, would not see the invoice as simple paperwork. They would treat it as a statement about what truly existed and when it came to existence. The law required that financial records reflect physical reality. But the transaction had already moved ahead. The invoice had been posted, and the entry recorded. The contract had been activated. Customs filings would follow. Michael knew that it no longer depended on him alone. Too many steps, too many hands, too many rules in different countries. He remained responsible, yet much of what would happen next was beyond his direct control.

Jakub, by contrast, experienced this unease in a more physical way. Every measurement he wrote on the plan was a promise that might last longer than him. Each bolt he tightened or screw he fastened had a weight he couldn't fully explain. He was simply in a role responsible for making the machine work. In that sense, he was one of the most honest people in a world full of complex systems and paperwork. Michael dealt with numbers, documents, and intentions. Jakub dealt only with results. The machine either worked or it did not.

On the day the container ship departed from the Port of Oakland, Michael remained in the logistics room longer than necessary, his fingers tracing the details of the shipping documents, as if he could will the outcome into clarity. He softly read the description aloud: "Semiconductor lithography system, including installation services." He paused. Installation services. This was not merely a line item or a footnote. It marked a decisive point that could change how the tax rules would apply in practice.

"SilPol Fab, a Polish semiconductor plant," remarked the young Head of Warehouse operations, "will be responsible for settling all necessary taxes in Poland."

Should VAT be recognized at the point of shipment, upon installation, or at final acceptance? No individual could yet fully answer this question. Only the law would attempt to do so, and only partially succeed.

Jakub, in Warsaw, received the preliminary shipping notification hours later. He read the short email and then closed his eyes. He felt chill, even though the office was warm. The message was not just about when the equipment would arrive. It meant that soon it would be on him to make it work. The dates on the paper were one thing; the reality of installation was another. He knew the machine would not behave exactly as planned, and that small problems would become his problems. His confidence and his doubts pulled in opposite directions, a tension he felt clearly in his body.

Michael stared at his screen and just felt the weight of it all pressing down. The sale was large enough to shift the company's quarterly outlook. But he wasn't sure he could fully grasp what he had just achieved. Success was visible and close but not yet secured. Payment still had to be received.

Meanwhile, Jakub walked back and forth in the Warsaw office, tracing the lines of the blueprint with his finger. He pictured people lifting the machine, cables carrying power, and sensors lighting up one by one. Jakub had just joined Nano Source, and with every step and plan, he felt the pressure to get things right. He still did not know how the system would behave outside the drawings and tests, but he trusted the design and his own skill to make it behave as intended.

Michael got up and made his way to the window. Across the Bay, ships were docked, and cranes moved with the flow of business. He thought about the container with the lithography system crossing the Atlantic like a giant ship. He pictured Jakub, tall and careful, waiting alone in a Gdansk warehouse of the customer for a delivery already recorded in books. Michael realized again that all the laws he studied and followed could only offer rough predictions of behavior, never fully capture it.

Jakub paused in the empty room. He tapped his fingers while thinking about Michael, the invoice, the customer, and the group of people who would evaluate his work without ever seeing him. It was the reason all of them were connected. He felt a bond with Michael that he couldn't explain, a connection made from anticipation, anxiety, and the common understanding that sending something across a border was never just logistics. It meant obligations and responsibilities that did not disappear once the shipment left the port.

In the silence, each man in his own office faced the same challenge. They had to balance business, law, and their own ethics. The invoice promised profit, but also accountability.

1.3 THE BIRTH OF NEUTRALITY

Sciences Po, Paris 1957

Morning light entered the tall windows of the Sciences Po lecture hall and fell across the benches. The room showed its age. It smelled lightly of dust and old books, like many long-used academic buildings. The wooden floor made soft noises, adding to the feeling of a place shaped by years of study.

As the students settled into their seats, the hall's informal ambiance fostered a reflective mood, inviting minds to engage deeply with the lessons ahead. Light and shadow moved across the lecture hall, showing the shape and size of the room. The sunlight felt warm, the wooden benches were rough to the touch, and the faint smell of paper and dust filled the air. Together, these small details made the space feel calm and familiar, a place where serious study and discussion naturally took place.

Professor Elise Moreau tied her gray hair back. As she stepped up to the lectern, the room was quiet. She adjusted her glasses and looked at the crowd. She carried herself with the disciplined gravity of someone who had watched Europe fracture twice in her lifetime and was determined to rebuild it with words.

"Mesdames et messieurs," she began, her voice steady but not cold, "we gather here to discuss a word that did not exist in our fiscal vocabulary twenty years ago. Neutrality."

She paused and looked at her students. Young men with short hair and ambition, young women with notebooks and defiance. Among them, near the back, sat a tall blonde woman, foreign-looking. She listened very carefully, more than most people there. Her name was Sofia Lindberg, a Swedish postgraduate studying the integration of postwar European economies. She would one day work for the European Commission, though that morning she did not yet know that the very concept of neutrality would become her lifelong obsession.

Elise continued: “Before the war, taxation was a weapon of sovereignty. Each nation guarded it like a relic. But sovereignty, like honor, has become a costly luxury. Europe is bleeding. We need cooperation. And so, gentlemen, ladies, in the ashes of protectionism, a new principle rises. Neutrality.”

Her chalk scratched the word on the blackboard:

NEUTRALITÉ

(Neither favors nor punishes.)

“The idea,” she said, “is that the tax shall not interfere with trade. It shall not determine outcomes or confer advantage. It should simply remain neutral.”

The students murmured, uncertain whether a tax could ever be neutral. Taxes were born of necessity, not virtue. Taxes inherently carry moral and political weight, often reflecting the priorities and interests of those in power. The notion that a tax could be neutral implies a detachment from these influences, suggesting a tax system governed by fairness and impartiality rather than strategic advantage. Yet Elise's tone suggested that neutrality might somehow absolve Europe of its past wrongdoings. Her emphasis on neutrality as a virtue hints at a broader aspiration. To redefine taxation as a means of stabilizing economic relations without perpetuating historical grievances or inequalities. This vision, while ambitious, raises questions about the feasibility of completely depoliticizing fiscal policy in a world where economic decisions are invariably intertwined with sovereignty and national interest.

Sofia leaned forward, holding her pencil above her notebook. The word "neutral" seemed both simple and deep to her.

She thought of her father, who worked as a customs officer in Malmö. He spent many years checking boxes of French wine and German machines, discussing tariffs like a priest talks about beliefs.

Europe was made up of many competing bureaucracies. But in this Paris hall, someone imagined a fair tax that no border could change.

Elise turned, and her eyes, bright, gray, severe, fell on Sofia.

"Mademoiselle," she said suddenly, "you are from Sweden, no?"

Sofia nodded, surprised.

"Tell me," Elise continued, "do you believe in neutrality? Your country stays neutral in war. But in business, can you stay neutral when competing?"

There was a pause. Sofia hesitated, then answered softly: "Perhaps neutrality is not peace. Perhaps it is only the absence of visible conflict."

Elise smiled, faintly. "Then you will understand our task."

After the lecture, Elise walked down the corridor, her heels echoing. Behind her, the students broke into small groups, talking like sparks from a dying fire.

Neutrality was a new word, but the idea was old. Since 1945, France had been dealing with destruction and rebuilding. The Marshall Plan brought American dollars to ports, factories, and government offices, but Europe still felt hurt. Every country wanted to grow, but none wanted to lose control.

In the Ministry of Finance, Elise had once been part of a small committee tasked with designing a "modern consumption tax."

She remembered it like the smell of ink and tiredness. Long nights in a gray Paris office, with cigarette smoke in the light of desk lamps, and debates about invoices, credits, and the tricky idea of neutrality.

Lauré once talked about "A tax that sees through things."

He said, "it would be transparent, invisible, and fair. Like truth; if truth were ever measurable."

They had all laughed then, but Elise had felt the gravity of his words. A tax that sees through things… the idea haunted her. It meant a tax without bias, without favoritism, without politics.

A tax that would one day become Europe's constitution.

Elise returned to the podium. The chalk trembled slightly in her hand, not from weakness but because she was sure of herself.

"Let us imagine," she said, "a merchant who buys a chair in Lyon, works on it in Milan, and sells it in Amsterdam. Under the old system, each border, each step, each nation would take its bite. By the time the chair reached the buyer, the price was high because of many taxes."

She drew a simple chain on the board:

Manufacturer → Wholesaler → Retailer → Consumer.

"In our new system," she explained, "each part adds value and pays tax only on that value. The merchant may reclaim the tax he paid before. No more cumulative burden. The tax no longer favors integration nor fragmentation. It observes, records, and passes on. It is, in theory, neutral."

The students were taking notes furiously. Elise's tone darkened.

"Yet neutrality," she said, "is demanding. It needs fairness in actions. One mistake, one indulgence to national interest, and neutrality turns into dishonesty."

The room became quiet. She thought about how politicians still tried to change the new tax to help local businesses. Customs officers held onto their small areas of power. Neutrality was not born of goodwill but of exhaustion.

She added, "Europe did not invent neutrality because it was wise. It invented it because it was tired."

That evening, Sofia wrote in her journal:

'Neutrality - a beautiful word for a tired continent. France, Germany, Italy, all pretending to build something moral out of the debris of their own guilt. Yet perhaps that is the only way to build anything lasting.'

She had stayed after class to speak with Elise, who told her of the early VAT experiments in France. By cautiously introducing the tax on gasoline and cigarettes first, bureaucrats were effectively testing the waters, aware that any misstep could break public trust or destabilize the system. How they were creating an elaborate system that could easily fall apart. Of a complex, delicate structure, where each component must fit perfectly to function without breaking. This experiment was not merely administrative but symbolic of a broader societal attempt to innovate and adapt within constraints, reflecting the broader theme of measured progress amid uncertainty and the weight of historical legacies.

"VAT is not a tax," Elise had said. "It's a mirror. It reflects what we are willing to declare."

Sofia had smiled politely, not yet grasping that this was more than a metaphor.

Paris 1967

A decade later, Europe had changed. The Common Market had been signed. Trucks crossed borders with less friction, and VAT was becoming common everywhere.

Elise, now older and thinner, sat in her office surrounded by stacks of Directives. The Sixth Directive was being drafted, and she was one of its ghost authors. Each paragraph she wrote was an act of faith; that neutrality could be legislated, that fairness could be standardized.

She often thought of the courtroom cases that would one day test these words. Already, whispers circulated among lawyers about what constituted "consideration."

The first case would be *Tolsma*, a street organ player in the Netherlands who played music on the public road and received donations. The tax authority claimed he was providing a paid service. He insisted that he was simply playing music and accepting whatever people chose to give.

Elise pictured the man standing in the street, playing his instrument and hoping someone might drop a coin into his hat. The wind shook the streetlamps above him. She wondered whether the law's idea of neutrality, its refusal to take account of personal circumstances, intentions, or hardship, and its insistence on treating everyone only through abstract legal categories, could really reach someone like him.

The Court ultimately decided that he was not providing a service for payment, because there was no clear exchange between the music and the money. People gave what they wished, if anything at all. The situation did not fit the legal definition of a transaction.

The judgment suggested that legal neutrality meant sticking closely to formal definitions and exact rules, rather than responding to sympathy or moral feeling.

Years later, reading the decision again, Elise wrote in the margin: "Perhaps being neutral means not caring, not because the law is cruel, but because it must look away from individual lives in order to remain fair to everyone."

Brussels, 1993

Sofia, now in her forties and a rising figure in the Commission's VAT unit, read *Tolsma* at her desk in Brussels. The office had the smell of bureaucracy, paper, ink, and computers running.

She underlined the phrase "direct link between service and consideration."

It fascinated her. The Court was teaching Europe how to think in symmetry. Every act, every payment, every intention must align like an equation.

But deep down, she felt an unease. As if Europe were building a system that measured perfection but ignored life.

She thought of Elise's phrase, "VAT is a mirror." If so, what did it now reflect? Not the artisan or the merchant, but spreadsheets, invoices, and digital records. Neutrality had become mechanical.

Later that week, she attended a conference on the "Principle of Fiscal Neutrality." The speakers quoted *Fonderie Officine Riunite*, *Tolsma*, *Marks & Spencer*, each praising the Court's consistency.

Sofia tried to take notes but ended up drawing instead. She drew a small organ player without a face, with coins floating around him like snow.

That night, unable to sleep, she walked through the empty streets of Brussels. The cobblestones glistened under the rain, and the lamplight reflected off puddles like sheets of glass. She thought of all the people VAT had rendered invisible. Street performers, artisans, teachers paid in kindness.

Neutrality had promised fairness, but it also demanded detachment.

"In the pursuit of equal treatment," she thought, "we have banished compassion."

She wondered whether Elise had foreseen this.

When she returned to her small apartment near Place Jourdan, she found an old letter among her files. Elise's handwriting, delicate but firm.

"Remember, Sofia," it read, "neutrality is not absence of judgment. It is judgment perfected. The danger is when perfection replaces understanding."

She read it twice, then folded it back carefully.

The passage highlighted a profound distinction in the concept of neutrality, emphasizing that it does not imply the absence of judgment but rather the refinement and perfection of judgment. This suggests that true neutrality requires an active, deliberate process of evaluating information with clarity and precision, rather than passively withholding opinion or avoiding decisions. The warning against perfection replacing understanding underscores the risk that an excessive focus on flawless judgment can hinder genuine comprehension, implying that striving for an unattainable ideal may obscure the nuanced realities that understanding demands.

It invites reflection on the balance between critical evaluation and empathetic insight. It suggests that neutrality, when practiced correctly, involves a mature form of discernment that integrates both objectivity and depth of perception. However, this balance is delicate; the pursuit of perfect neutrality should not lead to detachment or intellectual rigidity that prevents meaningful engagement with complex issues. Instead, neutrality should serve as a foundation for thoughtful analysis that acknowledges complexity without succumbing to indecision or superficiality.

Elise's Last Lecture

Paris, 1978. The Sciences Po once again.

Elise, now frail and white-haired, stood before a smaller crowd. Her voice had grown soft but not uncertain.

"Neutrality," she said, "was born from exhaustion. But it lives by vigilance. Every belief turns into a lie if left unprotected."

She spoke of *Fonderie Officine Riunite*, a case from before the internal market, where an Italian company imported goods into Germany and then installed them. The issue was whether VAT could be charged twice, once on import, and again on the installation. The Court held that such double taxation violated the principle enshrined in Article 95 of the EC Treaty. If a domestic operation is taxed only once, the same cross-border operation must be treated the same way.

Elise gave a sad smile.

"Even being neutral has its limits. How interesting. We want perfect systems, but they always face human boundaries."

After the talk, she stayed behind, watching dust settle on the desks. She sensed that her work had succeeded, too well. The law was no longer fragile. It was eternal. And yet, she missed the fragility.

In 1979, Sofia visited Elise in her modest Paris apartment. Case reports stood in uneven towers along the walls, some so old their spines had softened to cloth. A pot of tea had gone cold on the table between them, untouched since Sofia arrived.

"Elise," Sofia said gently, "Europe owes you more than it knows."

Elise only smiled, the kind of smile that answered nothing.

"Europe owes itself honesty. But tell me, Sofia, do they still believe in neutrality in Brussels?"

"Yes," Sofia said. "Though I sometimes think we worship it like an idol."

"Then be careful," Elise whispered. "Idols demand sacrifice."

Sofia said nothing to that. She wrote it down later, on the train back to Brussels, in the same notebook where she kept the things Elise said that sounded like warnings dressed as compliments.

When Sofia left that evening, Elise pressed into her hand a folded note. It contained only a single sentence: 'When the law becomes indifferent to human difference, neutrality can feel cold.'

Brussels, 2002 The New Neutrality

Years passed. Sofia became Director of Indirect Taxation. Technology invaded taxation. Digital invoices, automated refunds, algorithms classifying transactions faster than any auditor could read them.

VAT neutrality, once a guiding principle designed to ensure fairness and uniformity, had now been fully codified into automated systems. These algorithms executed tax rules with mechanical precision, indifferent to national interests or political pressures, yet equally incapable of accounting for the nuanced realities behind transactions.

Sofia observed the growing discord among nations, each fiercely debating the meanings of complex legal terms like "fixed establishment," "place of supply," "economic reality." The principles Elise had built to unify Europe were now fracturing under the weight of interpretive complexity and conflicting national priorities.

She chaired a meeting one afternoon when a young policy analyst quoted *Tolsma* to justify a digital services rule. "There must be a direct link between service and consideration," he said proudly.

Sofia smiled but said nothing. In her mind, she saw again the street organ player, playing to a crowd that listened but did not pay.

In the digital world, everyone played and everyone listened, yet no one knew who paid whom.

Neutrality, she thought, had become too perfect to see imperfection.

If Zola had written of tax, he might have called it La Machine. The system of neutrality, including offices, servers, and auditors, worked smoothly and predictably, like a well-functioning machine.

Sofia, walking through the Berlaymont corridors late one evening, felt that same mechanical pulse. The Commission's heart beat in ceaseless, mechanical cadence. No crime, no drama, just the steady hum of administration.

But behind that hum, she felt the presence of Elise, Lauré, and other dreamers after the war, who had created neutrality as a belief in reason.

Now, as the machine perfected reason, something human was being erased.

"Zola saw miners and factories," Sofia thought. "We have tax engines. Both crush men the same way. Invisibly, through necessity."

Sciences Po, Paris, 2015, A Return

Decades later, Sofia returned to Paris as guest lecturer. The lecture hall had been renovated. There were new LED lights and digital projectors, but the windows were the same. She could almost see Elise standing there, chalk in hand.

Her lecture was titled "Neutrality in the Digital Age."

She began softly: "In the past, neutrality came from war. It meant fairness, with no nation or person getting special treatment. Today, neutrality faces a new challenge: algorithms, platforms, and online markets without borders."

She projected a slide showing *Tolsma* and *Berlin Chemie* side by side - the street organ player and the multinational. Two extremes of the same principle.

"Between them lies our failure," she said. "The poor man who gave music freely, and the rich company that structures control invisibly, both untaxed, both justified by neutrality."

The students shifted uneasily. Sofia paused, looking at their faces, young, idealistic, impatient.

"Neutrality," she said finally, "was meant to make us fair. But perhaps fairness, once abstracted, becomes sterile."

A student raised a hand. "Madame Lindberg, are you saying VAT is immoral?"

Sofia smiled. "No. I am saying that morality without empathy is machinery. VAT is perfect but it no longer feels."

That evening, she walked through the courtyard, where the plane trees made soft sounds in the autumn wind. The bells rang six times. She thought of Elise, of her final letter, of how neutrality had become cold.

Neutrality had been Europe's great compromise, between justice and survival, between unity and control. It had done what no army or parliament could. It made nations behave. But it also made them forget that acting properly isn't the same as being good.

Sofia looked up at the sky and whispered, "Elise, your neutrality saved us. But what will save neutrality from itself?"

In a square not far from the Sciences Po, a man played an old barrel organ. The tune was cheerful but weary, echoing against the stone façades. People passed, some smiling, some indifferent. A few coins fell into his hat.

A young law student paused, listening. She took out her phone, filmed a few seconds, and posted it online with the caption: #TaxableOrNot?

Within hours, comments flooded in. Jokes, legal citations, debates about consideration and supply. The organ player remained unaware. He kept turning the crank, and his music blended into the city's noise.

And somewhere, far away in Brussels, Sofia's computer pinged with a new alert:

> 'Digital services – user interaction monetization. Classification pending'

She stared at the screen, then at the window beyond, where the rain traced silent paths down the glass.

The system worked perfectly.

The man, the music, and the audience would not be recorded together.

Neutrality, a cold and elegant force, had succeeded.

1.4 THE MOMENT OF VALUE

The invoice lay on the table like a misplaced artifact, a document born in another legal universe. Marta stared at it, hands still, focus fixed. She had seen hundreds of invoices from foreign suppliers, some sloppy, some naïve, some shameless, but this one had a particular wrongness that troubled her. It was the way the numbers dissolved into each other without any recognition of borders: "Semiconductor lithography system. Installation included. $32,000,000." A single line. A bundled price. As if goods and services existed in the same moment, in the same place, in the same tax reality.

Michael, sitting opposite her, had not noticed her disturbance. Yet his shoulders were tense, his red cheeks betrayed his embarrassment. His laptop was covered with stickers: Rolling Stones, 49ers, Golden State Warriors, "I paused my game to be here" and others... He had flown in from California to "clarify the situation," as his email had said. But clarity, in this room, would not come easily.

He began with the tone of a man who has repeated a script many times.

"The sale occurred in the United States," he said. "Title passes on shipment. Our accounting system books revenue at dispatch. This follows U.S. GAAP principles. The customer here, the Polish SilPol Fab, they paid import VAT, right? So from our perspective, everything is covered. The value was recognized when the goods left our warehouse."

His voice expected agreement. He was waiting for some affirmation that never arrived.

Marta did not answer. She preferred silence to premature correction. Silence had power. It forced the other person to hear his own words again, as if the room's acoustics revealed the flaws in logic.

Michael moved on. "I mean, look, the equipment came in. Polish customs assessed import VAT. The Fab paid it. They deducted it. Everything is in motion. I don't see the problem."

People often get confused about VAT. They think it is about owning goods, shipping, or accounting. But VAT is different. It isn't like Generally Accepted Accounting Principles (GAAP) or revenue recognition. It has its own rules. VAT operates under a distinct set of regulations that govern its calculation, collection, and reporting, separate from standard accounting frameworks. Businesses charge VAT on their sales (output tax) and reclaim VAT paid on their purchases (input tax), remitting the difference to tax authorities. This system requires careful compliance with specific VAT rules, which vary by jurisdiction, making it crucial for businesses to understand VAT's unique mechanisms and not confuse it with general accounting standards or revenue recognition criteria.

She finally spoke, softly. "They paid import VAT, yes. They deducted it, yes. But did they own the goods?"

Michael looked puzzled. "Well… they got them."

"That is not the same."

Her words were clear and simple. No blame, no drama. Just stating a fact.

He looked down at the invoice again.

"But we shipped it to them. They accepted delivery at the port."

Marta looked from the invoice to him.

"You sent equipment that needs to be installed. It's just one supply. Installation is necessary. A semiconductor lithography module needs to be set up and adjusted before use. According to EU VAT law, the supply location is where the installation happens, not where it is shipped from."

Her words felt like a subtle decision, not just an explanation. Michael blinked, as if hearing a language he half-understood. He kept trying.

"I understand that the installation is technically a separate service," he said. "Our subsidiary provides it, we reimburse them, they invoice us… all internal transactions. From that perspective, the only external supply to SilPol Fab should be the equipment itself, right?

But I want to make sure I'm not missing how that interacts with Polish VAT and customs rules."

Marta found comfort in thinking about legal details. That always calmed her. Just sending goods does not mean there is a supply. The Court of Justice had said so more than once. Substance over form. Look at the real purpose, what it actually does, because it matters more than what it's named. Installation that creates operational capability absorbs the underlying goods into a single supply. In such cases, the place of supply becomes the place of installation. It became taxable here, in Poland, on Polish soil, under Polish VAT rules.

After reflecting on the situation, she responded with a question: "When did installation finish?"

Michael hesitated.

"Uh… three months after importation. There were delays. The cleanroom wasn't ready. That wasn't our fault. The equipment had to sit in storage for six weeks, then be moved in stages. And final calibration, look, these are extremely sensitive components. You don't just plug them in. But still, that doesn't change the sale."

"It changes the tax point, the time of taxation." She said.

He shook his head.

"The tax point occurred when we issued the invoice in the U.S."

"No," she said, quietly. "That is not the tax point for a supply with installation."

Her voice was like a judge speaking quietly. It was polite but final.

Michael began tapping anxiously at his laptop.

"Our ERP system recognizes the sale at shipment. Payment terms start then.

Revenue is recognized. Isn't VAT supposed to follow that? Tax follows revenue, right?"

"VAT follows consumption," she said. "Revenue follows accounting rules. They are different."

Michael looked at her as if she had told him gravity worked differently in Europe. He realized he had oversimplified. Shipment might not dictate the timing of revenue when installation affected the transfer of control. VAT timing could also differ depending on whether the supply was considered one combined service or separable components.

Marta continued,

"When installation is essential, the supply is not complete until the equipment is usable. Not when it crosses the border. Not when your system prints an invoice. Not when revenue is recognized in your general ledger. Usability is the moment of value. Economic reality governs, not shipment documents."

The room was quiet again. Outside, the winter evening in Warsaw made the light look grey through the blinds.

Michael tried to regain his balance. He shifted in his chair, the kind of small movement people make when they sense the ground beneath them is no longer firm.

"But SilPol Fab already paid the import VAT," he said, trying to find something solid. "Doesn't that mean the authorities got what they wanted? The tax was paid."

Marta did not answer immediately. She flipped the invoice over on the table between them, ran a finger down the single line, and then looked up.

"Tax was paid," she said. "But it was paid on the wrong value."

Michael frowned. "The wrong value?"

She leaned back.

"Your invoice bundled everything together. Equipment. Transport. Installation. One price. From a customs perspective, that single number represented the value of the goods."

She paused, letting the silence do some of the work.

"But installation happened after the machine crossed the border," she continued. "Under EU customs law, post-importation services must be excluded from the customs value. They are not negotiable. They are not optional. Customs value stops at the border."

Michael looked back at the invoice. He had seen it a hundred times before. It had always felt efficient. Clean.

"So because we bundled it," he said slowly, "they treated everything as if it were the machine itself."

"Yes," Marta replied. "They had no choice. A single figure creates a presumption. And that presumption falls on you to prove them wrong."

He exhaled. "But customers prefer simplicity. One invoice. One payment."

"Customs does not," she said calmly.

Michael rubbed his temples.

"Still, SilPol Fab deducted the VAT. They wanted the machine running. They didn't complain. Why would they?"

"Because they paid tax on goods they did not yet own," Marta said.

He went still.

"The equipment belonged to you at import," she went on. "SilPol Fab paid import VAT on a value that included installation services carried out later, in Poland, by your Polish technicians.

Services that should never have crossed the customs line in the first place.

Incorrect customs valuation means underpayment of customs duty if the installation was offshore, or overpayment if included wrongly. Here, it meant overpayment of import VAT.

The VAT the Fab deducted, though they weren't the economic owner."

Michael stared at the table. The pieces were aligning now, but not comfortably.

"How could they not own them? They ordered and received them. So the law doesn't care that the machine was delivered?"

"It cares," Marta said, "but not in the way you expect. VAT may treat the supply as one economic whole. Customs law does not. Customs law draws a hard line at the border."

She tapped the invoice again. "When you cross that line with a bundled price, you drag services across with the goods. And customs law pushes back."

He swallowed.

"So that means…?"

"That the law ignores convenience," she finished. "And preference. And intention. It looks only at what can be proven, line by line."

The room was quiet again for a moment.

Michael finally nodded.

"So what do we do?"

"We separate what was always separate in reality," Marta said. "The machine. And the work done after it arrived."

He leaned back, eyes closed.

"For years," he said, "this felt clean. Efficient."

"It was," Marta replied gently. "Just not correct."

"Economic ownership arises when benefits and risks transfer. Your contract says title passes after installation is complete. So at importation, they were not the owners. They were importers of record only because your logistics agents told them to be. They paid VAT on goods still owned by Nano Source Corporation."

Michael blinked again. The concept struck him as absurd.

"Why would it matter who owns the goods? I thought VAT wasn't supposed to be a cost for businesses."

Marta looked at him. Non-EU multinationals often claim to understand VAT well and frequently emphasize its neutrality, especially when they make mistakes…. as if being neutral removed responsibilities.

"Neutrality does not erase conditions," she said. "Only owners or persons acquiring the power to dispose may deduct VAT. At importation, the SilPol Fab had neither."

"But they needed the equipment. At the end, they paid for it."

"They did not yet bear the risks. They could not use it at that point in time. They were custodians, not owners."

Michael stared at the invoice again, as if hoping it might change its content.

Marta crossed her arms again, her voice calm.

"This touches the core issue. When does value arise? On shipment? On importation? On completion? VAT law examines reality. In *Budimex*, the Court recognized that acceptance certifies completion for certain construction services. Completion is the key point. Not billing. Not partial delivery. Completion."

Michael tried desperately to keep up.

"So… are we saying the tax point is when installation finished?"

Marta spoke softly.

"For a supply with installation, yes. Unless payment is received earlier.

Was payment received?"

"No," he admitted. "They pay after acceptance testing."

"Then the supply occurred upon completion of installation. The tax point is there. Not in the U.S. Not at importation. Here, three months later."

"And the VAT base?" he asked.

Marta said, "We need to tax the whole supply, which includes goods and installation, here in Poland. But your invoice wrongly combined them for customs, so the import VAT was paid on a higher amount than necessary. Also, Poland hasn't received VAT for the local supply with installation."

"So, too much tax was paid at the border and too little inland?"

Marta nodded once. "In essence."

He exhaled shakily. "This is… complicated."

"VAT often is," she said.

He looked at her with a kind of confused respect.

"How do you keep all this straight?"

She answered simply, "I listen to what the supply is trying to be."

Michael blinked. "Supplies don't try to be anything."

"Sometimes they do," she said.

For a moment, he wondered whether she was being metaphorical or literal. With VAT, it could be either.

The table was covered with records like emails, shipping instructions, and customs forms. These forms were filled out by agents who probably did not understand the deal or its purpose. The equipment's value was confusing.

It was recorded in the U.S., taxed at the Polish border, used in Poland months later, and neither the importer nor the installer paid for it when it mattered.

Marta walked around the table, lightly touching the papers.

"We also need to think about where the supply is," she said.

It seemed like a small comment, but it changed everything. Michael muttered, with frustration in his voice.

"I thought we just covered that. Didn't we?" he said, with irritation barely contained.

"We acknowledged it," she said. "But we have not yet confronted its consequence. By treating shipment as the supply, you treated the place of supply as the United States. But the true supply is here, in Poland. This means your U.S. invoice didn't include EU VAT requirements. There should have been a Polish taxable supply. SilPol Fab should have handled Polish VAT under reverse charge for everything, goods and installation, because they got a supply with installation in Poland."

Michael closed his eyes briefly. "So… the import VAT was unnecessary?"

"Not unnecessary," Marta said. "But misaligned. The import VAT should have been calculated on the customs value of the goods alone. Not the installation. And more importantly, it was paid by SilPol even though SilPol was not the economic owner of the goods at import."

"They deducted it."

"That is precisely the problem," she replied. "The right to deduct import VAT belongs to the person who imports the goods for the purposes of their own taxable transactions. Here, the goods were imported on behalf of your U.S. company. SilPol paid the VAT, but the economic supply happened later, when the goods were installed and accepted after testing."

"So the tax point was split," Michael said slowly.

"Yes. Import VAT at the border, on the goods alone, by the company that actually owned them at that moment. Then, a separate domestic taxable supply should have followed in Poland. That second step never happened."

"And because we didn't do that?..."

"Poland appears to have lost VAT," she said. "Think of it like this. Tax was paid at the border and then reclaimed, but the sale that should have replaced it inside Poland never happened on paper. So the system sees an empty space where tax should be. The system shows a gap, and that gap is treated as a loss."

Then she added, "Which is enough for the tax authorities to question the transaction. Apparent loss is sufficient to open an audit. Actual loss is not required."

Marta looked at Michael calmly. "There's also a timing issue. You booked the revenue and issued an invoice months before the supply actually took place. In itself, issuing an invoice doesn't automatically create a VAT obligation here. Under Polish law, VAT becomes due at the earliest moment when the supply occurs, payment is received, or an invoice is issued in compliance with local VAT rules. Your invoice, sent before installation and without following Polish VAT requirements, was only an internal accounting record… it reflected intent, not a taxable event. From Poland's perspective, nothing taxable had happened yet. Until the goods were installed, or until payment was actually received under Polish VAT rules, it wasn't a tax event here. It was just paperwork."

Michael muttered, "In the U.S., we would never think about it this way."

"I know," she said. "That is why we are here."

They spent hours walking through the timeline. Shipment date. Import date. Removal from customs storage. Partial installation. Cleanroom delays. Calibration failures. Re-installation attempts. Acceptance protocol signed only after the third round of testing. Each moment held a different type of value. Economic value, functional value, customs value, VAT value. None aligned.

Michael eventually pressed his palms flat on the table.

"So what went wrong?"

Marta answered,

"Nothing went wrong. Reality went forward. Your paperwork did not follow."

He stared at her, absorbing the sentence.

She went on without waiting for an argument.

"And now we must reconstruct the moment of value."

He asked, in a near whisper,

"And when was that moment?"

"Completion," she said. "It always was."

Her confidence made him uncomfortable. He used to believe the invoice was the crucial point, when numbers were clear, when responsibilities were set, and when value was defined. But in this system, she seemed to say that value came from completing the task. Setting it up. Getting it to work. Approval. That was when VAT acknowledged the supply. Michael was very confused about the differences she talked about between EU VAT Law and Polish national rules. When it comes to when ownership of goods is transferred, supply is more than just what national law says. The CJEU's ruling in the *Shipping and Forwarding Enterprise Safe* case clarifies that "supply of goods" does not hinge on the procedural transfer of ownership but encompasses any transfer of tangible property that empowers the recipient to dispose of it as if they were the owner.

Thus, the recipient assumes the position of the former owner regarding rights and powers over the goods.

This approach aligns with the principle that VAT recognition depends on the economic reality, control, and disposal rights, rather than solely on formal ownership transfer. Just as VAT acknowledges supply upon task completion and approval, the supply of goods is established when the recipient obtains effective control, regardless of national ownership procedures.

"There is another layer." Marta continued. "The *Evita-K* case. Its reasoning. The Court did not focus on formal ownership, or on signatures, or even on final acceptance. It focused on economic capacity. On whether the recipient had obtained the power to dispose of the goods as if they were the owner. Not merely because the goods were present, but because the recipient could use them, bear their risks, or integrate them into their activity."

"So acceptance doesn't define the supply?" Michael asked.

Marta gave a soft, sympathetic smile.

"Not entirely. Acceptance is often used as a practical proxy, but the existence of supply depends on economic reality. In *Evita-K*, the Court emphasized that even after supply occurs, the right to deduct VAT can be conditional, for example, on providing required documentation or fulfilling procedural obligations. That's the layer that matters for your case. SilPol Fab may have paid import VAT, but whether they could fully deduct it depended on whether they truly held economic control and satisfied all national conditions."

She added, "*Evita-K* shows that subtle point. The right to deduct VAT borne on the acquisition can be conditional. In that case, the deduction depended on providing identification and registration information for the bovine animals. Applied here, it raises a similar question; even if SilPol Fab imported the goods and paid the import VAT before formal acceptance, was the deduction fully allowable?

Could national law have conditioned the deduction on formal acceptance, or on confirmation that the economic control of the equipment had effectively passed?"

Michael's eyes widened in horror.

"Earlier? Not later?"

"Yes. The law doesn't always follow what feels logical."

"But acceptance didn't happen until the very end."

"That is *Budimex* logic," she said. "There, acceptance fixes the tax point because nothing of economic value passes before completion. *Evita-K* asks a different question."

She leaned forward.

"Who actually held the power over the goods on importation?"

Michael swallowed. "SilPol imported them. They paid the import VAT."

"They did," she agreed. "But import VAT can only be deducted by the party who imports the goods for their own taxable activity, which requires economic ownership, not merely making a payment. Paying import VAT does not automatically create a deduction right if the goods were never under your economic control."

He went still.

"So, the deduction could have been premature," she continued in a measured tone. "And that's why the invoice, acceptance, and the allocation between goods and installation matter. Because VAT law follows economic reality and conditional entitlement, not just logistics or paperwork."

Michael closed his eyes briefly, trying to absorb it.

"*Evita-K* isn't about acceptance alone," Marta said. "It's about control, rights, and conditions for deduction. If SilPol Fab never truly had the power to dispose of the equipment, or if they failed a condition before deduction, the law may not recognize their VAT claim. And that changes everything, the tax point, the deduction, and the timing of supply."

Michael tried to recall the installation report.

"There were partial calibrations. Diagnostic runs. Environmental stabilization tests."

"Usability," she said.

"But they were just tests."

"Tests can be use," she said.

He leaned back, overwhelmed. "So the tax point is either the acceptance date or one of the earlier testing dates?"

Marta nodded. "Exactly. And we must determine which logically prevails."

"But how? How do you decide that?" he asked.

Marta looked toward the window, as though drawing on something older, something jurisprudential.

"The law decides it. The supply reveals it. Our task is only to watch."

The office lights made the room look clean and bright, shining on the polished table. Papers were everywhere. The coffee was cold. There was a feeling of legal uncertainty in the air. But Marta seemed calm in this uncertainty. She was okay with not having all the answers. Michael was not.

He asked suddenly,

"Are we in trouble? Is this… serious?"

Marta did not answer quickly. She considered her words.

"It is significant," she said. "But significance is not guilt."

That was the closest she came to reassurance.

He swallowed. "What will the tax authority conclude?"

Marta moved back a bit, stepping away from the main conversation. Her presence softened, but her influence lingered.

"We do not know."

Marta closed a folder gently, aligning its edges with meticulous precision.

"The audit is ongoing. We must gather more evidence. Review the installation schedule. Examine whether the Fab derived actual economic utility before acceptance. Review the customs entry. Request the internal contract between your U.S. entity and your Polish subsidiary. Determine if the Polish subsidiary's role was subcontractor or independent service provider. Clarify whether SilPol Fab ever bore risk."

Michael looked defeated.

"Can't you just… give an answer?"

She looked at him kindly.

"VAT law rarely gives answers. It gives frameworks. The rest is interpretation."

"And the tax authorities?" he asked.

She answered with judicial serenity.

"We will interpret too."

Silence settled over the room like fresh snow.

Michael stared at his hands.

"We really thought import VAT settled everything."

"It settled something," she said. "Not everything."

"And economic ownership… we never considered that. We assumed the customer owns what they receive."

Sofia's voice entered in Marta's mind, remembering their long conversations in

Stockholm, almost a whisper. She quoted her: “Ownership is not reception. Ownership is risk.”

Michael nodded slowly, absorbing another truth he had never been taught.

Marta stood, signaling the end of the meeting. Michael rose immediately, as if dismissed by a judge.

Marta sat back for a moment and watched him with a gentle curiosity, as if she could see him trying to change his way of thinking.

He gathered his laptop and documents, movements heavy with the weight of new knowledge.

Before he reached the door, Marta added one last sentence, delivered with the subtle force that shaped the entire day.

“Value arises when the supply becomes real. Not when we wish it to be. Not when we invoice it. When it becomes real.”

Michael turned, looking at her with a mixture of respect and exhaustion.

“And when is that?”

She said simply, “That is the question.”

He walked out of the room slowly, and the bright corridor surrounded him.

Marta stood up and looked at the empty doorway. 'He won't get any sleep tonight.' She collected the leftover documents. 'And neither will the law,' she thought.

The audit remained open, unresolved, its conclusions suspended like an unfinished judicial reasoning awaiting the final premise.

And somewhere, between shipment and installation, between importation and acceptance, between form and substance, the true moment of value waited. Patient and still unnamed.

1.5 HOW CJEU OPINIONS SHAPE VAT DOCTRINE

For several days after the meeting, everything was quiet in the investigation, at least on the surface. Sometimes quiet is violent. Internally, emails were coming in from all directions. Some were short, some were worried, but none saw the big picture. Michael personally stepped in, sending polite follow-up emails, using more careful language each time, but receiving clear responses proved difficult. The internal tax team worked intensively to prepare the files and questions for the next round with Marta.

But under all the paperwork, something deeper was shifting.

On the other side, Marta felt pressure in her chest. She sensed that the case was about to go into new areas not often explored in domestic audits. This one was no longer just about invoices, customs value, and the timing of supply. It was about interpretation. And interpretation, when pushed hard enough, inevitably challenges the limits of authority.

She had seen it before. When the administration wanted one result, the courts delivered another, and everyone quietly pretended the gap did not exist. EU VAT law lived permanently in that tension. A system meant to be the same everywhere, but with decisions that didn't always match what countries did.

The current case had that same hidden complexity. Installation services. Composite supplies. Customs valuation. Economic ownership. Tax point. In *Aktiebolaget NN* Advocate General had spoken with confidence about goods supplied with installation, establishing taxation at the place where the equipment was made operational. It assumed a certain coherence that the supplier delivering the machinery was also the one, directly or indirectly, bringing it to life on the customer's site. The judgment worked because the facts were tidy. Delivery and installation pointed in the same direction.

Here, they did not.

The installation had been carried out by the Polish subsidiary, not the U.S. parent that stood as supplier of record. Legally separate. Operationally entangled. The Advocate General in *Aktiebolaget NN* had warned against formalism, urging that VAT follow economic reality rather than contractual choreography. But economic reality itself had become slippery.

Whose reality mattered?

Then there was *DSV*. A case about transit, rejected goods, and a customs debt that survived even after the goods left and re-entered the system. The Court had confirmed not only the duty, but also the denial of import VAT deduction, on the ground that *DSV* was neither importer nor owner of the goods. VAT had been paid, undeniably. But it had attached to the wrong person. And once paid, it could not be reclaimed without unravelling the logic that made the system work.

Two judgments. Two clean answers. And yet, placed side by side, they refused to align with the Nano Source case.

If *Aktiebolaget NN* insisted on coherence between delivery and installation, *DSV* showed what happened when coherence broke. Tax could crystallize without a corresponding right, leaving payment "stuck" in the system. Marta could already see the argument forming. If the installation were treated as performed by the local subsidiary and the customer had already paid import VAT before accepting the goods, treating the installation as part of the supply of goods could complicate the import VAT allocation, while treating it as a separate locally supplied service might shift registration, liability, and input VAT recovery, creating a complex interplay that the law does not explicitly reconcile.

She knew what would come next. Someone would invoke the Advocate General's opinions, carefully reasoned, balanced, and persuasive. They would be quoted when helpful and set aside when not. They always were. Because they asked the uncomfortable questions. Whether VAT could tolerate payment without entitlement, whether substance could be separated from structure, whether a system built on neutrality could survive cases where neutrality demanded contradiction.

And Marta knew that once those questions were on the table, this was no longer a routine audit. It was a stress test of the system itself.

She suspected that the Nano Source case had crossed into territory where ordinary audit logic no longer sufficed. It was the kind of situation that called for the discipline of an Advocate General's reasoning. Not in name, but in method. Competing interpretations could all claim internal consistency, and only a careful reconstruction of first principles could expose where coherence truly lay.

After three days, Marta gave a call to Sofia, which was unusual for her. She emailed her the case study and organized an online discussion. She activated the camera on her laptop with the calm confidence of someone whose thoughts had had time to ferment.

Marta smiled as Sofia's face appeared on the screen.

"Good to see you," she said. "You look like you've been thinking."

Sofia laughed softly. "I have. I couldn't let this case go. It's not what it looks like."

Marta raised an eyebrow, intrigued.

Sofia set her notebook on the desk in front of her.

"You mentioned something last time," she continued. "You said, 'We must reconstruct the moment of value.' I've been turning that over ever since. Because in VAT law, value isn't just economic. It's interpretative. And interpretation isn't neutral, it has direction. It has power structures behind it."

Marta frowned slightly. "But how do we know which interpretation is correct? Everyone seems to read the same contract differently."

Sofia leaned back. "That's where sincerity comes in."

"Sincerity?" Marta repeated.

Sofia nodded. "Yes. Not good faith, which is subjective. Not fairness. VAT assumes sincerity. It assumes that when businesses describe a transaction, they are trying to map reality, not optimize across legal silos. That's the starting point. The law presumes you're telling it what actually happened, even if the law doesn't like the outcome."

Marta thought for a moment. "So the system trusts the description first, and only later do we check whether it aligns with legal coherence."

"Exactly," Sofia said. "And that's why we reconstruct value carefully. Because it's not enough to accept invoices or contracts at face value. We have to see if what's being represented matches economic reality."

Marta closed the file and leaned back slightly.

"You're saying we'll defend the interpretation that justifies the assessment?"

Sofia inclined her head slightly.

"That is often how it begins. But that is not how it must end."

Marta looked up. "You're thinking like an Advocate General."

Sofia smiled, not denying it.

"Because this is precisely the kind of case where an opinion must slow the system down."

There was a thoughtful silence between them, deliberate and measured.

"You know," she said, "none of this is conceptually new. We've seen it before. Installation blurs movement. Customs valuation blurs timing. Acceptance blurs ownership. The difficulty is that each rule works perfectly well on its own."

Sofia nodded. "And breaks when you line them up."

Marta allowed herself a thin smile. "Exactly. Take the supply itself. The goods are here. Installed. Bolted to the floor. But contractually, ownership and disposal stay with the supplier until acceptance. So the first question is unavoidable. Does physical installation override a contractual transfer of ownership?"

"And if it doesn't," Sofia added, "then no supply of goods exists yet, no matter how tangible the equipment looks."

"Which pushes everything else forward," Marta said. "Chargeability. Tax point.

If acceptance is the act that completes the supply commercially, can we really say VAT becomes chargeable before that?"

She shook her head slightly. "*Budimex* answers a timing question but only once a supply exists. It doesn't tell us to invent one."

There was a pause.

"And then there's import VAT," Marta continued. "Which is where people get impatient. VAT was paid. At the border. On the full value. Goods and installation. Everyone wants that to settle the matter."

"But it can't," Sofia said quietly. "Because import VAT and domestic VAT are legally distinct events. One happens because goods cross a border. The other happens because a taxable supply exists. EU law never said one can replace the other."

Marta leaned back. "And worse," she said, "the import VAT was paid before any supply of goods could exist under the contract. Which raises the uncomfortable question… VAT paid on what, exactly?"

"On importation," Sofia replied. "Not on a supply. And that difference matters when we get to deduction."

Marta nodded. "*DSV* makes that painfully clear. Payment is not enough. Deduction follows use in one's own taxable activity. And that presupposes a supply that has actually taken place."

She glanced down at the file again. "So if, at the moment deduction is claimed, ownership hasn't transferred, disposal rights haven't passed, and acceptance hasn't happened, then legally, however artificial it feels, there is nothing to deduct against."

"And the invoice doesn't save it," Sofia said. "A non-EU commercial invoice used for customs valuation can't suddenly become a VAT invoice for a domestic supply that doesn't yet exist."

"No," Marta agreed. "Customs accepts anticipated value. VAT doesn't."

They were silent for a moment.

"And there's another layer," Marta added.

"The Polish subsidiary isn't just helping. It creates a fixed establishment. That pulls the US company into direct VAT liability here."

"Which means domestic VAT could be charged to the US company, not just reverse-charged to the customer," Sofia added.

"And that's before we even reach enforcement," Marta said finally. "Because even if we say there is a domestic supply, the supplier is outside the Union. Not registered. Not charging VAT. Not enforceable."

She looked directly at Sofia now.

"So the system faces its hardest question. Do we protect neutrality by letting deduction flow anyway, or do we protect structure, even if that leaves the customer carrying VAT they can't recover?"

Sofia didn't answer immediately.

"I think," she said at last, "that an Advocate General would refuse to resolve that tension by shortcut. No treating import VAT as a substitute. No letting enforcement gaps rewrite the definition of supply."

Marta exhaled slowly. "So the suggestion isn't to pick a side."

"No," Sofia said. "It's to force the Court to say which value governs the system. Neutrality, or legal coherence. Because this case sits exactly at the point where you can't have both without changing the law."

Marta looked back at the falling snow.

"And until the Court answers," she said, "the uncomfortable truth remains."

"That VAT can be owed by the US company," Sofia finished, "because its fixed establishment makes it liable, even if import VAT was already paid. Reputationally, and financially, the stakes for the customer and parent company are real."

"That VAT can be paid," Sofia finished, "without being legally due, and that EU law doesn't always tell us how to make that fair."

Marta smiled softly. "Then that," she said, "is the real question we send upstairs."

The next day's meeting with Michael Torres was scheduled for late morning, but he arrived early, visibly tired, holding a binder so stuffed it looked ready to burst. He greeted everyone with forced cheerfulness but without the previous week's naïveté.

Inside the offices of the Polish Tax Authority, the room smelled faintly of ink and coffee. Marta sat at the far end of the conference table, her posture immaculate, her eyes scanning the documents spread before her with meticulous precision. Even when she was quiet, she seemed to have a strong, calm authority. She was careful and understood every detail on every page.

Michael sat across from her, moving in his chair and fixing his cufflinks for the fourth time that morning. Jakub, Michael's lead engineer, arrived just in time. He was there too, but quieter, leaning against a wall. His presence was like a grounded reminder of logic in the room. The three of them had been there for hours, going through timelines, invoices, and installation reports.

"The issue," Marta said calmly, "is not just about money changing hands. It's about which tax was collected, who collected it, what it was based on, and under which legal provision."

Michael leaned forward. “Isn’t that what the import VAT covered? They paid it. The State received money. What more do you need?”

Marta remained silent, allowing the words to settle.

“No. Legally and in terms of VAT, the correct VAT has not been collected. Let me explain.”

She lifted a folder, opening it with calm deliberation.

“You must distinguish between import VAT and domestic VAT. They are distinct taxes, governed by distinct provisions, payable by different persons, on different bases, and producing different legal consequences.”

Michael frowned. “Different taxes? It’s all VAT, isn’t it?”

“Legally, yes. Economically, no.”

Her look was sharp.

“Import VAT arises at the moment the goods cross the border. Its base is the customs value of the goods alone, not including post-importation services such as installation. Domestic VAT, in contrast, arises when a supply occurs within Polish territory. For a complex supply with installation, that is when the installation is complete and the equipment is usable. The base for domestic VAT includes both goods and installation. These taxes are complementary but not interchangeable. You cannot satisfy domestic VAT obligations simply by paying import VAT.”

Michael leaned back, exhaling.

"So the fact that SilPol paid import VAT doesn't mean the correct tax was collected."

"Exactly," Marta said. "Even if the State 'got its money', it did not get the correct tax." She tapped her pen against the table for emphasis. "The law does not measure compliance by receipt alone. Compliance is measured by who owes the tax, at what time, and on what value."

With her voice calm but firm voice, she continued.

"From the moment the equipment crossed the border, SilPol acted as importer of record. They paid VAT on the total invoice value, which included installation services. That was legally excessive. Import VAT cannot include services performed after importation. The customs code and valuation rules are clear. Only the goods themselves form the customs base.

By including installation, the import VAT was artificially inflated."

Michael's eyes widened. "So, they paid too much at import, and not enough domestic VAT?"

Marta nodded. "Precisely. The money has changed hands, but the tax nexus has not been respected. Legal consequences arise. The State is entitled to domestic VAT on completion, Nano Source Corp. may be liable for output VAT in Poland, and SilPol Fab cannot deduct import VAT to satisfy domestic VAT obligations because it is not yet the economic owner."

Michael shook his head slowly.

"It seems impossible to follow. The customer paid. Isn't that enough?"

She gave him a measured look.

"VAT is not a transactional convenience. It is a legal framework. The State's interest is collection of the correct tax, not merely receipt of funds. This distinction is why the audit continues." She paused, allowing the weight of her words to settle. "The import VAT is one layer. Domestic VAT is another. Both must align with the law."

And she added, "When what is said does not match what is done, like in this case, just getting money is not enough to satisfy legal obligations. The law cares about correctness, not convenience."

Michael exhaled. "So… we're in trouble…"

"Not yet," Marta said. "We are in the process of analysis.

The problem is the gap between seeming to follow the rules and actually being correct legally."

She got up and walked to the window, looking at the icy streets. "Consider this," she said. "If SilPol had been the economic owner at import, and if the customs value had reflected only the goods, excluding installation, then the import VAT would have been properly assessed. The subsequent supply with installation could then have been analyzed separately, with chargeability arising only once the supply was actually completed under the contract."

She turned back to him. "In that scenario, each tax event would have followed its own legal logic, and the right to deduct would have rested on a completed domestic supply. What happened instead is that the transaction collapsed several distinct moments into one, import, supply, completion, and acceptance and that is what created misalignment at every step."

Michael's hand rested on the edge of the table.

"I think I see it. The State received money… but it is the wrong money in legal terms. The tax points are off. Ownership, place of supply, value… they don't match."

Marta nodded. "Correct. The law cares about sequence and substance. Payment alone cannot substitute for legal compliance."

She returned to the table, picking up a document.

"Now consider place of supply. Article 36 of the VAT Directive is explicit. The place of supply of goods installed in a Member State is where the installation occurs. The U.S. invoice and Nano Source Corp.'s accounting do not reflect this. They treat the supply as exported, taxed elsewhere, or neutralized. But under EU law, the supply was Polish from the moment the equipment became operational in the Fab."

Michael looked down at the papers.

"So our invoice, issued in the U.S., misrepresented the place of supply?"

"Yes. The invoice treats this as a shipment of goods, but under EU VAT rules, when a supply includes installation or assembly, the place of supply is where the installation actually occurs, here, in Poland. That's the key."

"This is not a case of a simple cross-border sale of goods," she continued. "The equipment was not merely delivered. It was installed, commissioned, and made operational on Polish territory. That pulls the entire supply into Poland for VAT purposes."

"In such cases," she added, "the law does not automatically shift liability to the customer under reverse charge. Absent a specific statutory mechanism, the supplier of the installed goods remains responsible for accounting for Polish VAT."

"That responsibility does not disappear simply because the invoice was issued from the United States, or because a Polish entity assisted with installation."

"It also affects timing," she said. "*Budimex* shows that for complex supplies with installation, the tax point arises at completion, not shipment."

"So shipping the goods doesn't create the supply?" Michael frowned.

"Exactly," Marta said. "The supply occurs where the goods are installed and usable. In a composite transaction like this, the installation component pulls the place of supply to Poland. Even if ownership and invoicing happen elsewhere, the taxable event happens where the goods are made operational."

Michael exhaled. "So all compliance obligations, VAT registration, invoicing, and reporting should have been assessed by reference to where the installation was completed and who controlled the supply, not merely by reference to where the invoice was issued or who paid import VAT."

"Yes," Marta replied. "Ignoring this creates misalignment at every step. Import VAT on goods, domestic VAT on the composite supply, and potential penalties. The law treats installation as the trigger for domestic taxation. The law distinguishes between import VAT and domestic VAT.

They fall under distinct legal provisions, with different taxable persons, different bases, and different consequences. Payment of one does not extinguish liability for the other."

She paused, letting the complexity sink in.

"The State might seem happy because it has money, but it hasn't collected the right tax. That's what our audit is about."

Michael slumped back, hands over his face. "We did not know. Our system… it is designed for GAAP, not EU VAT law."

Marta's expression remained neutral.

"Ignorance does not negate the legal requirement. But it does illustrate the challenge of cross-border transactions. Law does not bend to familiarity."

"And when interpretation diverges from power, the divergence becomes evident. You perceived compliance because money was transferred. The law sees non-compliance because the correct taxable event was not observed."

Michael looked up.

"So what happens next?"

Marta tapped a pen.

"Next, we must map chronologically each stage. Shipment, import, partial installation, acceptance, invoicing, payment. We must determine where legal obligations were triggered and whether each taxable person, Nano Source Corp. U.S., Nano Source Poland, and SilPol, acted correctly under VAT law. Until this mapping is complete, the audit remains unresolved."

Michael swallowed.

"So, hypothetically, could the State demand domestic VAT, even though import VAT was paid?"

"Yes," Marta said. "Because import VAT does not substitute domestic VAT. The correct tax has not been collected. Payment at import does not erase the obligation arising from the actual supply in Poland."

"It is the systemic logic of VAT. The tax point, the place of supply, the taxable person, and the taxable base must all align. Where they do not, money changing hands is insufficient."

Michael buried his face in his hands.

"All this because we issued a bundled invoice and shipped before installation."

Marta remained calm, allowing the weight of that truth to settle in the room. She had no need to criticize. Legal clarity was more powerful than any criticism.

"The Advocate General's voice," she said finally, almost to herself, "reminds us that law is interpretation, and compliance is measured against interpretation, not merely power or payment. When interpretation diverges from the perceived act of paying, the consequences may be invisible, yet they are binding."

Michael peeked through his fingers.

"So what is the risk if we proceed as-is?"

Marta's tone remained judicial, calm, unyielding.

"The risk is that domestic VAT may be assessed retroactively, penalties and interest may apply, and reputational impact will follow. But the deeper lesson is conceptual, apparent compliance does not equal legal compliance. The State may have money, but it does not have the correct tax."

"It is subtle, but fundamental. Import VAT is the wrong legal instrument for the domestic supply of installed goods. Only completion creates the taxable supply in Poland. The law distinguishes between what was paid and what was owed."

Michael nodded slowly, exhausted but attentive.

"I think I understand, conceptually. But practically… what do we do now?"

Marta gathered her documents.

"We continue the audit. We request further evidence, clarify the contract between Nano Source U.S. and Nano Source Poland, review the installation logs, and map the timeline of value. Until then, the question remains open. The divergence between legal interpretation and financial power is unresolved."

Outside, the winter fog got thicker, and the office lights flickered, shining on shiny surfaces. The room felt caught between being clear and being unsure, between money received and taxes owed, between shipping and using.

Michael stood, attempting to process months of invoices, hours of installation, and layers of legal principle. He felt a rare humility.

"So even if the State 'got its money,' it did not get the correct tax."

"Precisely," Marta said, her calm eyes fixed on him, still brilliant and calm. "The law measures correctness, not receipt."

The conference room was quiet, except for the buzzing lights and the faint noise from the tax office. Outside, Warsaw was gray and calm. And in this calm, one main question remained. What happens when interpretation is different from how the law is applied in practice?

No answer had yet emerged. The Advocate General's voice had spoken through logic, through principle, through the measured brilliance of observation. But judgment remained pending, the audit unresolved. The law waited, patient and exacting, for the correct moment of recognition, the moment when interpretation and fiscal reality would converge, if ever.

Michael and Jakub left the room shortly thereafter, minds heavy with the weight of complexity.

Marta remained behind, stacking papers with precision, listening to the hum of compliance and the echoes of principle, the Advocate General's voice alive in every thought.

And somewhere, between import and installation, between apparent compliance and correct tax, the law held its unyielding position, silent but authoritative, awaiting the day when interpretive reasoning and administrative action might finally align.

Marta closed the file after the first audit session, but one detail kept returning like an unresolved equation. The way the installation work was coordinated. The subsidiary insisted it merely executed instructions from the U.S. parent, while the parent styled the subsidiary's work as an internal logistical convenience. Neither version aligned neatly with VAT law.

Back at her desk, she reviewed the correspondence. Project timelines approved in California. Engineering decisions originating abroad. Local technicians dispatched at the parent's request. The more she traced the flows of work, the more the question sharpened itself: "Where, for VAT purposes, did the real supplier sit?"

While looking over the installation schedule, Marta remembered something Jakub, the lead engineer from Nano Source Polish subsidiary, had said during a technical meeting: "Engineering starts with what works, not just what is written." At that time, it was about assembly details. But now, Marta found Jakub's words very relevant.

That was when the fixed establishment issue surfaced naturally. Not as theory, but as a necessary lens. It wasn't just a theory. It was needed to understand the situation. If the parent company used the Polish subsidiary's people and resources as its own, the whole VAT analysis changed. The *Dong Yang* judgment, once abstract, suddenly became decisive.

PART II - THE PLACES THAT DON'T EXIST

The hidden geography of fixed establishments and cross-border fictions

2.1 DEFINING TAX PRESENCE

The question would not let go of her. Where, for VAT purposes, did the real supplier sit?

Michael's argument from their last meeting kept resurfacing, uninvited. The parent company used the Polish subsidiary's people and resources - surely that made it something. Marta turned the claim over for the better part of a week before she let herself answer it.

It was not a question of legal form, but of operational reality, the same logic the Court had articulated decades earlier in *DFDS*, where a subsidiary acting exclusively for its parent, using the parent's resources under the parent's control, was held to constitute the parent's own fixed establishment. *Dong Yang*, more recent, had not invented that idea. It had simply told her how to recognize it when she saw it. This was not a question of legal form, but of operational reality. The very logic articulated decades earlier in *DFDS*, where the Court held that a subsidiary acting exclusively for its parent, using its resources under the parent's control, could constitute the parent's fixed establishment. The *Dong Yang* judgment recently became decisive not because it created the concept, but because it defined when and how it could be recognized.

Another meeting with Nano Source. Marta sat at the long conference table. The morning light was pale and gray on invoices and contract pages. Michael Torres sat across from her. He rubbed his forehead and whispered something to himself. He looked upset and frustrated. Jakub entered the room and gave a brief nod to both of them, not looking up. His phone buzzed. He leaned against the window frame and read the message in silence.

'Call me ASAP – VAT audit on the equipment.'

– Paweł

Pawel from SilPol Fab.

The room smelled faintly of coffee and uncertainty.

"Let's start with the basics," Marta said, calm but precise.

"You'll remember the note I sent last week. I outlined some preliminary observations. Today, we are not discussing import VAT or rules for selling equipment with installation. We're not questioning whether a Nano Source subsidiary exists on paper. What we're examining is something subtler… When a subsidiary actually qualifies as a fixed establishment for VAT purposes."

Michael looked worried.

"So… if the authorities say our Polish subsidiary is a fixed establishment, we'd be liable for all Polish VAT? Penalties? Interest?"

"Potentially." Marta responded, "That's why this functional test matters. The question is not whether the subsidiary acts independently, but whether the parent company has, through that subsidiary, a stable structure in Poland capable of receiving and using supplies?"

Michael blinked, trying to keep pace.

"I… I thought that was obvious. If you have an office, staff, a mailing address, surely that counts. They coordinate installation. They supervise locally. They manage logistics..."

Marta shook her head, her voice judicial, measured.

"Form without substance is irrelevant. Mere coordination alone does not create a fixed establishment. But sustained operational use of local staff and infrastructure by the parent may. The Court of Justice addressed this very issue in *Dong Yang Electronics*. A 'fixed establishment' requires stable arrangements, human and technical resources capable of independent operation, decision-making, and risk assumption."

Michael leaned forward, frustration visible. "But our subsidiary has staff. It has a desk. Phones. A registered office. How can that not be enough? Uhm"

"So… we're liable anyway? Even though the subsidiary is doing all the local work?"

"Yes," Marta said calmly.

"The subsidiary is operational, not fiscal. It cannot generate domestic VAT obligations for the parent. Obligations remains with Nano Source Corp. And that includes VAT, reporting, and any penalties or interest arising from non-compliance."

Michael ran a hand over his face.

"So all this import VAT, our bundled invoices… it doesn't protect us?"

"Import VAT is separate," Marta replied, "It applies because goods cross the border. Domestic VAT arises from the actual supply of goods and installation. Payment of one does not extinguish liability for the other. The authorities are looking at the parent company as the taxable person."

"The Court has repeatedly said that mere presence, without autonomy and operational control, does not create a fixed establishment. In *Dong Yang*, the entity had an office and employees who only acted as an agent for the parent. It could not make decisions, issue invoices, or assume liability independently. Form existed; substance did not."

Michael frowned.

"So, an office can exist in reality but not exist legally?"

"In VAT terms, yes," Marta said. "The 'place that does not exist' is exactly that. An arrangement that seems to exist formally but is incapable of creating a taxable presence. The parent company cannot hide behind a letterhead. It must demonstrate that the subsidiary can act as a taxable person in its own right if it is to be considered a fixed establishment."

Marta stepped closer to the table, her tone calm, measured.

"Think of it as functional geography. The law does not map space merely by lines on a lease agreement. It maps capabilities, autonomy, and use. If the office cannot receive and utilize supplies in its own name, it is a phantom office.

A fiction. A place that does not exist for VAT purposes."

Michael leaned back, exhaling slowly.

"I don't follow… So, our Polish subsidiary… they can't just be our fixed establishment because we say they are?"

Marta nodded. "Correct. But we are discussing Nano Source Corp.'s presence in Poland. Regarding the formal incorporation of a Polish subsidiary, it does not automatically create VAT nexus for Nano Source Corp. The Court examines the economic reality. Who decides? Who assumes risk? Who can act without direct parent intervention? These questions determine whether a fixed establishment exists."

She picked up a file, flipping to a diagram of Nano Source's Polish office.

"Look at this. Three employees. A rented desk. Technical support provided to the U.S. parent. They cannot issue invoices independently. They cannot commit to contracts. Their budget is allocated by the headquarters. By form, they exist. By substance…" Marta paused, searching for the right word.

"They are not a ghost, they are a body without a name. And VAT law looks at bodies, not letterheads."

Michael rubbed his temples.

"So for VAT purposes, they are invisible."

"Invisible but not irrelevant," Marta said.

Their presence matters only in terms of where supply occurs and which entity may be deemed the taxable person. But if they are a phantom office, the parent company remains the taxable person in the jurisdiction where supplies are received and used.

"This is where fiction and substance collide," she continued. "Many companies assume that registration equals presence. But registration is a formality, not functionality."

She leaned forward, tapping the table once for emphasis.

"The law ignores letterhead. It examines operational capacity."

Marta let the silence settle before continuing.

"Let's consider a hypothetical. Your U.S. parent ships semiconductor equipment to the Polish subsidiary for installation at the Fab. The subsidiary merely receives instructions, coordinates with local contractors, and reports to headquarters."

She looked directly at him.

"They cannot invoice in their own name, but they act continuously under the parent's authority, executing supplies that the parent could not perform without them."

A pause.

"Are they a fixed establishment? Legally? Economically?"

She shook her head.

"No. Phantom."

Michael's eyes widened.

"But they handle logistics. They interact with customs. They handle installation."

"Supervision does not equate to autonomy," Marta replied calmly.

The law, she explained, asked could the subsidiary receive and use supplies in its own name? Could it create domestic VAT liability independently? Could it assume the legal consequences of supply?

"If the answer is no," she said, "formal presence is irrelevant."

She reached for another file.

"*Dong Yang Electronics* confirmed this."

The entity had a physical office and staff, but all activity was controlled by the parent. The Court ruled that mere office space and nominal employees do not create a fixed establishment.

"Substance is decisive." Marta said. "Form is illusion."

Michael slumped back in his chair.

"So, paperwork can lie. Leases, emails, org charts… they can mislead tax authorities."

"Exactly," Marta said. "Which is why audits exist."

Authorities look beyond appearances. They seek the reality of operations.

"The test is functional," she added. "Does the subsidiary have decision-making power? Does it bear risk? Can it act as an independent entity in the market?"

She did not wait for an answer.

"If the answer is no, it is a phantom office."

Marta opened a new document, showing Michael a map with arrows and dotted lines.

"Observe this. The parent company issues instructions. The subsidiary coordinates with third-party installers. Contracts remain in the parent's name. Payments flow from the U.S. entity."

She traced one of the arrows with her finger.

"The subsidiary's involvement is administrative. The law may recognize it as a fixed establishment precisely because the parent uses it as one."

Michael followed the diagram in silence.

"So for VAT purposes," he said finally, "the parent is liable, not the subsidiary."

"Yes," Marta replied. Calm, precise. "The fixed establishment concept does not exist to simplify corporate reporting."

She paused.

"It exists to determine where VAT arises and who bears it."

Her voice softened slightly.

"And this is crucial for cross-border supplies. A fixed establishment is not about whether the subsidiary is independent. It is about whether the parent has made the subsidiary's people and infrastructure its own."

She closed the file.

"But the Court has repeatedly emphasized substance. The ghost office can generate invoices, occupy space, hire employees, but if it lacks economic autonomy, it does not create a fixed establishment."

"So all of our assumptions about Polish VAT obligations may be wrong if we assume the subsidiary itself is the fixed establishment?"

Marta nodded.

"Exactly. If the subsidiary lacks autonomy, it may not be the fixed establishment, but that does not end the analysis."

She paused.

"It shifts it to the parent."

All VAT obligations, reverse charge, and reporting remain with the parent. The law does not recognize the office unless it has operational capacity sufficient to act independently.

She leaned forward.

"Consider it another layer of the hidden geography of VAT," Marta said. "Official addresses exist on maps. Tax authorities see them."

She let the sentence hang.

"But operational reality may place the taxable presence elsewhere entirely."

Michael sounded almost defeated.

"So it's possible to have an office, pay rent, have employees, and still… legally, it does not exist?"

Marta's eyes were calm, unyielding.

"Exactly. Or rather, it may not exist in the way companies expect it to."

The Court in *Dong Yang* was clear. Form without substance is irrelevant for VAT purposes. You may occupy space, hire staff, and issue reports. None of that creates a fixed establishment of the subsidiary unless there is capacity to act independently and assume legal and economic responsibility.

"This matters," Marta continued, "because a VAT fixed establishment is the legal gateway but not always for the entity you think."

Only if it exists can the subsidiary be treated as the taxable person, liable for domestic VAT and able to issue invoices that the customer can deduct. If it does not, the analysis does not end. It shifts.

Michael exhaled.

"And what happens if the tax authority believes it exists?"

"There could be conflict."

"Yes," Marta said, judicial and measured.

"Which is why functional analysis is crucial. Contracts, staff autonomy, budgetary control, and operational decision-making. These were the elements that mattered not to prove the subsidiary's independence, but to assess how its resources are actually used."

"If the subsidiary were a VAT Fixed Establishment," she explained, "then Polish VAT on the supply of goods and installation could be charged through the subsidiary, and the domestic customer could deduct it."

She paused.

"But if the subsidiary lacks autonomy, and its people and infrastructure are used to carry out the parent's supplies, the conclusion may be different."

"Without that status, the U.S. parent remains the taxable person. And if it performs supplies in Poland through those local resources, the parent itself may be regarded as having a fixed establishment here."

The Court's guidance was consistent. Mere supervision, coordination, or administrative tasks performed locally were insufficient. What mattered was decision-making power, risk assumption, and the capacity to receive and use supplies in the entity's own name and whose name that capacity truly served.

Michael leaned back, staring at the ceiling.

"So the Phantom Office isn't a place you can see on a map."

He thought for a moment.

"It's a place defined by what it can do, and by who uses it."

Marta nodded. "Correct."

Phantom offices existed in paperwork, not in law. But a phantom subsidiary could still determine a very real fixed establishment, not for itself, but for its parent. For VAT purposes, the question was never whether the office existed, but whether its human and technical resources were placed at the disposal of the taxable person carrying out the supply.

"That is why," Marta said, "in your case, even if SilPol paid import VAT or the subsidiary coordinated installation, Polish VAT treatment hinges entirely on the parent's status as a taxable person."

She added, more softly, almost to herself: "And yet the phantom can still create illusions, apparent compliance, perceived presence, false tax points."

She looked back at Michael.

"But reality determines who is liable for VAT, who can deduct it, and whether a domestic supply is correctly recognized."

Her tone remained steady.

"That is why your assumptions about Polish VAT, your treatment of the subsidiary, and your assessment of obligations may all be flawed. Recognition of a fixed establishment changes who the law treats as responsible."

She paused.

"But your subsidiary is not that fixed establishment, at least not in its own name."

Michael muttered,

"So what do we do now? How do we fix the phantom problem?"

Marta leaned back in her chair, calm and judicial.

"We document reality. We analyze operational capacity. Not to prove the subsidiary's independence but to understand how its resources are actually used."

She enumerated the steps without emphasis.

"We map contracts, budgets, authority, and decision-making power. We ask who truly directs the work, who assumes the risk, and for whose benefit the activity is carried out. Only then could the subsidiary be treated as a VAT fixed establishment and domestic VAT obligations correctly allocated."

Until then, any assumption based solely on legal form was unreliable.

"And remember," she added, "a phantom office may appear to exist, may coordinate daily activity, may occupy space yet still matter profoundly for VAT."

Michael sat back, silent. For the first time, he understood the paradox. A place can exist legally but not for VAT. A company can have offices and staff and still shift VAT responsibility elsewhere.

Reality mattered more than paper. Substance defeated form.

Without a fixed establishment of the subsidiary, the parent did not escape liability. On the contrary, it became exposed. If the Polish resources were used to carry out the parent's supplies, the parent remained the taxable person, possibly with a fixed establishment grounded precisely in those local operations.

Marta let the point settle.

"And that," she said softly, "is the hidden geography of fixed establishments."

Some places exist on maps, but not in law. Others exist in law only because of what is done there, and for whom. VAT obligations, chargeability, and deduction rights depend on substance, not perception.

Outside, Warsaw's winter light faded, the city gray and still.

Inside the office, the unspoken truth lingered. Not all places that exist are real in VAT law. Not all offices create taxable persons. But some create taxable presence for someone else.

Until functional autonomy is proven, the law ignores them.

Michael exhaled, a slow, weary sound.

"Then everything we thought about our Polish subsidiary… it may be wrong."

Marta nodded once, precisely, judicially.

"Until proven otherwise, it is a phantom."

That meant domestic VAT was the parent's responsibility. Domestic VAT could not simply be pushed onto SilPol. Deduction claims, invoicing logic, and compliance obligations had to be reassessed by reference to Nano Source as the taxable person, and to whether its Polish operations amounted to a fixed establishment in fact.

"And the fiction persists," she concluded, "until substance is established."

Until then, the law treated the office as a place that did not exist. It asked who used it, and to do what.

The room fell silent. The lesson was learnt, unambiguously.

Reality.

Autonomy.

Functional capacity.

These were the coordinates of VAT law. Paper and perception were secondary. And somewhere, Nano Source's subsidiary waited for either recognition or continued invisibility.

The office had never been empty. It had simply been misnamed. What appeared as support was, on closer inspection, structure. What was described as coordination was, in practice, execution. VAT law did not ask whether the subsidiary existed on paper. It asked whether the parent had learned to operate through it. And once that question was asked, the phantom began to take shape.

2.2 BUSINESS PRESENCE, RESIDENCY, AND TAX JURISDICTION

Marta arrived at her office before the sun was up in Warsaw. The frost on the window sparkled a little, but inside, it was warm and silent. There were no phone calls and no interruptions. No urgent emails. Just her desk, organized folders, and the low sound of a radio playing somewhere in the background. Today, the challenge was abstract but pressing. Fixed establishments, invisible presence, and the hidden geography of cross-border VAT.

On her desk were files of new cases she had gathered over the past weeks. These included contracts, technical diagrams, invoices, and notes about two example companies, which she called Company A and Company B. Both companies provided digital services to EU customers. They did not have large offices or many staff in Poland, where their services were used. They claimed to have a small presence, using cross-border service delivery and centralized reporting.

Marta poured herself a cup of coffee and opened her notebook. The lines were already covered with dense annotations from previous cases: *Dong Yang Electronics* (C-547/18), *Welmory* (C-605/12), and more recent clarifications from *Berlin Chemie (C-333/20)* and *Cabot Plastics* (C-232/22). She looked at the paper and began to write her analysis.

"Definition of fixed establishment," she murmured to herself, while looking at articles 11-13 in Council Implementing Regulation 282/2011 and relevant recitals. The regulation was clear, permanence, structure, and capacity were decisive. A mere postal address, a registered office, or incorporation as a subsidiary did not suffice. The entity must possess human and technical resources capable of receiving and using or supplying services independently.

She began mapping Company A's operations. A Cypriot digital services provider. It supplied analytics tools to customers across the EU, including Poland, Germany, and France. Contracts were executed electronically. Payments flowed through a single centralized bank account. The servers were located across various cloud platforms, with none being physically located in the Member States of consumption. No staff were stationed locally. All support was outsourced to remote contractors acting under instructions from Cyprus.

Marta sketched a diagram in her notebook. She did this not as an art project but to help with legal analysis. On one side, she placed the registered office in Cyprus, the legal address of Company A, and the minimal contact details provided to customers. On the other, she drew the lines connecting the Cyprus office to EU customers, dashed arrows indicating that all decision-making, contract execution, and operational control originated in Cyprus. She noted: 'Legal form exists. Operational substance in Member States absent.'

Turning to the question of VAT presence, she recalled the CJEU's ruling in *Dong Yang Electronics*. The Court emphasized that a fixed establishment does not arise simply because a subsidiary exists. What mattered was the functional capacity. Could the local entity make decisions, assume liability, or act in its own name? For the organizational structure of Company A, the answer was no. The remote contractors could coordinate service delivery, but they could not enter into contracts, accept payment, or assume responsibility independently.

Marta jotted in the margin: 'Phantom presence. Formal address and minimal operational role cannot create fixed establishment. Substance over form.' She underlined it twice, knowing it would be central in her internal memo.

She moved to Company B, a larger digital services supplier with a complex cross-border footprint. It maintained minimal office space in several EU countries, but all operational decisions were centralized. The offices were staffed with administrative assistants, whose role was limited to forwarding requests to headquarters. Technical support was performed remotely; invoicing and risk management remained in the home office.

Again, Marta drew a functional map. Unlike Company A, Company B had a physical presence, but the presence was not autonomous. Decision-making power rested entirely at headquarters. Here too, the phantom office principle applied. Physical footprint alone does not create a fixed establishment.

She reflected on the doctrine from *Berlin Chemie* and *Cabot Plastics*. Even where technical infrastructure exists, if human resources are insufficient to assume independent responsibility, the entity cannot qualify as a fixed establishment. The Court had consistently reaffirmed that autonomy and operational capacity are decisive, not mere occupancy or nominal staffing.

Her pen moved to the question of cross-border digital services. Company A's Cypriot base delivered services to customers in multiple EU Member States. Payments were centralized. Servers were remote. Could VAT presence be recognized where consumption occurred? She wrote: 'Place of supply determined by customer location (Art. 58–59 VAT Directive). OSS[1]/MOSS[2] filings satisfy reporting, but absence of local fixed establishment confirmed.'

She considered scenarios. What if a Member State argued that remote technical support constituted a fixed establishment? Marta jotted notes:

- Staff must have functional capacity to receive and use supplies.
- Ability to contract or make binding decisions locally is decisive.
- Coordination alone does not create VAT presence.
- Mere marketing, technical assistance, or customer liaison does not equal fixed establishment.

She paused, sipping coffee, considering the implications. A company could make money all over the EU and show up in customer records everywhere. But it might not have to pay VAT. She found it interesting that a business could be active in many places but only legally exist in one.

[1] The One Stop Shop (OSS) is an EU VAT simplification scheme that allows businesses supplying cross-border goods and services to EU consumers to declare and pay VAT due in multiple Member States through a single VAT return submitted in one Member State.

[2] The Mini One Stop Shop (MOSS) was an EU VAT scheme, introduced in 2015 and replaced by OSS in 2021, which enabled suppliers of telecommunications, broadcasting, and electronically supplied services to report and remit VAT for multiple Member States via a single electronic portal.

Returning to Company B, she reflected on its quasi-physical presence in multiple countries. Staff were administrative, incapable of independent decisions, but offices were rented, equipment installed. Marta noted: 'Operational footprint exists but functional autonomy absent. Fixed establishment not recognized. Phantom offices multiply, but legal recognition requires capacity.'

Her pen traced lines from the offices to customers, from payments to OSS filings. She annotated: 'OSS simplifies reporting; it does not erase legal responsibilities. Simply having offices or staff in a country does not count as a real fixed establishment. Legal recognition requires actual functional independence. Having an FE matters because it defines who the tax authorities can hold responsible for VAT. Without it, a "local" office is invisible for VAT purposes.'

Marta's mind turned to drafting her internal memo. She structured her argument:

1. Definition and Criteria of Fixed Establishment
    - Permanence of arrangements
    - Human and technical resources
    - Functional capacity to act independently
2. Subsidiary vs Fixed Establishment
    - Incorporation insufficient
    - Minimal local presence insufficient
    - Case law: *Dong Yang* C-547/18, *Berlin Chemie* C-333/20, *Cabot Plastics* C-232/22
3. Digital Services and Phantom Presence
    - Place of supply = customer location (Art. 58–59)
    - OSS reporting = reporting convenience, not elimination of VAT liability

- Remote services can create VAT obligations without fixed establishment

4. Functional Analysis for VAT Presence
   - Decision-making authority
   - Ability to contract independently
   - Control over technical and human resources
   - Coordination alone does not suffice
5. Practical Implications
   - Cross-border digital companies may appear "everywhere"
   - Legal recognition requires substance in the Member State
   - Phantom presence can mislead accounting and auditing, but law prioritizes functional reality

Marta paused, reviewing the internal diagrams. The visual contrast between paper maps and functional maps captured the essence: **legal presence is not geography; it is capacity**. A company could rent offices, hire staff, and claim local presence, but without autonomy, it remained a phantom in the eyes of VAT law.

She wrote a note in the margin: 'Verify actual decision-making power, functional capacity, and operational independence. The mere existence of premises or staff does not create taxable presence.'

Her thoughts turned to OSS compliance. Many companies misunderstood it. Filing via OSS did not exempt them from scrutiny. A Member State could examine records, trace operational activities, and challenge claimed absence of establishment if functional capacity existed locally. Marta noted: 'OSS makes reporting easier, but it should not hide phantom presence from legal examination.'

She returned to the central paradox, which is that companies can be everywhere, but legally nowhere. Revenue could flow from multiple Member States, consumption occurred physically (or virtually) in those jurisdictions, yet the companies could claim no fixed establishment. Marta's notes reflected the tension:

- Economic footprint ≠ legal presence
- Operational substance required for VAT recognition
- Phantom presence must be dissected carefully in audits
- Phantom offices and subsidiaries may exist on paper but not create VAT presence
- Fixed establishment requires functional autonomy, human and technical resources, and decision-making capacity
- Digital services delivered cross-border remain taxable at the place of consumption, regardless of claimed absence of establishment
- OSS reporting is a mechanism of convenience, not a legal protection
- Auditors must focus on economic reality, not formal registration or minimal footprint

Marta sat back in her chair and looked at the city through frosty glass. Warsaw was gray and quiet. Inside, she imagined a complex world of representative offices, cross-border services, and digital footprints.

For now, the companies were everywhere and nowhere. But the law remained firm and patient. Functional capacity, decision-making, and economic substance were the coordinates it relied upon. Marta's job was to trace these lines, expose the phantom, and align legal recognition with reality.

She closed her notebook, satisfied with the framework set out for cases of companies A and B.

Her final task was to prepare and consolidate her conclusions regarding the Nano Source case for the next stage with Michael, once he returned.

The internal memo was not ready, yet her notes were structured, reasoned, and grounded in CJEU jurisprudence, reflecting all the nuances they had discussed.

Taxable supply, chargeability, import versus domestic VAT, the right to deduct, timing of acceptance, and the limits of non-established suppliers. Michael would return, and the dialogue would begin. But Marta already understood the core. Legal and economic realities, not formal labels or invoices, defined VAT obligations. The interplay between import VAT, domestic supply, and functional use had to be considered carefully. Payment, installation, and control were critical, not just contractual clauses or the flow of paperwork. And yet, she reminded herself, enforcement against Nano Source, the non-established U.S. company, was effectively impossible, leaving practical compliance and deduction questions open.

In her office, Marta was ready. She thought about the rules for legal presence and responsibility, not about borders, offices, or spreadsheets. The rules for VAT in Europe were complex, and she was figuring them out. She was learning where obligations start, where deductions are allowed, and where the law must be followed, no matter how things look.

2.3 WHO SUPPLIES THE INSTALLATION WORK?

Marta got to her office early again. She had already set up the files she needed for the day. The Nano Source US sales contract, the subsidiary's service agreement, invoices, and notes on import VAT, domestic VAT, and the allocation of risk.

Her mind returned to the essential question. Who truly controlled the installation, and who bore the economic risk while it was being performed? Reading contracts was one thing but interpreting the flow of value and control was another. Formal arrangements could suggest clarity, but the substance often told a different story. The Nano Source transaction lay open before her. The U.S. parent sold semiconductor equipment to SilPol Fab in Poland, issuing a single invoice covering both goods and installation. SilPol Fab had already paid import VAT on the full value, even though the Polish subsidiary, managed by Michael, would carry out the actual installation. Jakub, the engineer employed by the subsidiary, was scheduled to assemble and commission the equipment, but legal and functional ownership, operational control, and risk remained intertwined in complex ways.

Marta drew a diagram. The flow of equipment from the United States, into Poland, through customs, and into the SilPol Fab's facility. Alongside, she noted the flow of responsibility. The parent company formally contracted to supply and install. The Polish subsidiary executing the service, i.e., Jakub performing the technical work. Payments were layered. The U.S. parent invoiced SilPol Fab, and the subsidiary invoiced the parent for services rendered.

She paused. Risk. Who bore it at each stage? The goods were imported by SilPol Fab; import VAT was paid upon receipt. Risk for the equipment during shipping rested with SilPol Fab, but who bore operational risk during installation? Jakub was the one physically handling the machines, adjusting settings, and testing functions. In essence, the economic reality placed operational control and incidental risk in the hands of the local engineer, even though formally, the U.S. parent retained contractual obligations.

Marta scribbled a note: 'Economic ownership vs contractual ownership is critical for VAT. Substance prevails.' She recalled that the tax point and VAT treatment must reflect actual supply and consumption, not just the invoice lines. She highlighted: 'Invoice is both evidence and illusion.'

Next, Marta examined the contracts. The parent's contract to SilPol Fab described delivery and installation as a single package. The Polish subsidiary's internal agreement framed the installation as a service supplied to the parent, to be invoiced separately. From a formal perspective, the U.S. parent was the supplier; the Polish subsidiary was a contractor. But Marta's analysis required substance: Jakub's performance, and the subsidiary's operational capacity, were decisive for VAT treatment.

She drew a functional map:

- Parent company: contractual supplier, invoicing entity, assumes formal legal risk.
- Polish subsidiary: executes service, supervises installation, employs Jakub and two other engineers.
- Jakub: performs installation, controls equipment on-site, interacts with SilPol Fab staff.

Marta noted: 'For VAT purposes, performance is tied to the entity executing the work and controlling risk, not the entity issuing the invoice. Place of supply may diverge from invoice origin.'

She turned to import VAT. Paid by SilPol Fab, the Polish tax authorities received revenue at the point of import. Yet domestic VAT could arise when installation services were performed. Marta's pen traced lines between payment flows, noting: 'Import VAT $\neq$ domestic VAT.

Distinct legal provisions, paid by different persons, on different bases.

Revenue collected ≠ correct tax'.

Even if the state had "received the money," the legal incidence of VAT depended on who actually supplied the installation locally.

Her mind focused on the bundled invoice issue. The U.S. parent had issued a single invoice covering equipment and installation. Could it be argued that VAT was paid upon importation since the invoice included installation charges? Marta's internal note read: 'Bundling does not alter substance. Import VAT, even if calculated on a bundled customs value, applies only to the importation of goods and cannot be treated as VAT on installation services. The installation, physically carried out in Poland by a subsidiary acting as subcontractor, forms part of the supply invoiced by the U.S. parent to the customer. Any VAT consequences for that service must be assessed separately under domestic VAT rules and cannot be cured by import VAT paid at the border.'

She paused to recall CJEU guidance: the place of supply of goods supplied with installation or assembly services can be determined by whether the service is essential to the good and where the service is performed. Jakub's work, installing and testing the semiconductor equipment, took place entirely in Poland. Therefore, even though the invoice originated abroad, the service element is supplied locally, and the installation cannot be ignored for VAT purposes.

Marta annotated the contracts further, contrasting formal assignment vs functional reality:

- Contract: Parent supplies equipment + installation to Fab.
- Internal assignment: Subsidiary supplies installation service to Parent.
- Reality: Subsidiary executes, Jakub performs, Fab receives service.
- Risk allocation: Parent's formal contract does not alter operational control.

Her pen flew across the page, creating a visual schema: the U.S. parent as a contractual node, the subsidiary as operational executor, Jakub as hands-on performer, SilPol Fab as ultimate recipient and importer. She wrote: 'VAT treatment must follow the functional path of risk and performance, not contractual fiction.'

She reflected on tax point issues. When did value arise? The invoice issued by the U.S. parent did not match the time of actual performance. Payment may have occurred months before Jakub's installation work. Marta wrote: 'Moment of value: when service is performed, when risk transferred, when customer accepts the installation. Invoice alone insufficient.'

She considered possible scenarios for audit:

- Formal invoice only: Parent issues invoice covering goods + installation; VAT treatment applied incorrectly if relying solely on import VAT.
- Functional reality recognized: Subsidiary performs installation, domestic VAT applies to the service supplied in Poland, risk and control with Jakub and subsidiary.
- Hybrid reporting: Parent invoiced for entire bundle; subsidiary reimbursed internally. Tax authorities must adjust VAT reporting to reflect actual performance and risk.

Marta jotted a summary for her memo: 'Audit risk: misallocation of VAT, incorrect invoicing, failure to account for domestic VAT on local service. Substance must prevail over form. Risk for the tax authorities if not challenging single bundled invoice.'

She returned to Jakub's role. In legal terms, he was an employee of the subsidiary. Functionally, he executed all technical activities, assumed operational control, and mitigated risks during installation.

Marta's note read: 'Jakub = functional supplier. His actions define VAT liability in Poland. Parent's formal invoice is secondary. Risk resides with executor.'

Her mind wandered to a related consideration. Payment flows. The subsidiary invoiced the parent, which in turn billed the Fab. Did this circular payment affect VAT incidence? Marta shook her head. Substance dictated VAT, not flow of money. She wrote: 'Payment to subsidiary ≠ VAT recognition. Performance location and risk ownership decisive.'

Marta paused to draft internal diagrams, marking:

- Goods shipped from U.S. to Poland. Import VAT paid by Fab.
- Installation performed in Poland by Jakub / subsidiary. Domestic VAT applicable.
- Parent invoices SilPol Fab. Formal contract only, may mislead authorities if taken at face value.
- Subsidiary invoices parent. Reflects actual supply of service, functional reality for VAT.

She added a note: 'Invoice = evidence + illusion. Must reconcile contractual form with operational reality.'

She reflected on CJEU principles again. The Court consistently emphasizes substance over form, economic reality over mere legal assignment, and functional capacity over invoice labels. Marta highlighted *Budimex* in her notes: 'economic and commercial realities form a fundamental criterion for the application of the common system of VAT. Hence, VAT recognized where service performed, risk controlled, and benefit received.'

By late evening, Marta's memo had taken shape. It mapped roles, performance, risk, and VAT implications clearly.

She reviewed her conclusions:

- Installation performed locally by subsidiary / Jakub.
- Risk during installation resides with subsidiary / on-site engineer.
- Import VAT covers goods only, paid on goods and installation by SilPol Fab.
- Domestic VAT arises on local installation service.
- Bundled invoice cannot substitute correct VAT treatment.
- Misallocated VAT if we rely solely on U.S. invoice.
- Functional reality dictates legal recognition for VAT purposes.

Leaning back, Marta sipped her tea. The case was complex, but her diagrams and notes revealed the hidden aspects of responsibility and VAT. The invoice alone was insufficient to capture reality; Jakub's hands and decisions had determined operational risk and the place of supply.

Tomorrow, Michael would return, armed with new arguments and evidence. Marta would need to translate this functional analysis into a coherent argument. Risk and performance drive VAT recognition, not contractual fiction. For now, she allowed herself a moment of clarity. In the world of cross-border semiconductor installations, the engineer who performs defines the tax point, and the entity that controls risk determines local VAT obligations.

2.4 WHEN CORPORATE STRUCTURE REPLACES REALITY

The conference room in Warsaw's tax office was quiet, almost oppressively so, as Marta laid out the folders on the long table. Soft winter light came through the window blinds, shining on the contracts, invoices, and flowcharts she had carefully prepared. Today, she was no longer alone, and her views were likely to get questioned. Michael, the CFO of the U.S. parent, would join shortly, accompanied by two external advisors.

When they entered, Marta stood back and watched. Michael seemed calm and a bit distant, like he was used to being in tax audit meetings. The advisors bore laptops and thick folders, ready to argue the formalistic side of the transaction. Marta had been thinking about the details for weeks. She focused on the main issues, on substance over form, and wondered if the meeting could align the U.S. view with Polish VAT law.

Michael began, his tone neutral but deliberate:

"We understand the Polish authorities have questions regarding the installation services. Let's review the facts as we see them. The U.S. parent is the supplier. We issued the invoice covering both equipment and installation. The contract specifies that we are responsible for delivery and commissioning."

One of the advisors adjusted his glasses before interjecting, his tone careful, deliberate:

"That framing is important," he said. "Because it reflects how Nano Source structured the transaction across all relevant dimensions, contractually, operationally, and financially."

He gestured toward the invoice.

"Before we move into any discussion of substantive VAT outcomes, we think it's important to frame the issue correctly," he said.

"Nano Source Corp. is not disputing that EU VAT law exists, nor that Member States may apply it where the statutory conditions are met.

Our position is narrower, and more precise."

He paused briefly.

"First, Nano Source Corp. is a U.S. entity with no incorporation, no assets, and no decision-making personnel in the European Union. Any VAT obligation would therefore have to be grounded in a legally recognizable fixed establishment, or in a clear statutory registration obligation applicable to non-EU suppliers. Without this, the assessment might be just theoretical, and enforcement and penalties raise serious concerns about proportionality and proper legal procedures."

He continued, more deliberately.

"Second, the contractual and accounting framework matters. The parent company is the sole contracting party with SilPol Fab. It bears the full performance obligation under the contract, including delivery and commissioning. The subsidiary does not contract, does not price, does not assume commercial risk, and does not interact with the customer in its own name."

He folded his hands.

"The parties expressly excluded the CISG, the international convention governing contracts for the sale of goods, and selected Californian law. Under that law, and under ASC 606, revenue recognition follows transfer of control, not physical performance. Control remains with the U.S. parent until formal acceptance by the customer. The Polish entity does not control the supply, cannot redirect it, and cannot substitute performance. It merely executes instructions."

He added carefully: "From a VAT characterization perspective, the single invoice line does not determine the nature of the supply. EU law itself is clear that economic reality prevails over invoicing technique. Here, the equipment is fully manufactured, independently functional, and has a standalone market value. Installation is time-limited, non-continuous, and technically separable. Customers may, and in other transactions do, use third-party integrators."

He tapped the contract.

"Importantly, SilPol Fab acted as importer of record and paid import VAT. Re-characterizing the transaction in a way that creates additional VAT obligations for the supplier risks double taxation, contrary to VAT neutrality principles. At a minimum, this context precludes penalties or retroactive reassessment."

Finally, he concluded calmly:

"In short, Nano Source structured its transactions consistently with U.S. law, international contracting standards, and industry practice. If a different VAT characterization is now proposed, it must overcome the absence of a fixed establishment, respect legitimate expectations, and satisfy proportionality, particularly given the practical limits on enforcement against a non-EU entity. This is not a case of evasion but of a cross-border transaction."

Marta remained silent, observing. She made a note in her journal: 'The structure is coherent within its own legal system: exclusion of CISG, Californian law, parent as sole contracting party, centralized control. From a U.S. legal and accounting standpoint, the framework is internally consistent. The question is not whether the structure is valid but whether it answers the VAT questions EU law actually asks.'

She began outlining what she called, not a recharacterization, but a functional map:

- Equipment manufactured and shipped from the U.S., SilPol Fab acts as importer of record and pays import VAT.
- Installation physically carried out by Jakub, employed by the Polish subsidiary.
- The parent company contracts with SilPol Fab; the subsidiary invoices parent for installation support.

"Mr. Torres," she began carefully, "I understand your position. Your invoice and contractual allocation of responsibility are clear, and from a Californian law and the U.S. accounting standards perspective, the logic is consistent. My task, however, is narrower."

Michael nodded slightly, inviting her to continue.

"Under EU VAT law," Marta said, "the decisive questions are not who bears contractual risk in the abstract, but how the supply is characterized and where the relevant functions are carried out. That analysis is separate from revenue recognition or governing commercial law."

Michael raised an eyebrow.

"But we did not hide anything. The parent remains fully responsible. The subsidiary has no authority vis-à-vis the customer."

"I don't dispute that," Marta replied. "And I am not suggesting the subsidiary contracts or prices. But VAT law looks at operational reality when determining the place of supply, particularly for installation-related activities."

An advisor attempted a counterpoint:

"But even then, installation does not automatically create a taxable presence. There is no fixed establishment. No autonomy. No capacity to supply services independently."

Marta nodded.

"That is indeed the critical point, and it's not assumed away. Fixed establishment requires permanence and functional independence. *Titanium* and *Berlin Chemie* make clear that contractual links and ownership alone are insufficient."

She paused, choosing her words.

"However, those same cases also confirm that the physical performance of services matters for place-of-supply analysis, even where no fixed establishment ultimately exists. The question I'm examining for now is not whether Nano Source has a fixed establishment but whether the installation element, as performed, establishes a taxable service in Poland, and if so, who is regarded as supplying it for VAT purposes."

Michael frowned, exchanging a glance with his advisors.

"So you're not saying our structure is irrelevant?"

"No," Marta replied calmly. "I'm saying it is relevant but not determinative. The exclusion of CISG, the choice of Californian law, the bundled invoice… All of these explain intent and allocation of risk. They do not, by themselves, answer how EU VAT law allocates taxing rights when the installation services are physically carried out in a Member State."

She drew two arrows on her pad, deliberately this time with question marks.

The first concerned the goods. They had entered the Union, and import VAT had been paid by SilPol Fab. That point was settled.

The second concerned the installation. It had been carried out physically in Poland, but its characterization and its allocation within the transaction remained unresolved.

Taken together, the two points reinforced her conclusion. The origin of the invoice and the law chosen by the parties were secondary. Functional execution is primary.

"At this stage," she concluded, "the analysis remains about classification and consequences, not accusations. And I fully recognize that even if VAT were theoretically due, enforcement, penalties, and retroactivity raise separate and serious questions."

Michael leaned back, exchanging a glance with his advisors.

"Alright. So we're talking exposure, not wrongdoing. We're trying to understand exposure. How much do you believe is owed?"

She made one final note to herself: 'This is not civil litigation logic. This is settlement terrain. Liability, enforceability, proportionality, three different battles.'

2.5 WHO EXERCISES ECONOMIC POWER OVER THE SUPPLY?

As the meeting progressed, the focus moved away from contracts and invoices to something less tangible. The mechanics of control. Not control in the corporate sense, but in the operational sense. How decisions were made, how tasks were completed, and who was responsible in practice.

Michael and his advisors emphasized centralization. Project planning, timelines, quality standards, and escalation protocols all originated in the United States. Oversight was continuous, documented, and contractually reinforced. From their perspective, the Polish subsidiary was an extension. Executing instructions, not exercising judgment.

Marta acknowledged the coherence of that model. It reflected how multinational groups often organized risk and accountability. Yet VAT law, she knew, did not ask where oversight resided in theory. It asked how control manifested at the point of performance.

She reframed the issue internally, not as a contradiction but as a tension:

- The parent set parameters, approved milestones, and bore contractual liability.
- The subsidiary employed the personnel, maintained the local infrastructure, and absorbed immediate operational friction.
- Jakub executed the installation, resolved technical issues on site, interacted with the customer, and managed day-to-day contingencies.

This was not a question of independence in the corporate sense. It was about proximity to action. Remote supervision shaped outcomes, but it couldn't replace the need for decisions made on the spot, in the factory. This practical judgment, however limited, had a big impact.

From the advisors' standpoint, this distinction felt artificial. Under U.S. accounting and legal principles, responsibility followed control, and control followed contractual allocation. Marta understood that logic. But under EU VAT principles, the analysis followed a different approach.

Autonomy was not measured by who approved budgets or signed contracts, but by who commanded resources at the moment the service was rendered.

The room became quieter as the implications became clearer. The discussion was no longer about whether Nano Source had acted improperly. It was about whether the structure they had chosen produced VAT consequences they had not fully anticipated.

When the conversation turned to resolution, the tone shifted. The idea of a pragmatic settlement surfaced, not as an admission, but as a way to contain uncertainty. Marta outlined the contours carefully. Import VAT already paid would stand. The installation element required separate consideration. Penalties and interest were governed by statutory rules, but proportionality mattered.

Privately, she noted the familiar pattern. Anglo-Saxon negotiation instincts meeting a civil-law framework that tolerated settlement only up to a point.

Later, as she drafted her internal summary, the case began to change shape. The amounts involved were substantial, and the questions extended beyond this transaction alone. Issues of characterization, attribution, and deduction were present in different areas.

At that moment, the possibility of an easy resolution seemed unlikely. What had begun as a technical review was now framed as a matter of principle. And once seen that way, the issue moved away from an easy conclusion to an assessment made with possible litigation in mind.

When Michael left the Polish tax office after the heated two-hour meeting, he believed, perhaps naively, that the most difficult part of the audit had already taken place. He had made what he considered a fair offer: "Tell us how much you want us to pay? We want to settle and move on." It was the American way of resolving regulatory friction, the logic of closing files and limiting exposure.

But Polish tax procedure did not work that way. A settlement was not a handshake or a negotiation. It was the outcome of a formal process, framed by the Tax Ordinance and the VAT Act. The inspectors did not have the discretionary mandate to simply "name a number." Even if they had been inclined to find a pragmatic middle ground, their jurisdiction was constrained by statutory obligations. To correct the past, determine the tax, and protect the integrity of the system.

So, while Michael and his advisors spent the next weeks waiting for what they imagined would be a settlement proposal, Marta was doing what the law required. She was drafting a formal tax assessment. Not an accusation, and not a punishment, simply the legal reconstruction of what the supplies were, as the Polish VAT Act understands economic reality.

Her analysis forced her deeper into the facts than even the meeting had revealed. The more she examined the commercial documents, the installation protocols, the intercompany instructions, the more the picture sharpened. The Polish subsidiary was more than a mere auxiliary support unit. It was deeply embedded in the performance of the installation. Meanwhile, the US parent company had structured the contract in a way that left the Polish Fab paying import VAT on equipment it arguably did not yet own, pending acceptance. These were not small details. They were the main questions that would decide if the right to deduct was possible at all.

Eight weeks after the meeting, Michael was surprised to find the tax assessment on his desk.

The wording was clinical, but the implications were extraordinary:

- VAT due on installation services performed in Poland;
- late-payment interest;
- potential VAT registration obligation for the US parent;
- questions regarding the SilPol Fab's deduction of import VAT;
- and an implicit warning that the chain of supplies might not align with economic reality.

To Michael, this felt like an escalation. To Marta, it was simply procedure.

The assessment opened the door to the next phase. The taxpayer's objections, the authority's response, and, if no understanding was reached, the possibility of litigation.

In accordance with the Tax Ordinance, Nano Source Corp. lodged a formal objection to the tax assessment within the statutory time limit. The objection did not dispute the amounts involved. They questioned the legal basis. The timing of the supply, the identification of the taxable person, and the interaction between import VAT and domestic VAT under the Directive.

Both sides soon realized their disagreement was not just about facts. It was also about deeper issues and ideas. This audit touched the heart of EU VAT's most subtle doctrines. These include abuse, fixed establishment, neutrality, and economic reality.

The case was no longer a misunderstanding.

It was to become a legal conflict.

TAX ASSESSMENT DECISION

(Decyzja określająca zobowiązanie podatkowe – nieostateczna)

Issuing authority:
Head of the Mazovian Tax Office
(Naczelnik Mazowieckiego Urzędu Skarbowego)

Date: 14 November 2025

Case reference: KAS/US/MZ/443-217/2025

I. Legal Basis

Pursuant to:

- Article 21 §1 point 1, Articles 122, 187 §1, 191, 193 and 210 §1 of the Act of 29 August 1997, Tax Ordinance (Ordynacja podatkowa),
- Articles 5(1), 7(1), 19a, 22(1)(2), 29a, 86, 88, 96 and 106b of the Act of 11 March 2004 on Goods and Services Tax (Ustawa o podatku od towarów i usług),
- Articles 14 and 36 of Council Directive 2006/112/EC of 28 November 2006 on the common system of value added tax,
- Relevant case law of the Court of Justice of the European Union,

the Head of the Mazovian Tax Office, after conducting tax proceedings, hereby determines the VAT consequences of the transaction described below.

II. Parties

1. Nano Source Corp., a company incorporated under the laws of the United States of America, registered office: California, USA.
2. SilPol Fab sp. z o.o., VAT-registered entity established in Poland.

3. Nano Source Poland sp. z o.o., Polish subsidiary of Nano Source Corp.

III. Subject of the Decision

This decision concerns the VAT consequences of a transaction executed in 2025 involving the supply of semiconductor manufacturing equipment together with installation, assembly, testing, and commissioning services, documented by a single invoice issued by Nano Source Corp. in the amount of:

- USD 32,000,000
  (approximately EUR 28,000,000 / PLN 125,000,000).

IV. Findings of Fact

Based on the evidence collected in the proceedings, including contracts, invoices, customs documentation, installation protocols, intercompany agreements, and witness statements, the authority establishes that:

1. The equipment was transported from outside the European Union and physically delivered to the premises of SilPol Fab sp. z o.o. in Poland.
2. SilPol Fab sp. z o.o. acted as importer of record, and import VAT was paid at the time of customs clearance.
3. Installation, assembly, testing, and commissioning of the equipment were performed in Poland, at the customer's premises.
4. The installation activities were carried out by personnel employed by Nano Source Poland sp. z o.o., a subsidiary of Nano Source Corp. The activities were directed and supervised centrally by Nano Source Corp., and economically integrated into the supply invoiced by Nano Source Corp.

5. The installation constituted an essential element of the supply and was necessary for the equipment to perform its intended function.
6. Nano Source Corp. issued a single bundled invoice covering both the equipment and installation services, without a reverse-charge notation.
7. Nano Source Corp. was not registered for VAT in Poland at the time of the transaction and did not charge Polish VAT..
8. The Polish purchaser did not declare VAT under the reverse-charge mechanism in respect of the installation services.

V. Legal Assessment

1. Characterization of the Supply

Pursuant to Article 7(1) of the VAT Act and Article 14 of Directive 2006/112/EC, a supply of goods occurs where the right to dispose of tangible property as owner is transferred.

The authority finds that the delivery of the equipment and the installation, assembly, testing and commissioning activities form a single composite supply for VAT purposes.

The installation activities were not ancillary or optional. From the perspective of the purchaser, the economic objective of the transaction was to acquire fully operational equipment, not merely the physical delivery of machinery. The supply would have been incomplete and devoid of economic value without installation.

In accordance with the established jurisprudence of the Court of Justice of the European Union, supplies which are economically indivisible and whose elements are inseparable must be treated as a single supply for VAT purposes.

Artificial separation of the transaction into a supply of goods and a supply of services is therefore inadmissible. This applies irrespective of whether individual elements of the supply could, in isolation, be classified as services for VAT purposes.

2. Place of Supply

Pursuant to Article 36 of Directive 2006/112/EC, implemented in Poland under Article 22(1)(2) of the VAT Act, the place of supply of goods which are installed or assembled by or on behalf of the supplier is the place where the installation or assembly takes place. For these purposes, installation carried out by personnel of a subsidiary acting under the supplier's direction constitutes installation 'on behalf of the supplier' within the meaning of Article 36 of the Directive.

As the installation and commissioning of the equipment took place in Poland, the place of supply of the entire composite transaction is Poland.

The fact that the goods were imported from outside the European Union does not alter this conclusion.

3. Taxable Person and Chargeability

Nano Source Corp., as the supplier of the composite supply of goods with installation, acted as the taxable person within the meaning of Article 15 of the VAT Act.

In the present case, installation and commissioning coincided with the moment at which the purchaser obtained the right to dispose of the equipment as owner in economic terms.

The description of the transaction in the commercial invoice and customs documentation does not determine its VAT treatment, which must be assessed on the basis of economic reality.

4. VAT Registration Obligation

By carrying out a taxable supply located in Poland, Nano Source Corp. was obliged to register for VAT in Poland in accordance with Article 96 of the VAT

Act, charge Polish VAT on the transaction, and submit VAT returns.

Nano Source Corp. failed to fulfil these obligations.

5. Import VAT

The import VAT paid by SilPol Fab sp. z o.o. constitutes a tax due under customs regulations as a consequence of the importation of goods.

Import VAT is legally distinct from VAT due on a domestic taxable supply. Payment of import VAT does not eliminate or substitute the obligation to account for VAT due on a supply taxable in Poland.

VI. Determination of VAT Due

The taxable base of the supply, pursuant to Article 29a of the VAT Act, is the full contractual consideration:

- PLN 125,000,000 (approximately EUR 28,000,000)

VAT due at the rate of 23% amounts to:

- PLN 28,750,000 (approximately EUR 6,440,000)

VII. Interest on Tax Arrears

Pursuant to Article 56 §1 of the Tax Ordinance, statutory interest on tax arrears is due from the day following the date on which the VAT became payable.

Indicative interest calculated as at the date of issuance of this decision amounts to:

PLN 2,400,000 (approximately EUR 540,000)

VIII. Additional Consequences

In light of the findings, the authority notes that:

- The incorrect VAT settlement exposed SilPol Fab sp. z o.o. to cash-flow costs and legal uncertainty regarding import VAT deduction.
- The manner of transaction structuring and invoicing may constitute an infringement of fiscal obligations subject to separate penal-fiscal proceedings.
- The reputational and operational risks arising from the irregularities may have affected the customer's tax position and compliance standing.

IX. Determination

The Head of the Mazovian Tax Office hereby determines that:

1. Nano Source Corp. carried out a taxable supply of goods with installation in Poland.
2. The place of supply was Poland pursuant to Article 22(1)(2) of the VAT Act.
3. Nano Source Corp. was obliged to register for VAT in Poland and charge Polish VAT.
4. VAT in the amount of PLN 28,750,000 (approx. EUR 6,440,000) is due, together with statutory interest.

X. Instruction

Pursuant to Article 200 §1 of the Tax Ordinance, the parties are entitled to submit objections and evidence within 14 days from the date of service of this decision.

Issued by:
Marta Bogacka
VAT Inspector
Mazovian Voivodeship Tax Office
National Revenue Administration

Michael's reaction to the assessment was immediate but measured. The amount assessed against Nano Source, while unwelcome, was not in itself destabilizing. Interest and penalties were manageable. The company could absorb them without material financial difficulty. What concerned him and his advisors, far more, was what the assessment implied rather than what it demanded.

Within days, the issue moved beyond Warsaw. Calls were arranged with VAT specialists in Amsterdam, Düsseldorf, and Brussels. The tax assessment was read not as a local enforcement act, but as a legal thesis. A reconstruction of the transaction that, if correct, reverberated far beyond Poland.

The more closely it was analyzed, the clearer it became that the Polish authority's position was internally consistent, carefully reasoned, and grounded in existing case law. And yet, it rested on fault lines that EU VAT law has never fully resolved.

At its core, the dispute was no longer about compliance. It was about classification.

Was there, in legal terms, a taxable supply of goods at the moment the equipment crossed the Polish border, even though ownership and the right to dispose as owner were contractually suspended until formal acceptance? Could physical delivery and installation suffice to trigger a supply under Article 14 of the VAT Directive, or did contractual acceptance remain decisive for the very existence of the taxable event?

If acceptance marked completion of the supply, could VAT nevertheless be treated as chargeable earlier, under national rules, without violating Articles 63 and 66 of the Directive? Or would such an approach collapse the distinction, so carefully drawn by the Court, between the existence of a supply and its chargeability?

The tax assessment also exposed a deeper structural mismatch. Import VAT had been paid, lawfully, definitively, and in full at a point in time when, under the same assessment, no domestic taxable supply of goods had yet occurred.

This raised a question that went well beyond Nano Source. Whether VAT paid at import could be regarded as "due or paid" within the meaning of Articles 167 and 168 if, in substance and law, the downstream supply had not yet come into existence.

That question was not academic. It went directly to SilPol Fab's right to deduct. The assessment did not formally deny the deduction, but it cast a long shadow over it. If import VAT was paid before any taxable supply existed, and if the supplier was neither established nor registered in Poland, on what legal basis did the customer's right to deduct truly rest?

Here, the dispute ceased to be bilateral. The reputational and operational risk shifted decisively toward the Polish customer. SilPol Fab had acted in good faith, followed the customs process presented to it, and borne VAT economically. Yet the assessment suggested implicitly but unmistakably that the integrity of the deduction depended on a chain of supplies whose legal alignment was now in doubt.

The role of the Polish subsidiary sharpened the problem further. Installation was not incidental. It was essential, inseparable from the functionality of the equipment, and performed by employees under the subsidiary's control. The authority did not assert the existence of a fixed establishment outright, but its reasoning moved deliberately along that edge. The message was subtle but clear. Corporate form and contractual allocation could not, by themselves, neutralize functional reality.

What troubled Michael's advisors most was not that the Polish authority had reached a conclusion but that, in reaching it, Marta had touched questions that EU law still answers only in fragments. Neutrality versus enforceability. Paid VAT versus legally chargeable VAT. Contractual ownership versus economic disposal. Import VAT as a distinct taxable event versus a precursor to domestic supply.

The procedural path that followed was orthodox, almost mechanical. Nano

Source lodged a formal objection to the tax assessment, not in pursuit of financial relief, but to challenge the legal premises on which the reconstruction rested. The objection worked its way through the administrative hierarchy, narrowing with each iteration. Peripheral issues fell away. What remained were questions of principle.

By the time the case reached the Voivodeship Administrative Court, it was evident that existing jurisprudence provided guidance, but not closure. Each pointed in a direction, but none resolved the constellation as a whole.

The judges recognized the pattern immediately. This was not a disagreement about facts. It was a disagreement about how the VAT system holds together when importation, suspended ownership, non-EU suppliers, and local installation intersect.

Invoking Article 267 TFEU, the court paused the case and referred a set of questions to the Court of Justice. They were technical in form, restrained in number but profound in consequence. They asked, in essence, whether EU VAT law permits a system in which VAT may be paid without a supply, deducted without chargeability, and enforced against one party because another lies beyond reach.

When the order for reference was transmitted to Luxembourg, the character of the case changed irrevocably. It was no longer about Nano Source's assessment, nor about Poland's audit practice. It became part of the slow constitutional dialogue of the VAT system itself.

A dispute that began with an installation schedule and a bundled invoice had reached the place where European tax law confronts its own unresolved architecture. Not through confrontation, but through interpretation.

And there, without personal biases, commercial impatience, and administrative pragmatism, it would be decided not by what seemed fair or reasonable, but by what the law could ultimately support.

PART III: THE HUMAN MAP OF THE SINGLE MARKET

How people live within systems designed for abstraction

3.1 HOW TAX AUDITS RECONSTRUCT TRANSACTIONS

The meeting did not end with a handshake. It ended with something far more ambiguous. A silence that was both promising and threatening. Michael's final words were 'Tell us the number. We want to settle this and move on'. But it was an offer the legal universe was unwilling to accept.

Marta knew immediately that the case could not be closed. Not with a number. Not with an apology. Not with an Anglo-Saxon instinct for commercial pragmatism. Polish VAT law did not negotiate with the same fluidity as Californian contracts.

It marched along statutory pathways carved by directives, regulations, and judgments from Luxembourg.

The system did not bend to the intentions of the parties. It bent only to its own internal logic.

But that was not the only reason she couldn't give him a number.

Something in the case did not fit, and the more she examined the file over the following days, the more the pieces resisted alignment. The customs value included charges that clearly should not have been there. The installation services had been performed in Poland but invoiced as if they had occurred in California. The Polish Fab had deducted import VAT despite not yet being the economic owner of the equipment at the moment of release. And the US parent, operating through its Polish subsidiary, might or might not have had a fixed establishment, depending on how one weighed the contradictory views of *Dong Yang*, *Berlin Chemie*, and *Titanium*.

In domestic terms, the situation was messy. In EU terms, it was a clash of ideas.

Under the framework of Directive 2006/112/EC, VAT is not classified as a transactional tax in the conventional sense. It is neither imposed by a governmental mandate nor is it a result of the taxpayer's consent. It arises automatically and impersonally when legally defined conditions are met. The taxable event, chargeability, taxable base, and liable person are all determined by law. Neither the taxpayer's willingness to pay nor the authority's appetite for pragmatism can alter that sequence.

This characteristic is often misunderstood by those accustomed to systems in which tax assessments function as starting points for negotiation. In EU VAT, the assessment is the end of a process of legal qualification, not the opening bid. Marta reflected that Michael's offer implicitly assumed that the authority possessed something it did not. The power to trade certainty for expediency. But VAT law does not belong to the authority. It belongs to the system. The inspector is not a party to a dispute in the contractual sense; she is an organ tasked with identifying and declaring legal reality as defined by statute and interpreted by the Court of Justice.

Once facts are established, the law applies. There is no margin for compromise.

This structural rigidity is reinforced rather than softened by the Polish administrative tradition. Article 120 of the Polish Tax Ordinance codifies the principle of legality. Tax authorities act on the basis of and within the limits of the law. This is not an abstract maxim. It is an operational constraint.

An inspector who knowingly deviates from the correct legal outcome, even in the name of pragmatism, violates the constitutional principle of legality. The legality principle is not balanced against efficiency or commercial reasonableness. It overrides them.

Marta knew that even if she were personally convinced that a negotiated payment would "solve" the issue, such a solution would be legally void. Any settlement not grounded in correct legal classification would be vulnerable to being cancelled by supervisory authorities, by administrative courts, or by the Supreme Audit Office. Worse, it would undermine uniformity, the very value VAT is designed to protect.

In civil-law systems, and particularly in Polish tax law, discretion exists only where the statute explicitly grants it. VAT grants none in matters of classification.

There is absence of a true "settlement" mechanism in VAT. There are procedural instruments that resemble settlement, voluntary corrections, reduced penalties, waiver of interest in limited circumstances, but these operate after the taxable position has been correctly determined. They are relief mechanisms, not substitutes for getting the law applied first.

Michael's request skipped the essential step. He sought a number before the transaction had been legally defined.

The Existence of a Taxable Supply

Under Article 2(1)(a) of the VAT Directive, VAT applies to supplies of goods effected for consideration within the territory of a Member State. Article 14(1) defines a supply of goods as the transfer of the right to dispose of tangible property as owner. That definition is autonomous, detached from national civil-law concepts, and deliberately functional. The Court established this early, most famously in *Safe* (C-320/88), where it held that VAT looks not to formal title but to economic control.

But *Safe* also imposed a discipline. Functional does not mean presumptive. Physical delivery is relevant, but not conclusive. The right to dispose as owner requires that the recipient obtain, in economic terms, the power to use the goods as if they were their own.

In Nano Source's case, the equipment was physically delivered to Poland and installed at the Fab's premises. On that fact alone, one might be tempted to infer that a supply of goods had occurred. Yet the contract complicated that conclusion. Ownership and more importantly, the right to dispose, was contractually suspended until formal acceptance following installation and commissioning. Until that moment, the Fab could neither deploy the equipment commercially nor assume the risks associated with ownership.

This distinction mattered. The Court had repeatedly warned against collapsing physical presence into legal completion. In *Kollroß and Wirtl* (C-660/16 and C-661/16), the Court rejected the notion that VAT consequences could arise where contractual mechanisms prevented the customer from acquiring the power to dispose of the goods as owner.

When delivery ultimately does not occur, the question is whether the purchasers are entitled to retain the right to deduct VAT already paid. The Court held that the right to deduct cannot be maintained if the underlying supply ultimately fails to materialize, but the purchaser should not bear the economic burden of VAT.

The taxable event required more than presence; it required completion in an economic sense.

Marta wrote in her notebook: 'Physical delivery evidences potential.
Acceptance confers disposal.'

This was not just a small difference in meaning. It determined whether a supply of goods existed at all, and if not, whether import VAT could be connected to a downstream taxable transaction.

If the existence of a supply was uncertain, its timing was even more so.

Article 63 of the Directive provides that VAT becomes chargeable when the supply is completed. Article 66 allows Member States limited flexibility, but they must not separate chargeability from completion where completion is contractually defined.

The Court addressed this tension directly in *Budimex* (C-224/18). There, it accepted that where a contract makes formal acceptance the constitutive act of completion, VAT cannot be treated as chargeable before that acceptance occurs. *Budimex* concerned construction services, but the reasoning extended beyond services alone. The Court recognized that contractual structures can legitimately define when a supply is completed, provided they reflect commercial reality.

In Nano Source's case, acceptance was not decorative. It was operational. The equipment could not be used, resold, or integrated into production until installation and testing were completed. Acceptance marked not only contractual completion, but economic readiness.

If that was so, Marta asked herself, how could VAT be chargeable earlier, whether at import or upon installation?

This question forced her to distinguish between two events that were often mixed up in practice. Importation and domestic supply.

Article 2(1)(d) treats importation as a distinct taxable event. Articles 30 and 70 tie import VAT to the moment goods cross into the customs territory of the Union. That event is independent of any subsequent domestic supply.

This independence was not academic. It meant that VAT paid when importing goods could not automatically be considered as VAT paid for a later sale. The two taxes have different purposes, happen at different times, and apply to different events.

In Nano Source's transaction, the import value declared included charges relating to installation services to be performed after importation. That inclusion had inflated the import VAT base. The Fab had paid that VAT and deducted it.

From a revenue perspective, the State had been paid. From a legal perspective, however, the payment raised a deeper problem. Could VAT paid at import give rise to a right of deduction if no taxable supply yet existed under Article 14?

Marta returned to the Court's insistence that deduction is conditional, not automatic. Import VAT and domestic VAT are similar but not substitutable.

Articles 167 and 168 of the Directive establish the right to deduct, but only where VAT is due or paid in respect of a taxable supply. The Court has consistently distinguished between VAT that is merely paid and VAT that is legally chargeable.

In *VSTR* (C-587/10), the Court reaffirmed that VAT rights depend on the objective existence of a taxable transaction, a principle developed in its case law on deduction, according to which the right to deduct presupposes that the underlying transaction is subject to VAT. In *Senatex* (C-518/14), it allowed correction of formal invoicing defects but only where the substantive conditions for deduction were satisfied. Formalism could be cured; the absence of a taxable supply could not.

Marta underlined a passage from *Senatex* in her notebook: '...the fundamental principle of the neutrality of VAT requires deduction of input VAT to be allowed if the substantive requirements are satisfied, even if the taxable persons have failed to comply with some formal conditions.'

Formal requirements cannot override economic reality.

Here, the Fab had deducted import VAT at a time when, under the contract and arguably under Article 14, no domestic supply of goods had yet occurred. Ownership was suspended. Economic disposal was absent. The equipment was not yet used for taxable outputs.

Was the VAT "due or paid" in respect of a taxable supply? Or was it paid prematurely, detached from any completed transaction?

This was a question that Polish law could not answer alone. It was systemic.

Layered onto this already complex structure was the issue of installation service and territoriality.

The installation services were physically performed in Poland by an engineer employed by the Polish subsidiary. Even if considered separately, services consisting of the physical installation of equipment are supplied where the activities are actually carried out, under the specific place-of-supply rules. On any analysis, the place of supply for the installation was Poland.

The U.S. parent's attempt to contractually assume responsibility for installation did not change that. VAT law attributes services to performance, not to billing strategy. The subsidiary invoiced the parent, but that intercompany allocation did not relocate the service.

This created a further mismatch. Domestic VAT was due on installation services performed in Poland, regardless of how they were invoiced. Import VAT did not discharge that obligation.

Marta wrote: 'One transaction, two taxes, neither interchangeable'

At this point, Marta confronted a question she had initially tried to avoid. Intent.

She did not reach for abuse lightly. The *Halifax* doctrine is not a blunt instrument. It requires two cumulative elements. A transaction resulting in a tax advantage contrary to the purpose of the Directive, and an essential aim of obtaining that advantage.

Here, the structure had not eliminated VAT altogether. Import VAT had been paid. Yet the structure had displaced domestic VAT, distorted timing, and transferred enforcement risk onto the Polish customer.

Was that sufficient to suggest abuse?

Marta was cautious. She noted that centralized invoicing, deferred acceptance, and contractual allocation of risk are common and often legitimate. Optimization is not abuse. But *Halifax* warned that compliance with formal requirements cannot justify outcomes that defeat the purpose of the VAT system.

The question, then, was not whether Nano Source intended to evade tax, but whether the structure produced effects the VAT system could not accept. Particularly where enforcement against a non-established supplier was impracticable.

Each of these legal questions can only be answered with a yes or no. There is no middle ground. If a number had been negotiated, it would have hidden unresolved issues and made things seem certain when they were not. This is exactly what VAT law aims to avoid. The main reason a settlement could not be reached was outside of Poland.

VAT is harmonized not merely in rate structures, but in logic. The Court of Justice has consistently emphasized the necessity of uniform application to prevent competitive distortions and the fragmentation of the internal market. This is why autonomous EU concepts such as "supply of goods," "economic ownership," and "right to deduct" override national civil-law classifications.

If Marta were to accept a negotiated outcome that implicitly tolerated:

- import VAT standing in for domestic VAT,
- deferred acceptance being ignored for chargeability purposes,
- or deduction being allowed without a completed supply,

She would create a significant disruption within the system.

Every similarly structured transaction would point to this case as precedent. Uniformity would not change through legislation, but through administrative tolerance.

VAT neutrality is not achieved by making sure "some tax" is paid. It is achieved by ensuring that the correct tax is paid, by the correct person, at the correct time, with the correct consequences. Any deviation from this approach compromises principle for convenience, thereby undermining neutrality.

Michael and his advisors emphasized good faith. The structure was disclosed. Import VAT was paid. There was no concealment. No artificial invoices. No missing revenue.

All true. All irrelevant to the core problem. But the intent and good faith could not save the case.

VAT liability is not based on moral blame. It is based on factual conditions. The Court has explicitly stated that even genuine errors do not establish rights when substantive conditions are not satisfied. Conversely, even aggressive planning may be tolerated where it respects the law's purpose.

Marta wrote: 'Good faith explains behavior. It does not redefine transactions.'

This was not a case of fraud. But it might be a case of misalignment so deep that correction could not occur without judicial guidance.

One of the most troubling parts of the case was the right to deduct import VAT. This made settling the case very risky.

Deduction serves as the cornerstone of VAT neutrality, but it is subject to certain conditions. It assumes that VAT has been accurately applied to a taxable transaction. When this assumption fails, the deduction is at risk. And this is not as a form of punishment, but just a natural consequence.

If acceptance defined the completion of the supply, and if acceptance had not yet occurred at import, then SilPol Fab's deduction rested on a legal fiction. To allow that fiction to persist just because it's easier would weaken the whole deduction system itself.

Marta knew what was at risk. If the deduction were to be maintained solely on the basis of VAT neutrality, the distinction between chargeable and non-chargeable VAT would become meaningless.

At this point, Marta articulated, first to herself, later in writing, the full reason the settlement was not merely impractical, but impossible.

EU VAT law is not remedial. It is constitutive.

It does not correct outcomes *ex post* based on fairness. It constitutes taxable reality *ex ante* based on defined conditions. Where those conditions are unclear, the system does not permit improvisation. It demands interpretation.

In common-law jurisdictions, disputes are frequently resolved through negotiated compromise, largely due to the legal system's acceptance of ambiguity. In contrast, places with civil-law systems see unclear rules as mistakes that need fixing. And in EU VAT, ambiguity is a threat to harmonization.

A settlement would have required the authority to:

- tolerate unresolved contradictions,
- accept a hybrid legal characterization,
- and prioritize closure over correctness.

The system does not allow that trade.

Marta also recognized something more subtle.

The settlement would have turned compliance into something negotiable for the powerful, but mandatory for everyone else. Nano Source had advisors, resources, and leverage. Smaller taxpayers would not. VAT law cannot operate on such asymmetry. Uniformity demands that like cases be treated alike, regardless of negotiating strength.

Thus, paradoxically, refusing settlement was not an act of rigidity. It was an act of equality.

Once Marta understood this, everything else happened naturally. The inevitable dispute had to go to court...

The unresolved questions were not Polish questions. They were European:

- Does deferred acceptance delay the completion of a supply for VAT?
- Can import VAT paid before completion support deduction?
- Can domestic installation be absorbed into an offshore supply by contract?
- How does neutrality operate where enforcement and classification diverge?

These were questions only the Court of Justice could answer authoritatively.

Administrative closure would have been a failure of responsibility. Judicial referral was not an escalation. It was compliance.

Late that evening, Marta closed her notebook and put her pen on top. She switched off her desk lamp. Files slept behind closed cabinets, indifferent witnesses to the day's certainties.

This one, she knew as she reached for her coat, would not close so easily. She felt no triumph. No adversarial satisfaction. Only clarity.

The audit had revealed no wrongdoing, but misalignment.

Not evasion, but friction between systems. Between contractual form and functional tax law, between commercial intuition and legal architecture.

Michael wanted a number. The law wanted an answer.

And until that answer was reached, no number, however reasonable, could end the case.

3.2 APPROVING THE DEAL AND OWNING THE CONSEQUENCES

Michael Torres had always believed that the role of a chief financial officer was to impose order on uncertainty. Not to eliminate risk as no serious leader thought that was possible. Instead, it was to name it, measure it, and place it within a framework that allowed the business to move forward without illusion. For most of his career, accounting standards had been his ally. They were predictable and disciplined. They followed the contract and the economic reality behind it.

VAT law did not.

He had sensed the gap when the first request came from the Polish tax authority. After his meeting with Marta, it was no longer a suspicion but a fact. The spreadsheets on Michael's laptop were organized according to U.S. GAAP, with deferred revenue schedules and performance obligations set out in clean, ordered columns. He understood every line and could defend every assumption, yet for the first time in years, he was not certain that this command of the numbers would protect him.

What troubled him was not the possibility of paying more tax. Nano Source was a large multinational, and after all, the amounts discussed in the audit were not existential. His discomfort stemmed from knowing that the company's core business model, which he had helped develop and defend, was being judged by a legal system that did not follow its logic.

Nano Source did not sell simple products. It manufactured complex equipment for producing semiconductors. Simply buying, shipping, and storing the equipment did not cover everything. Every unit was more of an ecosystem than a product. Hundreds of components, proprietary software, and calibration protocols meant an unavoidable waiting period, during which neither Nano Source nor its customers could be sure the machine would work as expected.

The company handled that uncertainty deliberately and, in Michael's view, honestly. Customers were not asked to take the risk blindly.

Instead, the equipment was shipped to the fab, installed by Nano Source engineers, and operated under controlled conditions for months. Sometimes close to a year. During that time, production was limited, outputs carefully measured, defects analyzed, tolerances refined. Only when the machine demonstrated that it could meet the customer's specifications did formal acceptance occur. Only then did title pass. Only then did Nano Source recognize revenue.

This was not an accounting trick. It was a reflection of reality as Michael understood it. Until acceptance, Nano Source bore the risk. Until acceptance, the customer had no obligation to pay the full purchase price. Until acceptance, the transaction was incomplete. GAAP captured this elegantly. Control had not transferred. Performance obligations remained open. Revenue stayed deferred.

For years, this model had been praised by auditors as conservative, even exemplary. It aligned legal form, commercial substance, and financial reporting. It let Nano Source compete globally without pushing customers into premature commitments. To Michael, it was a rational system in every meaningful way.

And yet, sitting in Warsaw, he saw that the very features that made the model attractive commercially were exactly what caused problems under EU VAT law.

VAT required more than simply determining when a sale was complete. It asked when and where value-creating activity occurred. It did not rely on acceptance or transfer of title. It relied on use, presence, and performance. And in Nano Source's model, those elements appeared long before acceptance ever took place.

The equipment, after all, was physically present in Poland for months. It was connected to the fab's infrastructure. It was powered on, calibrated, and tested. It produced output, even if limited.

Engineers, employees of the Polish subsidiary, worked on it daily, making decisions in real time, adjusting parameters, and interacting with the customer's technical staff.

From the perspective of VAT, something tangible and economically meaningful was happening on Polish territory.

Michael struggled with the implications of that observation. In his world, evaluation was not consumption. Testing was not use in the ordinary sense. Allowing a customer to run limited production to verify performance did not feel like delivering value in the way a completed sale did. It felt provisional, reversible, contingent. The equipment could still be returned. The transaction could still collapse. How, then, could tax law treat this period as a taxable reality?

And yet, the more he examined the logic Marta had outlined, without accusation, the more he saw that VAT law was not making a moral judgment. It was making a structural one. VAT was not interested in whether the transaction was final. It was interested in whether economic activity was taking place, whether resources were being used, whether services were being performed, and whether that activity occurred within its territorial jurisdiction.

The evaluation period, which GAAP treated as a prelude to a sale, VAT treated as a period of real economic interaction. The customer was using the imported equipment, however conditionally. The subsidiary was performing installation and commissioning services, however contractually framed. The territory served as a platform for that activity, even if its results were temporary.

The contrast made Michael uneasy. As CFO, he led the company's unified communications with investors, regulators, auditors, and tax authorities, where consistency was a vital survival mechanism. Yet here he was, facing a legal system that required recognition of a reality his financial statements explicitly denied.

By accepting the Polish authority's position, Nano Source would recognize that installation services in Poland were independently taxable, even though the local subsidiary provided them and then recharged the parent. From an accounting perspective, revenue was recognized upon acceptance, and intercompany services were eliminated on consolidation.

But Michael felt uneasy for another reason. The tax analysis treated the deal in terms of local value creation and operational presence. But the group's financial story emphasized a centralized grip and putting off finishing things. He knew these perspectives could coexist legally. What troubled him was how easily they could be read as competing explanations of the same reality. Analysts rarely traced the subtle differences between tax law and accounting standards, and regulators did not always respect the limits of their authority. And reputational risk, he had learned, often came not from real inconsistency but from the appearance of it.

What worried him more was the impact on the customer. SilPol Fab had paid import VAT on equipment it did not yet own, a detail Michael had dismissed as part of cross-border logistics. Now, after the Polish authority reconstructed the timeline, that detail carried far greater significance. If import VAT was paid before any domestic supply of goods occurred, what exactly did SilPol deduct, and on what basis? If that deduction were challenged, the impact on the customer could be far more damaging than any tax assessment against Nano Source itself.

Michael realized the audit went beyond compliance issues. It dealt with the fairness of the chain of transactions. Unlike corporate income tax, VAT operates across an entire chain of transactions, not within the accounts of one taxpayer. One party's ability to make deductions depended on another's liability to tax. One party's noncompliance could compromise another's position. The system was designed that way to ensure neutrality and self-enforcement. But in complex cross-border models like Nano Source's, that design increased uncertainty instead of reducing it.

As he thought about this, Michael realized the human element mattered more than abstract rules. GAAP was comfortable with distance. Decisions made at headquarters mattered. Risk allocated in contracts mattered. Control exercised through governance structures mattered.

VAT, by contrast, felt oddly local.

It focused on who was present, who dealt with customers, and who made day-to-day decisions.

In that sense, Jakub, the Polish engineer whose installation logs had become central to the audit, mattered more in the VAT analysis than any board resolution or master services agreement, even though he never negotiated contracts. He did not approve invoices. He did not decide when revenue would be recognized. And yet, from VAT perspective, his daily actions determined the taxable reality. He installed the equipment. He tested it. He adjusted it. He bore immediate technical risk. The law saw him as a functional node in the money-making system. If something went wrong, that was on him.

This thought bothered Michael more than he wanted to admit. It made clear that you couldn't just run things from the top office anymore. It suggested that the line between operational decisions and tax risks was thinner than he had thought. Decisions about evaluation length, staffing installations, and the autonomy of local engineers, choices made knowing the customer could still decide not to buy, were no longer just operational. They were legal decisions too.

As the hours passed, Michael's frustration slowly transformed into a more unsettling clarity. This was not simply a compliance problem or a quirk of Polish administration. It struck at the core of Nano Source's operating model. A model was built to handle uncertainty, technological risk, and the commercial realities of selling machines whose performance could not be guaranteed at delivery.

Nano Source did not sell finished products in the traditional sense. It sold potential. Each system it shipped carried years of research, millions in sunk costs, and an unproven relationship with a customer's manufacturing environment. No two fabs were alike. Temperature stability, clean-room standards, and upstream and downstream processes all affected whether the equipment would perform as expected. Expecting customers to accept it unconditionally at delivery would have been commercially absurd. Customers would reject the proposal upfront. Competitors that accepted it would fail.

Nano Source, by contrast, built its business around conditional deployment. It sent the equipment to client sites, installed and tested it on location, and marketed it as a solution to be evaluated, not as a finished product. During the evaluation phase, the customer could do small production runs. This was enough to check yield, consistency, and how well it fit with existing lines. Engineers monitored performance daily. Adjustments were made. Failures were diagnosed. Sometimes the machine passed. Sometimes it did not. In those cases, they had to take the equipment apart, pack it up again, and send it back. A costly process that preserved trust and long-term market credibility.

This model was not an accounting convenience but it was the only way Nano Source could operate in a complex sector. Acceptance wasn't just a formality. Acceptance was the commercial moment when uncertainty became value. Only then did ownership transfer. Only then did revenue crystallize. Only then did the transaction become irreversible.

Under U.S. GAAP, this logic was not merely accommodated but recognized as faithful representation. Performance obligations remained unfulfilled until acceptance. Control did not pass, and revenue remained deferred. The financial statements reflected the business's real operations.

But VAT law looked at the same reality differently.

The Polish audit forced Michael to see that, under EU VAT rules, Nano Source's core operational strengths, its willingness to absorb uncertainty and delay sales, could instead create VAT exposure. Local engineers exercising judgment, equipment running in production-like conditions, and prolonged on-site presence were exactly the factors that determined territorial VAT liability.

If installation and commissioning were taxed separately from the sale, these activities, once seen as mere preparation, began to take on a new role. Installation, testing, and commissioning were no longer merely steps toward a future transfer of ownership. They risked being reclassified as moments of taxable use in their own right.

The issue was not testing the equipment before sale, but that it became hard to tell when preparation ended, and economic use began. Once that boundary blurred, it became hard to tell when equipment was only temporarily on site and when it started operating. It didn't matter whether the machine was eventually sold, sold on acceptance, or returned.

And If that distinction disappeared, it created risk for the business model.

The consequences went beyond a single audit or contract. If VAT became due as soon as equipment started operating at a customer site, Nano Source would have to rethink how long machinery could stay in a Member State without triggering registration or reporting obligations. The company would need to reassess whether local subsidiaries or third parties could continue performing installation services without creating cross-border VAT liabilities. It would also have to decide whether customers could use the equipment for testing, calibration, or integration before ownership formally transferred. EU VAT law treats providing operational access as a taxable supply because it gives customers control similar to ownership, generating VAT liabilities that don't match the timing of the commercial deal.

Even more concerning was the effect on scale. Nano Source operated across Europe, delivering equipment under a variety of commercial arrangements. Some machines were sold and installed right away as part of the transaction. Some machines were sold and installed immediately, others were handled by third-party installers, and some were delivered on short trials with return options. This flexibility was central to how the business operated. Yet if the Polish authorities' reasoning prevailed, VAT would no longer apply at the moment of sale but would instead arise from local activity. Try-and-buy evaluation projects would be treated as taxable steps rather than neutral preparation for a sale. The moment the equipment crossed the border, it was subject to tax liabilities. Installation and commissioning, even when separate from any sale, may cause VAT obligations to fragment across jurisdictions. Sending engineers, keeping them on-site, and configuring machines awaiting acceptance all trigger potential local tax consequences. What had been designed as a scalable and modular business model now turned into a complex set of jurisdiction-specific compliance events to worry about.

What had once been seen as a smart commercial response to technological uncertainty now, under VAT rules, created legal risk.

Michael realized the Polish audit was not just about past compliance. It was testing whether Nano Source could survive the EU VAT rules without major changes. The stakes were strategic. If the company had to trim or rework the model to avoid VAT exposure, it would lose a key competitive advantage. If it took on broader VAT registration obligations, costs and compliance burdens would rise sharply. And if it tried to keep the status quo, it risked disputes cascading with both tax authorities and customers, whose own VAT positions depended on how Nano Source classified sales and transactions.

The problem seemed very hard to solve. It wasn't just about picking between two legal views but choosing between two ideas of how economic value is created. One idea said value appears only when something is accepted. The other idea said value grows slowly, wherever people use things and take action.

Nano Source became successful by handling uncertainty with patience, technology, and contracts. The audit showed that VAT rules were far less accommodating: they required classification, attribution, and taxation immediately, even while the commercial picture remained unclear.

Michael realized that, whatever the outcome of the Polish case, this issue would shadow Nano Source in its future operations. The evaluation-before-sale model was no longer just a business strategy. The case had become a legal issue across Nano Source's European operations, where contemporary VAT rules confronted modern technology and traditional tax principles.

And that, more than the size of the assessment itself, was what made the case impossible to resolve informally.

The dispute was about VAT treatment, whether it applied to installation services or the goods themselves. Paying an assessment would not resolve the underlying legal classification.

It would acknowledge it temporarily. The Polish authority was not seeking money alone. It was asserting a classification of reality. And that classification had consequences that extended beyond the immediate tax assessment.

Michael understood now why Marta had been unable to "give him a number" in the meeting. To do so would have implied that the issue was quantitative. It was not. It was existential. It was about law recognized events and their timing.

Michael closed his laptop. The issue wasn't GAAP versus VAT, or pragmatism versus European formalism. It was deeper. The company worked under different rulebooks, and following each framework's rules was necessary.

Generally accepted accounting principles would still guide Nano Source's financial reporting, and contracts would continue to assign risk, control, and responsibility under Californian law. But those rules would still tie human actions to places. They wouldn't care about business goals or detailed contracts. Evaluation periods, installation and commissioning work, interim storage, on-site testing, and other routine, intentionally modular services would remain points of friction. Not because they were abusive or artificial, but because they demonstrate alternative ways to characterize economic life and the distinctions between systems that describe it in fundamentally different ways.

Michael understood that the path forward would probably require some judicial explanation. He also knew that, whatever the Courts ultimately decided, the lesson would endure. In Europe, value did not wait patiently for ownership to transfer. It announced itself through use, presence, and performance. And the law, steadily but firmly, followed where people acted.

That realization did not resolve the dilemma. But it named it. And for a CFO, naming the problem was the first step toward living with it.

3.3 INSIDE A CROSS-BORDER VAT AUDIT

The conference room was silent.

The light spread evenly across the table, too white to be warm. The air smelled a little like a cleaning fluid and fresh paper. Chairs stood pushed in with bureaucratic precision, as if no one wished to admit they would soon be occupied. Along the wall, binders rested in mute formation, their spines identical, their contents sealed from view.

There was nothing overtly intimidating about the room. No symbols of authority, no theatrical weight. And yet it was unmistakably a place where narratives were tested, where facts were slowed down, examined, and fixed into record. A place where foreign companies were received politely, formally, and always on terms not entirely their own.

For a few moments longer, the room remained empty. Then, footsteps came down from the corridor, and the silence was about to end. The assessment was no longer being explained. It was being contested.

Marta arrived first, as she usually did. She laid out her notebook, the tax assessment summary, and a slim folder containing extracts of case law she knew she would not need to quote explicitly. This meeting was not about citations. It was about coherence. Or, more precisely, about the absence of it. It was also about record. About fixing, in a form that could later be reviewed by a court, what was agreed, what was contested, and what could not be reconciled administratively.

When Michael Torres entered with his advisors, the atmosphere shifted perceptibly. There was less defensiveness than in earlier meetings, but also less optimism. The tax assessment had already reframed the discussion. This was no longer about whether Polish VAT law applied in principle. It was about whether the legal system could accommodate the transaction at all without tearing itself apart.

Jakub arrived last, quietly taking a seat slightly apart from the others.

His presence was not symbolic. He had been asked to attend because the authority needed more than documents. It needed testimony that could confirm the facts beyond dispute. Everyone in the room understood that, even if no one said it aloud.

Marta opened the meeting without ceremony.

"We are here today," she said, "to address the observations reflected in the tax assessment and to hear your objections before they are finalized. The scope of this discussion is limited. We are not reopening questions already examined. We are focusing on the supply as it occurred. The delivery of equipment and the installation performed in Poland."

Michael nodded. He had learned, by now, that attempts to broaden the frame only delayed the inevitable.

"Understood," he replied. "We want to make sure the assessment accurately reflects the transaction as structured and executed."

Both Nano Source's objection and the authority's response accepted the factual record. What divided them was whether EU VAT law permitted those facts to be reconstructed in the way the assessment proposed.

"That is precisely the point," Marta said. "The difficulty is that structure and execution do not align neatly."

She let the sentence sit for a moment, then continued.

"The tax assessment proceeds from several findings that are not in dispute. First, the equipment was shipped from the United States to Poland and released for free circulation. Import VAT was paid by SilPol Fab. Second, installation was performed in Poland by personnel employed by Nano Source Polish subsidiary. Third, the U.S. parent invoiced SilPol Fab for a single amount covering both the equipment and the installation. These are facts."

One of the advisors leaned forward slightly.

"We agree with the factual outline."

"What is not resolved," Marta continued, "is how these facts should be characterized for VAT purposes without contradicting either the VAT Directive or settled jurisprudence."

Michael looked quickly at his team. This was something new. Earlier discussions had been about compliance failures. This sounded more like admitting there was a bigger problem.

Marta turned a page in her notebook.

"The assessment identifies VAT due on installation services performed in Poland. That conclusion follows directly from the place-of-supply rules for services and from the uncontested fact that the installation was physically carried out here. On that point, the authority's position is stable."

Michael responded carefully.

"We understand that position. Our concern is how that conclusion interacts with the rest of the transaction. The installation was not a standalone service. It was part of a single supply of equipment."

"Yes," Marta said, "and that is where the difficulty begins."

She did not say "problem" or "contradiction." She said "difficulty," as if naming it precisely might make it manageable.

"The VAT system does not give us the freedom to choose how to describe things," Marta said. "We need to decide if this is a single composite supply or multiple independent supplies. If the equipment and installation form one indivisible transaction, then VAT must treat them as one."

One of the advisors leaned forward.

"But installation does not cease to be ancillary merely because it is performed locally, or even by a subsidiary. The Court has been clear on that."

Marta nodded. "Correct. The fact that the installation was carried out by the Polish subsidiary does not, by itself, justify splitting the supply. What matters is whether those activities were performed on behalf of the supplier and formed an essential element of what the customer purchased."

She paused, then added carefully:

"That does not mean the installation disappears for VAT purposes. Between the subsidiary and the parent, it remains a taxable service."

Michael looked up. "But that service isn't taxed in Poland."

"Not automatically," Marta replied. "Under Article 44, it is taxable where the parent is established unless the parent is regarded as having a fixed establishment here capable of receiving those services."

She let that settle.

"And that," she said, "is why this case matters. Because the moment you say the subsidiary's resources belong to the parent for one purpose, you invite the question whether they belong to it for all of them."

No one spoke.

The difficulty was no longer whether VAT applied somewhere.

It was whether the law could draw the line once and stop there. If the parent can be treated as present in Poland for the purpose of delivering and installing the machine, then it may also be present for the purpose of receiving the services that made that delivery possible. Presence, once acknowledged, is difficult to contain.

Michael frowned. "The subsidiary acted on our instructions. Economically, we bore the risk."

Marta nodded. "That argument has been considered. The assessment does not deny that the parent bore contractual risk.

What it questions is whether contractual allocation alone is sufficient to override the functional reality of performance for VAT purposes."

She turned slightly toward Jakub.

"Mr. Kowalczyk," she said, "during the installation, who decided how technical issues were resolved on site?"

Jakub hesitated, then answered honestly.

"I did, within the technical parameters. I reported back, but decisions couldn't wait."

"And if installation had failed?"

"The subsidiary would have had to fix it. Practically, yes."

The answer was noted without comment. It did not need emphasis. Its value was in being ordinary.

Marta thanked him and turned back to Michael.

"This is not about second-guessing your internal arrangements," she said. "It is about identifying where the taxable activity took place. The VAT system is territorial. It attaches to acts, not intentions."

One of the advisors shifted in his chair.

"But the assessment goes further. It raises questions about the deduction of import VAT by SilPol Fab. That seems inconsistent with the finding that the goods were delivered to them."

Marta's expression tightened slightly. This was the most delicate point.

"The assessment does not deny that import VAT was correctly paid at the border," she said. "What it questions is whether, at that moment, SilPol Fab had acquired economic ownership of the equipment sufficient to justify deduction."

Michael reacted immediately.

"They had possession. They bore storage risk. They used the equipment."

"Yes," Marta replied. "But ownership for VAT purposes is not possession alone. It is the right to dispose of the goods as owner. The contract provided that acceptance and therefore transfer of ownership occurred only after installation and commissioning."

"That is standard in our industry," Michael said.

"I am aware," Marta replied. "The VAT consequences, however, are not standardized."

She paused, choosing her words carefully.

"If SilPol Fab did not yet have the right to dispose of the goods at the time of import, then the import VAT deduction is legally fragile. That does not mean it must be denied. It means its validity depends on how the supply is characterized as a whole."

The room was silent. This was no longer about a missed VAT registration or a misapplied rate. This was about mutually exclusive outcomes.

One advisor broke the silence.

"If the parent had registered for VAT in Poland, would that have resolved this?"

Marta did not answer immediately.

"Registration," she said finally, "was already required."

She paused, letting that land.

"Under Article 36, the supply of goods with installation is located where the installation takes place. That is Poland. On that basis alone, the U.S. parent was obliged to register and account for Polish VAT, regardless of whether it had a fixed establishment here."

Michael frowned slightly.

"Then what does the fixed establishment change?"

"Everything else," Marta replied.

She folded her hands.

"Registration answers the question of where VAT is due. Fixed establishment answers a different question. Through whom the supply is performed, and where the parent is functionally present for VAT purposes."

Michael leaned forward.

"You're saying registration wouldn't have closed the file."

"No," Marta said. "It would have opened a different one."

She continued carefully.

"If we stop at Article 36, we have a non-EU supplier obliged to register and charge Polish VAT on a supply located in Poland. That is uncomfortable, but administratively manageable. But once we examine how the installation was actually carried out, through a subsidiary whose personnel, infrastructure, and decision-making were essential to performance, the question inevitably arises whether those resources were merely assisting the parent, or whether they were, for VAT purposes, the parent's presence in Poland."

Michael understood immediately.

"Fixed establishment."

"Yes," Marta said. "And this is where the authority's difficulty becomes acute."

She looked around the table.

"If the subsidiary is treated as a fixed establishment, then the transaction is no longer just a foreign supplier registering late. The parent is treated as established in Poland for VAT purposes. That affects not only registration, but the internal consistency of the entire transaction. The import, the invoicing, the right to deduct, and who is regarded as performing and receiving services within the territory."

Michael exhaled slowly. "Berlin Chemie."

"And Dong Yang. And Titanium," Marta said. "Each warns us how carefully that step must be taken. None tells us how to avoid the consequences once it is."

For the first time, it was clear that the authority was not trying to resolve the tension.

It was mapping the fault line.

She looked around the table. "We are being pushed into a contradiction," Marta said. The assessment treats the transaction as a single supply of goods with installation, taxable in Poland in its entirety. Yet the system still has to explain how that liability is to be enforced, and how neutrality is preserved, when the supplier is not established here and the import VAT was paid before the supply legally came into existence. If we say there is no fixed establishment, then Nano Source remains a non-established supplier that was nevertheless obliged to register and charge Polish VAT on the full supply. That conclusion is legally coherent, but it leaves the import VAT paid by SilPol suspended in time, deducted before ownership passed."

She paused.

"If we say there is a fixed establishment, the chain realigns but only by treating the subsidiary's resources as those of the parent in a way recent case law approaches with great caution. Either way, the law forces consequences that do not sit comfortably together."

Michael sat back, the weight of it settling in.

"So what you're saying," he said slowly, "is that the assessment cannot fully resolve this because the law itself pulls in opposite directions."

Marta looked at him.

"Yes. And that is precisely why this discussion matters."

She continued, more quietly now.

"The tax authority was obliged to issue an assessment based on its best interpretation of the law. But it is equally obliged not to create systemic inconsistency. Where national authorities face such conflicts, the mechanism provided by the Treaties is judicial clarification."

One of the advisors exhaled.

"You're saying this was always headed to court."

"I'm saying," she replied carefully, "that the objections you've raised go beyond what an administrative authority can decide on its own."

Michael nodded slowly. There was no anger now, only recognition.

"So this meeting," he said, "is not about persuading you to change the assessment."

"It is," Marta answered, "to the extent that the assessment must accurately reflect both the facts and the legal arguments you are advancing."

She paused, then said it more simply.

"When your arguments point to problems the law itself doesn't answer clearly, I can't pretend they don't exist. I also can't fix them here."

She closed her notebook.

"What we do in this room," she said, "is make sure those problems are written down properly. So that if this goes further, no one can say they were ignored or misunderstood."

The room was quiet.

Michael nodded slowly. There was no frustration left in his face, only acceptance.

"So whatever happens next," he said, "it won't be because we didn't speak up."

Marta met his eyes. "No," she said. "It won't."

"The audit room exists for this reason.

Not to decide what the law should be, but to show clearly why it cannot decide alone."

As the meeting drew to a close, there was no sense of victory or defeat. Only the shared understanding that the case could no longer be settled administratively.

The binders were gathered. The room emptied. And in the silence that followed, the contours of a much larger legal question began to take shape. One that no audit room, however meticulous, could answer on its own.

By the end of the meeting, no one expected convergence. The objective was not to agree, but to ensure that disagreement was clear and followed the rules.

With the objection rejected in substance and the assessment upheld at the administrative level, judicial review became unavoidable. The issue was no longer just about one transaction. It was about how VAT law deals with importation, installation, and deferred ownership.

3.4 LEGAL QUALIFICATION

The decision arrived without any fuss. It came, as these things usually do, in a file.

The document was in a grey folder with the regional tax authority's logo. It didn't have any persuasive language or clear moral opinions. It used the precise and formal language of administration, with careful sentences and logical conclusions. However, it acknowledged, without making it explicit, that the authority had done all it could within its own jurisdiction.

Marta read it slowly, though she already knew its substance. She had helped shape it. Meanwhile, in California, Michael was examining the same decision from his own vantage point.

The Administrative Decision

The authority's decision began by fixing the frame. It rejected, explicitly and without hesitation, the notion that the transaction could be understood as a simple import followed by ancillary services. The sale and installation of the equipment were part of a single deal. They were negotiated, priced, and accepted together. This was not disputed.

What mattered was not how the transaction was described in contracts governed by Californian commercial law, nor how revenue was recognized under U.S. GAAP, but the moment at which, under EU VAT law, the purchaser acquired the right to dispose of the goods as owner. The authority concluded that this moment occurred only upon final acceptance of the equipment after installation at the Polish fab.

From that premise followed an uncomfortable implication. At the decisive moment of supply, the goods were already located in Poland. The place of supply of the goods was therefore Poland. In strict legal terms, the transaction had the characteristics of a domestic supply of goods subject to Polish VAT.

The decision did not shy away from stating this. It stated it plainly.

And then, almost immediately, it hesitated.

The supplier, Nano Source U.S., was established outside the European Union. It was not registered for VAT in Poland. It had not charged Polish VAT. No invoice reflecting a domestic supply existed. No mechanism for straightforward enforcement was available. The authority acknowledged, without embellishment, that while VAT law defined the transaction as domestic, the administrative reality rendered full enforcement uncertain.

This tension shaped everything that followed.

While the decision characterized the transaction as a domestic supply of goods with installation, taxable in Poland, it acknowledged the practical limits of enforcing that conclusion against a non-EU supplier that had not registered for VAT. The assessment therefore clarified VAT consequences where attribution and enforceability were clearest, while expressly preserving the broader legal characterization of the supply.

At the same time, it questioned the SilPol Fab's right to deduct import VAT paid at the border. If the economic ownership of the goods had not yet passed at import, the authority reasoned, then the Fab could not be said to have used the goods for its own taxable activities at that moment. The deduction, while not definitively denied, was declared open to reassessment.

The decision did not hesitate. It followed its legal reasoning to its conclusion and imposed Polish VAT on the full value of the transaction. It determined that Nano Source Corp. had carried out a taxable domestic supply of goods with installation in Poland and that Polish VAT was due on the full contractual consideration. Where the document grew cautious was not in defining the tax obligation, but in acknowledging the systemic consequences of that definition. Import VAT had been paid at the border by SilPol Fab, lawfully and in full, yet at a moment when the contractual right to dispose of the equipment as owner had not yet passed. The assessment agreed that the import VAT was due.

However, whether it could be deducted depended on how the domestic supply was defined and enforced. The result was not a compromise on liability, but a recognition that the VAT system, as applied to these facts, produced frictions that administrative enforcement alone could not resolve.

It was, in Marta's private assessment, a legally cautious document, careful not to overreach, careful not to collapse under its own logic. It resolved the immediate audit. It did not resolve the law.

Nano Source objected. The objection did not argue about the facts found in the assessment. Instead, they questioned the legal outcomes based on those facts, saying the authority described something it could not apply consistently.

The National Court

In the administrative court, the dispute was no longer just about numbers. The amounts mattered, of course, but they were no longer the main focus. What mattered was coherence.

Nano Source did not argue that the transaction escaped Polish VAT altogether. That argument had died in the audit room. Nor did it insist that the import VAT deduction must be preserved at all costs. Instead, its objection attacked the internal logic of the authority's position.

If, as the authority maintained, the supply of goods occurred only upon acceptance in Poland, then the supply was domestic. If the supply was domestic, then VAT was chargeable on the full value of the transaction. And if VAT was chargeable, then the system had to face the consequences comprising the registration, assessment, and enforcement against the supplier.

The authority could not, the company argued, accept the legal characterization of a domestic supply while refusing to follow it to its conclusion. Nor could it compensate for enforcement difficulties by fragmenting the transaction, taxing what was convenient, questioning what was already paid, and leaving the core supply legally unresolved.

The court listened carefully. The court did not question the authority's findings of fact, nor its legal classification of the transaction. It accepted that the delivery and installation of the equipment constituted a single composite supply of goods with installation, taxable in Poland, and that Nano Source Corp., as supplier, was in principle liable for Polish VAT on the full consideration. The difficulty lay elsewhere. The assessment simultaneously acknowledged that import VAT had been lawfully paid by the purchaser at a point in time when, under the same assessment, the right to dispose of the goods as owner had not yet arisen. The court observed that EU VAT law is structured as a sequence involving the existence of a taxable supply, the chargeability of tax, and the right of deduction. Each presupposes the other. A tax cannot be deducted before it is legally due, and a tax legally due cannot be rendered irrelevant because enforcement is complex. Faced with an assessment that was internally coherent yet systemically strained, the court concluded that national law did not provide the tools to reconcile these consequences without privileging one structural principle of VAT over another.

The VAT system, as harmonized at EU level, is built on a sequence. Chargeability, liability, deduction. Each presupposes the other. Import VAT is not a substitute for domestic VAT. Deduction is not a discretionary privilege adjusted to administrative convenience. Neutrality is not a policy preference but a structural principle.

Yet neutrality, the court observed, could not be pursued at the expense of legal coherence. If VAT was not legally due, it could not become due simply because it had been paid. If VAT was legally due, it could not be ignored simply because it was difficult to collect.

The court found itself unable to resolve this contradiction using national law alone, because any resolution would have required it to choose between mutually dependent elements of the VAT system that EU law treats as indivisible. Any answer it gave would privilege one value over another.

Neutrality over structure, or structure over neutrality. Either choice risked distorting the system beyond the facts of the case.

And so, the court acted as courts do when they have to interpret laws.

It referred the matter onward.

The Questions Referred

The referral to the Court of Justice did not ask who had acted in bad faith. It did not ask whether Nano Source had intended to avoid tax. It did not even ask whether the Polish authority had been right or wrong to issue the assessment.

Instead, the questions were reduced to their legal essence.

First, the referring court asked whether, under EU VAT law, import VAT may be deducted where goods are imported and tax is paid at customs, but the right to dispose of those goods as owner arises only later, upon acceptance after installation, and the domestic taxable supply is deemed to occur only at that later moment.

Second, it asked whether, where a single composite supply of goods with installation is deemed under Article 36 of the VAT Directive to take place in the Member State of installation, VAT must be charged and accounted for on the full consideration for that supply, notwithstanding the prior payment of import VAT by the purchaser.

Third, the court asked whether installation performed in that Member State by a subsidiary of a non-EU supplier, acting under the supplier's instructions and using its own personnel and infrastructure, may constitute a fixed establishment of the parent for VAT purposes, and if so, under what conditions. The question was framed narrowly, mindful of the Court's repeated warnings that a subsidiary does not, by its mere existence or economic dependence, constitute such an establishment.

Finally, and inevitably, the court asked whether a Member State may, consistently with the principles of neutrality and legal certainty, accept import VAT into its treasury while simultaneously requiring VAT to be charged on a domestic supply by a non-registered, non-EU supplier even where those obligations arise from the same transaction.

Beneath these carefully framed questions lay a deeper one, left deliberately unstated. Can neutrality survive where legality itself points in two directions at once.

This was the question Sofia had anticipated. Not a question of enforcement. Not a question of intent. A question of values.

The file left Poland without public attention. No one claimed victory. No one claimed defeat. The authority had acted within its competence. The taxpayer had exhausted its remedies. The national court had acknowledged its limits.

In Luxembourg, there would be no witnesses. No engineers. No CFOs. No auditors. Only documents, arguments, and a legal system forced to look at its own reflection.

And until that reflection was clarified, the uncomfortable truth remained, just as Marta had said it would.

That VAT could be paid without being legally due, and legally due without being collectable, and that the law, for all its precision, had not yet decided which of those discomforts it was willing to tolerate.

The referral order was signed without ceremony.

There was no hearing to mark the moment. No raised voices, no dramatic exchanges across a polished bench. The judges of the administrative court simply initialed the document, confirmed the wording of the questions, and closed the file. They noted, almost in passing, that the dispute could not be resolved by digging further into the facts. The facts were no longer in dispute.

What remained was law.

In its final paragraphs, the court recorded something close to resignation. The Polish tax authority had acted within the bounds of its competence. The taxpayer had structured its transaction in a way that was commercially coherent and formally consistent with its internal accounting. Yet the interaction between customs valuation, import VAT, domestic supply rules, and enforcement capacity produced results that the court could neither harmonize nor ignore.

The national system had reached its interpretive ceiling.

From this point forward, no additional evidence would be taken. No further clarification of what Jakub did on-site would matter. Not because it was irrelevant, but because its legal significance had already been exhausted. No spreadsheet could change the outcome. The only remaining task was to ask whether EU law itself contained an answer or whether the contradiction was embedded in the system's design.

The referral questions were framed with care, stripped of narrative, purged of context. Names disappeared. Poland became "the referring court." Nano Source became "a taxable person established in a third country." The SilPol Fab became "the purchaser." The installation became "ancillary activities performed prior to acceptance."

They were reduced to their legal essence.

1. Must Articles 14, 63, 66, 167 and 168 of Directive 2006/112/EC be interpreted as permitting the deduction of import VAT by a purchaser where the goods are imported into a Member State, import VAT is paid at customs, but the right to dispose of those goods as owner arises only at a later stage, upon acceptance following installation, and whether such a contractual deferral may constitute a permissible derogation under Article 66 for postponing the domestic taxable supply?
2. Where a single composite supply of goods with installation is deemed, pursuant to Article 36 of Directive 2006/112/EC, to take place in the Member State of installation, must EU VAT law be interpreted as requiring

that VAT be charged and accounted for on the full consideration for that supply, notwithstanding the prior payment of import VAT by the purchaser?

3. In circumstances where installation is performed in a Member State by a subsidiary of a non-EU supplier, acting under the supplier's instructions and using its own personnel and infrastructure, must Articles 44 and 192a of Directive 2006/112/EC be interpreted as allowing that subsidiary to constitute a fixed establishment of the parent for the purposes of the composite supply, and if so, under what conditions?
4. Where a non-EU supplier is found to have carried out a taxable domestic supply of goods with installation in a Member State but was not registered for VAT at the time of that supply, may the Member State, consistently with the principles of neutrality and legal certainty, accept the payment of import VAT by the purchaser while simultaneously requiring VAT to be charged on the domestic supply by the supplier?

Marta read the final wording one last time before it was dispatched.

She recognized the transformation. What had begun as a discussion about equipment, installation, and invoices had become a problem of architecture. Neutrality versus coherence. Deduction versus chargeability. Enforcement versus legality. The questions no longer belonged to Poland, or even to the parties.

They belonged to the system.

When the file left Warsaw, it did not carry testimony or intent with it. It carried only legal propositions, carefully arranged, waiting to be tested against principles laid down decades earlier.

And in Luxembourg, no one would ask what anyone meant to do.

No one would hear Jakub describe the installation, or Michael explain the accounting, or Marta defend the audit.

Because the next stage would take place in a setting where facts are assumed. People are not heard. Only the law speaks.

3.5 LITIGATION BUILT ON DOCUMENTS ALONE

The courtroom in Luxembourg was completely still, in a way that felt unsettling. Voices were measured, time was controlled. No witness stand existed. No cross-examinations. No engineers or CFOs or inspectors narrated their human complications. Before the Court of Justice of the European Union, cases arrived only as objects. Records, references, procedural histories, and questions of interpretation.

Marta had visited once before, years earlier, as part of a training program. What she remembered most was the silence. It was not like the silence in a waiting room. It was deeper and intentional, created by the institution. The Court of Justice of the European Union created order by setting boundaries. Everything unnecessary was kept out. Witnesses, emotions, factual disputes, even time itself seemed to stop at the door.

Here, the case no longer belonged to Nano Source, to the Polish tax authority, or even to Poland. It belonged to the Treaties.

The file that arrived from Warsaw was thin by the standards of national litigation. No transcripts of testimony. No cross-examinations. No diagrams of production lines or photographs of equipment bolted into clean-room floors. Those details had already done their work. They had brought the dispute to this point, but they would not follow it any further.

The Court would take those facts as given or, more precisely, it would take it for granted that the lower court had got them right.

From that moment on, the facts were frozen. That was the first harm built into the way EU cases are decided. It was a harm because, from that point on, the facts that shaped the outcome could no longer be questioned at the level where the final decision was made.

The judges would not ask whether Jakub truly supervised the installation, or whether the SilPol Fab's engineers relied on his instructions. They would not question the CFO's intentions, or whether the business model was clever, aggressive, or naïve. Those questions belonged to the realm of evidence, and evidence was a closed chapter.

What the Court would ask instead was far more abstract and risky. What must EU VAT law do when its internal values conflict?

In the courtroom, the parties would not sit across from one another. They would not even be present in the way they usually are. Their voices would be shared through written notes. These notes were sent months before. They were translated and summarized. The Polish government would speak not as an auditor, but as a guardian of fiscal coherence. The Commission would speak as the custodian of the system's internal logic. Other Member States might get involved because the issue affects their own administrative systems.

Nano Source itself would barely appear. Its name might be mentioned once or twice, but it would function more as a factual placeholder than as a protagonist. The Court did not decide cases between parties. It decided tensions within law.

This was the central paradox of preliminary rulings. They began with real disputes between real parties, but they were decided without examining the full facts. The specific details of each case no longer mattered. Only the legal relationships did.

The first relationship the Court would confront was between import VAT and domestic VAT, two concepts that, on paper, belonged to the same tax but behaved like distant relatives forced to share a surname.

Import VAT was created to make taxes fair. It made sure that goods coming into the Union had the same tax as goods already there. The approach was primarily focused on border regulations, methodical in its application, and somewhat accommodating in nature. If VAT was paid upon importation, the principle of neutrality suggests that it should be deductible. If not, the tax might become a cost instead of just being passed on.

Domestic VAT, by contrast, was territorial and functional. It is concerned not with the movement of goods, but with their presence. Who supplied? Where? When did the supply occur? What was important was not the movement of goods, but when economic value became something that could be taxed.

In the Nano Source case, these two logics collided head-on.

If the supply of goods was deemed to occur only upon acceptance, after installation, testing, and conditional use, then the import had preceded the supply. VAT had been paid at the border before the taxable event had legally come into existence. SilPol Fab had deducted import VAT on goods it did not yet own in an economic sense. The system had functioned, revenue had been collected, but coherence had fractured.

If, on the other hand, the supply was deemed to occur at import, then the installation services performed in Poland could not be ignored. They were not just a small part. Without them, the machine could not operate or produce value. And those services had been performed locally, through human agency, within the Polish territory.

Either way, something failed to align.

The Court was acutely aware that it could not solve this by appealing to fairness. Fairness was not a legal category in VAT law. Neutrality was closer, but neutrality itself was not absolute. It was a guiding principle, not a strict rule, and it existed in tension with the principle of legal certainty.

The Polish court's questions forced the issue with unusual clarity. They did not ask whether VAT should be payable. That much was obvious. They asked whether a tax system built on neutrality could accept outcomes that were economically neutral only by stretching its legal categories by allowing import VAT and reverse-charged services to produce a satisfactory result in practice, even though the underlying rules on place of supply, taxable person, and classification pointed elsewhere.

This was not an enforcement problem. It was a constitutional one.

The judges had encountered similar tensions before, though never in quite this form. In earlier cases, the Court had held that the right to deduct could not replace the obligation to pay output VAT, and that one taxable event could not be reshaped to correct another. Import VAT and domestic VAT were treated as distinct, each resting on its own legal basis and arising at a different moment.

Those cases, however, usually involved clearer allocations of responsibility. Here, responsibility became difficult to locate.

The supplier was established outside the European Union. It was not registered for VAT and had not charged VAT on the supply. In practice, it could not easily be required to do so retroactively. The customer, by contrast, had paid import VAT in good faith, following administrative guidance and relying on a customs valuation that later proved contested.

The State had received VAT. The question was whether it had received VAT in the form required by law.

The Court's task was not to fix the injustice of that situation. Its task was to say whether EU law allowed it to be fixed at all.

This was where the absence of witnesses mattered most.

No one would stand up to say that SilPol Fab could not have known. No one would testify that the customs broker had followed standard practice. No one would explain how multinational supply chains actually functioned in industries where installation and testing were inseparable from sale.

Those realities were frozen in the referral. They could not evolve. They could not plead.

Instead, the Court would focus on its own past decisions, looking for consistency instead of compassion.

The influence of *Halifax* was substantial, though not in the way Marta had first anticipated. This was not a case of artificial arrangements intended solely for the purpose of obtaining a tax advantage. The structure had commercial substance. The business model existed for reasons unrelated to VAT. The equipment was complex, the evaluation-before-sale period necessary, and the delayed acceptance commercially rational.

Earlier case law offered guidance, but not a direct solution. *Halifax* showed that VAT law is purposive, and that formal compliance cannot prevail where it undermines the objectives of the system. In the present case, however, no single objective clearly prevailed. The principle of neutrality pointed in one direction, while the need for legal coherence pointed in another.

Other judgments addressed related issues without resolving this conflict. *Budimex* spoke of moments of supply detached from payment. *FGSZ* warned against confusing economic use with legal ownership. *Berlin Chemie* cautioned against overextending the concept of fixed establishment merely to plug enforcement gaps.

The case law therefore provided guidance, but not an answer. Within those limits, the Court had to determine which consideration was more important.

Would it allow the deduction of import VAT to stand, even if the import was not the taxable moment of supply, in order to preserve neutrality and avoid cascading tax costs? Or would it insist on doctrinal purity, even if that meant accepting that VAT had been paid without legal basis and could not be reallocated without rewriting the Directive?

This was the kind of choice the Court disliked most. It was not because it was hard, but because it showed the limits of what the Court could decide.

The task of an Advocate General is first to clarify the problem before proposing a solution. Marta could almost anticipate the tone of such an Opinion. It would be careful and precise, identifying the difficulty without resolving it too quickly. It would avoid practical shortcuts that might hide the underlying contradiction. Taxable events would not be merged.

Supplies would not be reclassified simply to preserve the appearance of coherence.

Instead, the Opinion would likely frame the issue clearly. VAT law could not ensure perfect results in all cases of international trade. Its coherence depended on respecting its own rules, even when doing so exposed gaps.

The Court, when it came to judgment, would follow a similar discipline. It would not speak of injustice. It would speak of limits.

Marta understood then what it meant to decide cases without witnesses. The court did not listen to individual people because its task was not to correct personal unfairness. Its role was to preserve a legal structure that could be applied again and again, even if, in some individual cases, that structure led to outcomes that no one would prefer in a single case.

In that sense, the silence of the courtroom was not an absence. The silence was a rule.

The Nano Source case would end by clarifying the law, not by solving the business problem. It would explain what EU VAT law can and cannot do, even if that result did not fit commercial practice.

And when the judgment was finally read, months later, it would do what all such judgments did. It would answer the questions asked, not the questions felt.

The rest, the consequences, the adjustments, the incremental recalibrations of business models and administrative practice would unfold elsewhere, in offices and factories and future audits.

Outside the Court, life would resume.

Inside, the law would remain, pristine and indifferent, having spoken without ever listening.

3.6 EMAILS, CONTRACTS, AND THE MAKING OF EVIDENCE

No one ever touched the transaction.

Marta sat alone at a small table in a busy bar. She thought about it again as she listened to the conversations and the sound of glasses clinking. It was late, well past working hours, and she held a half-finished drink in her hand, barely noticing the groups of colleagues and strangers relaxing around her. The noise should have been distracting, but it made her feel more alone. Her thoughts felt empty, even though she was surrounded by people.

The Nano Source file lay open on her desk, not because she was rereading it, she no longer needed to. Keeping it open helped her stay connected to the case as it was, not as it might be simplified in her thoughts.

Steel, silicon, and carefully made parts worth millions of dollars traveled across the ocean. They entered the EU, were put together, adjusted, tested, and partially used. Machines had been powered up. Wafers had been etched. Production runs, however limited, had occurred. And yet the law, in its most decisive moments, had never laid a hand on any of it.

What the law had touched instead was paper. Or, more accurately now, data.

Invoices. Customs declarations. Shipping manifests. Internal instructions. Email chains. ERP timestamps. Acceptance certificates drafted, revised, postponed.

Every legal issue in the case arose from how the movement and use of the machines were recorded, not from what the machines actually did. The documents described the transactions in a particular way, and the law responded to those descriptions.

This was the invisible paper trail. In modern commerce, this division is common. What happens physically is one thing. What the systems record and treat as reality is another.

VAT law, Marta reflected, lived almost entirely in the second world.

The Polish audit had never asked how the machine worked. No one had questioned its technical sophistication or its necessity to the Fab's production. Those facts were inert from a legal perspective. What mattered was how the machine appeared in the administrative universe. When it was declared, who declared it, how it was valued, who invoiced whom, and at what moment responsibility was said to shift.

In theory, the paper trail was a mirror. In practice, it was a lens, sometimes shaping, distorting, or magnifying details, while rendering others invisible.

The import declaration was an example of this.

At the border, the goods entered Poland under a customs procedure for release for free circulation. The declarant was the Polish Fab. The customs value declared reflected the full amount invoiced by Nano Source, including not only the price of the equipment but also the costs contractually associated with its installation.

Strictly speaking, customs valuation law does not require that result. Under Article 72(b) of the Union Customs Code, costs relating to construction, assembly, maintenance, or technical assistance undertaken after importation are expressly excluded from the customs value. Installation carried out at the customer's premises within the EU does not, as such, form part of the value of the imported goods.

The inclusion of those costs was therefore stemmed not from evidentiary analysis, but from documentation. A single bundled invoice was presented, and the declaration followed its structure. From a customs perspective, the declaration was accepted and the goods were released. The system moved on.

From a VAT perspective, however, the ambiguity was there. Tax had been paid on a value that customs law did not insist upon, for a transaction whose legal character VAT law had not yet determined.

Import VAT had been assessed and paid on a value that implicitly assumed the goods were complete, usable, and economically transferred at the point of entry. Yet the commercial documentation told a different story. The sales contract deferred acceptance. Title, in economic terms if not formal ones, remained with Nano Source until months later. SilPol Fab could not freely dispose of the equipment. It could not resell it. It could not meaningfully exploit it beyond agreed testing parameters.

The customs declaration said "now". The contract said "not yet".

Between these positions, VAT law did not point clearly in one direction.

Marta had seen this tension before, but often not so clearly. The customs system was designed for certainty. A border demanded answers. Goods were either released or not. VAT, by contrast, was designed for continuity. It followed transactions across time, linking deduction and chargeability through a chain that assumed coherence at each step.

The invisible paper trail broke that assumption.

The invoice issued by Nano Source U.S. was the next link in the chain, and perhaps the most revealing. It was a single document, comprehensive and confident, bundling equipment and installation into a unified price. Thirty-two million dollars, payable under Californian law, CISG expressly excluded. The invoice did not distinguish between what was tangible and what was performed. It presented the transaction as a singular commercial act.

For U.S. GAAP purposes, this made sense. For internal management, it was elegant. For VAT law, it was provocative.

VAT did not like bundles unless they followed rules. It tolerated composite supplies when one element was clearly principal and the others merely ancillary. But in Nano Source's business model, installation was not decorative. It was transformative. Without it, the equipment was inert. Without local human intervention, no value could be realized.

Yet the invoice flattened this complexity. It told a story of centralized performance, of obligations discharged at parent level, of services flowing outward from the United States rather than emerging locally in Poland.

Marta had underlined the invoice date early in the audit. Not because it was wrong, but because it was too neat. It suggested finality where none yet existed. It fixed a moment in time that VAT law instinctively couldn't trust.

Then there were also the internal documents. These were not for the authorities, but they often had more proof than formal contracts.

Installation schedules circulated between teams. Emails from Jakub reporting unexpected calibration issues. Internal instructions authorizing limited production runs for testing purposes. Risk matrices identifying potential failures and escalation paths, all routed through the Polish subsidiary.

None of these documents spoke the language of VAT. None mentioned tax at all. And yet they mapped the transaction more faithfully than any invoice ever could.

They showed where decisions were made. They showed who exercised judgment. They showed where problems were solved.

They showed, in short, where the service was actually performed.

The paper trail was not a neat, straight line. It resembled a messy web. Some connections were official and strong, while others were casual and hard to see. The problem is that VAT law tends to cherry-pick. It focuses intensely on specific details while completely ignoring the bigger picture.

The narrow focus is what makes the law effective, but it's also what makes it fragile and easy to exploit.

In the Nano Source case, the authorities had initially pulled on the invoice thread, then the customs declaration, then the installation logs. Each time they checked, they found something different. The more they investigated, the more confusing things became.

This was not accidental. Modern business models were built on precisely this multiplicity. Functions were distributed. Responsibilities were layered. Legal form, accounting recognition, operational control, and economic risk rarely aligned perfectly.

The invisible paper trail allowed these misalignments to exist without immediate friction. Problems only arose when law demanded coherence.

The Polish Fab's deduction of import VAT was a perfect example.

On paper, the Fab was the importer. It had paid VAT. It had used the equipment in taxable activities. Deduction followed almost mechanically. The system rewarded compliance with procedure.

But when Marta and her colleagues began tracing the chain backward, the deduction lost its inevitability. Deduction was not a reward for payment. It was a result of chargeability. If the import was not the moment of supply, if economic ownership had not yet transferred, if the Fab was merely a temporary custodian of goods still owned, economically, by Nano Source, then what exactly had the Fab deducted?

The invisible paper trail offered no definitive answer. It contained contradictions without resolving them.

VAT law demanded resolution.

That demand exposed another uncomfortable truth. The paper trail did not merely record reality. It constructed it.

By choosing to declare the Fab as importer, Nano Source had shaped the VAT narrative at the border. By issuing a bundled invoice, it had shaped the narrative of performance. By deferring acceptance, it had shaped the narrative of ownership. Each choice was rational in isolation. Together, they produced a story the law struggled to read.

This was not abuse in the *Halifax* sense. There was no artificiality. No circularity. No transactions without economic purpose.

And yet the effect was similar. The system's categories were pushed to their limits.

Marta remembered a conversation with Sofia during one of their long discussions after work, when the case was still confined to national procedure.

"VAT assumes sincerity," Sofia had said. "Not good faith, that's different. Sincerity. It assumes that when businesses describe a transaction, they are trying to map reality, not optimize across legal silos."

"And when they don't?" Marta then asked.

"Then the system still tries to believe them. Until it can't."

The invisible paper trail was where that trust breaks.

The ERP systems used by Nano Source were global, uniform, and well-documented. They allocated costs, recognized revenue, tracked intercompany charges with a precision that auditors admired.

But they were not designed to answer VAT questions. They were designed to answer management's.

VAT wanted to know where value arose. The systems knew only where value was booked.

This distinction mattered profoundly.

When the Polish tax authority requested extracts from the ERP system, what it received were tables, not narratives. Numbers without context. The entries assumed the system was correct but did not explain why.

To the authority, this was frustrating. To the Court of Justice, it would be irrelevant.

The Court would not see the ERP system. It would see only the distilled facts presented by the referring court, facts already filtered through national legal categories. The invisible paper trail would be compressed into propositions.

That compression was not unbiased.

Once reduced to questions of law, the transaction became simple. The complicated process of importing, installing, testing, and waiting for approval turned into a step-by-step order. The paper trail, once all over the place, became organized.

And yet the contradictions remained.

This was why the Court's role was so clear. It could not fix the paper trail. It could not rewrite invoices or retroactively separate customs values. It could only say whether the law allowed the outcomes.

Marta saw now that the invisible paper trail was not merely evidentiary. It was constitutional. It was where national administrations, EU law, and global business models intersected without a shared grammar.

VAT law pretended that grammar existed. The Nano Source case showed this was not true.

There was always a temptation to solve these cases by choosing one document as more important than the others. To say that the invoice ruled, or the customs declaration, or the contract. That temptation was administrative, not judicial. It offered closure.

The Court would resist it.

Instead, the judgment would likely acknowledge that different documents served different functions. That customs law and VAT law, though intertwined, did not collapse into one another. That deduction followed from chargeability, not payment. That enforcement difficulties did not justify reclassification.

In doing so, the Court would leave a residue of discomfort.

Businesses would continue to structure transactions as Nano Source had. Customs declarations would continue to be made under pragmatic assumptions.

VAT would continue to be paid at borders, deducted downstream, and reconciled imperfectly with contractual reality.

The invisible paper trail would get more complicated, not clearer.

Marta finally closed the file. She realized that the real issue was not this case, but what it stood for. The law now relied more on how things were shown than on what actually happened. Following the law was judged by how well events were recorded, not by the events themselves.

The court would speak. Its words would be precise, careful, and incomplete.

And somewhere, in a factory in Poland, a machine would continue to run, indifferent to invoices, declarations, and judgments, creating value in a way the law could only ever approximate through paper it never truly saw.

3.7 TRACKING VAT THROUGH THE SUPPLY CHAIN

Value was the one word everyone used, and no one agreed on.

Marta noticed this early in the Nano Source file, long before the case became a set rule. The word "value" was everywhere. It was in contracts, financial models, customs declarations, and VAT returns. But each time, it meant something a bit different, depending on who used it and why.

For Michael Torres, value was about profit margins and growth. It was created through good design, engineering, global teamwork, and smart use of resources in a big company. Value was what justified Nano Source's business model. The ability to place immensely complex equipment in a customer's factory months before a sale was finalized, absorbing risk in exchange for long-term commercial certainty.

For the Polish Fab, value was more concrete. It lay in uptime, yield, and the gradual integration of new technology into fragile production flows. The machine mattered only insofar as it worked. Ownership, acceptance, and invoices were abstractions compared to the rhythm of wafers moving down a line.

For Marta, and for VAT law, value was something else entirely. It was not a number, nor a promise. It was an event. Or rather, a series of events that had to be located in time and space, attributed to actors, and translated into legal consequences.

The difficulty was that Nano Source's value chain didn't move in a straight line at all. It didn't flow neatly from production to sale to use. Components made in one factory could be sent to another facility for testing and then returned for modification, while some parts could be shipped directly to customers in a different country. At the same time, software updates could be deployed remotely, changing how the product was used before it even reached the next stage of production.

And VAT law, despite its complexity, continued to conceptualize chains.

The equipment at the center of the case was not sold in the traditional sense. It was deployed. Shipped across continents, installed in a live production environment, calibrated over months, modified in response to local conditions, and only then accepted and paid for definitively.

From a business perspective, this was not a bug. It was the core of Nano Source's competitive advantage.

The machines were very expensive, very specialized, and very important to a customer's business. They could not be sold like regular products. Customers needed proof, not promises. Nano Source needed proximity, not distance. The model collapsed if the company insisted on formal sales before functional integration.

So the company did what many high-technology suppliers did. It separated economic commitment from physical presence. The machine could be there without yet being sold. Value could be created without yet being realized.

This was where the value chain broke down.

In classical VAT logic, value was created by taxable supplies. Goods supplied, services performed. Each supply had a supplier and a recipient. Each had a place and a moment. The tax followed those coordinates.

Nano Source's model challenged that logic not by evading it, but by exceeding it.

Where, Marta asked herself, did value actually emerge?

Was it in the design laboratories in California, where engineers refined the technology over years? Was it in the factories where components were assembled? Was it at the Polish border, where the equipment entered the European Union and became available to an EU taxable person? Was it during installation, where local engineers solved real-world problems that no simulation could predict? Or was it only at acceptance, when the customer finally acknowledged that the machine met its needs?

Each answer was plausible. None was complete.

Michael truly believed that the most important thing was the complete, integrated whole. This included the machine and the knowledge of Nano Source's people. The installation was not just ancillary but a direct part of the product itself. Without it, there was no value at all.

From that perspective, centralizing the contract and the invoice made sense. The parent company bore the risk. If the machine failed, it would affect the parent's reputation. The subsidiary was an instrument, not an origin of value.

Marta did not dispute this. But VAT law did not ask who bore reputational risk. It asked who acted.

Jakub acted.

He made decisions on-site. He adapted installation procedures to the Fab's constraints. He interacted with local staff. He authorized temporary workarounds. He did not merely execute instructions, but he translated them into reality.

In doing so, he created something new. A functioning machine in a specific place.

VAT law, with its emphasis on economic reality, could not ignore that creation.

The problem was not that Nano Source misunderstood value. It was that VAT law understood it differently.

For VAT, value was not strategic. It was operational.

This divergence became obvious when Marta began mapping the internal flows within Nano Source. The intercompany agreements, including service arrangements and cost sharing, were very detailed. They showed how value moved up to the parent company.

But VAT law was suspicious of internal flows. It treated groups as constellations of separate persons, each responsible for their own supplies.

The Polish subsidiary, though economically subordinate, was legally autonomous. It employed Jakub. It controlled his time. It bore local operational costs. It invoiced the parent for services rendered.

In the value chain imagined by Nano Source, these were internal reallocations. In the value chain imagined by VAT law, they were supplies.

VAT law did not look at whether the arrangement reflected the economic reality in the broader sense but the fact that the subsidiary and the parent existed as distinct taxable persons.

Marta had learned early in her career that VAT did not care how a business felt about its internal organization. It cared only about whether activities could be identified, attributed, and taxed.

The value chain, then, was not a story told by the business. It was a reconstruction imposed by the law.

And that reconstruction was inevitably reductive.

The installation services, when isolated, looked like a taxable supply in Poland. They had a provider, a recipient, a place of performance. They could be priced, even if that price was not real.

But isolating them distorted the business reality. The services were inseparable from the goods. They were not optional. They were not independently marketable.

VAT law allows for composite supplies where one element is principal and the other ancillary. In Nano Source's case, the main part was clear. The goods were the core of the transaction. They couldn't be used without installation, and installation was pointless without the goods.

Yet that clarity did not solve the problem. Treating the installation as ancillary unified the supply but ignored the fact that performance took place locally through a separate entity.

Treating it as separate respected territorial execution, but fractured the transaction's economic unity.

The value chain could neither be cleanly split nor comfortably unified.

This was the dilemma that would later be sent to Luxembourg.

When Marta spoke with Sofia about it, they rarely used the word "value." They spoke instead of coherence.

"The system wants the value chain to line up," Sofia had said. "Customs, VAT, deduction, enforcement… they're all built on the assumption that value moves in a straight line."

"And when it doesn't?" Marta had asked.

"Then the law has to choose which fiction to preserve."

The import VAT paid by the Fab was a good example. From a cash perspective, the state had been paid. From a neutrality perspective, denying deduction felt punitive. From a structural perspective, allowing a deduction without a corresponding domestic supply felt inconsistent.

Where had the value been taxed? And where had it been created?

Nano Source's model blurred the answer deliberately, but not in a misleading way. The blurring was functional, not artificial.

This distinction mattered.

In *Halifax*, the Court had condemned structures designed solely to obtain tax advantages. In Nano Source's case, the structure existed for commercial reasons. The tax consequences were collateral.

Yet the system still struggled.

The value chain extended beyond Nano Source and the Fab. It reached into the architecture of the Single Market itself.

If the Court accepted that value could be created locally without triggering full domestic taxation of the goods, it preserved business flexibility but made the link between import VAT and domestic VAT weaker.

If it insisted that acceptance marked the moment of supply, it risked reclassifying imports retroactively as domestic supplies, destabilizing customs practice.

If it allowed enforcement convenience to dictate outcomes, VAT would cease to be neutral and become a tax shaped by who was easiest to target.

Each path privileged a different conception of value.

Marta saw now that the case was not about fixing an error. It was about deciding which version of the value chain EU VAT law would recognize.

- Would it follow physical transformation?
- Would it follow contractual risk?
- Would it follow economic ownership?
- Would it follow administrative practicability?

The law could not follow all of them.

This realization changed how Marta read the file. She stopped looking for mistakes and started looking for deeper issues. The main issue was between two different ideas of value.

One was managerial and global. It saw value as something designed centrally and realized over time. It justified long evaluation-before-sale periods, deferred sales, and integrated services.

The other was legal and territorial. It saw value as something crystallizing through acts performed in specific places by identifiable persons.

Neither was wrong. They were simply incompatible at certain points. VAT law had always lived with this tension, but the Nano Source case made it explicit.

The value chain was no longer just a metaphor. It was the battlefield.

Marta thought again of Jakub. His work was indispensable, yet invisible in the grand narratives of value creation. He did not design the machine.

He did not negotiate the contract. He did not invoice the customer. But without him, nothing would have happened.

VAT law saw him. U.S. GAAP did not.

This asymmetry explained much of Michael's frustration. From his perspective, VAT was misreading the business. From Marta's perspective, VAT was reading a different layer of reality.

The law was not blind to strategy. It was simply indifferent to it.

As the case moved toward the Court, the value chain would be flattened into questions. Abstracted. Sanitized. But beneath those questions lay a deeper issue. Whether EU VAT law could continue to function in a world where value was no longer created at a single point, but across time, space, and organizational boundaries.

The Court would not solve that problem. It could only respond to it.

Whatever the judgment, businesses like Nano Source would continue to operate as they did. Machines would be shipped, installed, tested, and sometimes returned. Value would be created before it was sold.

The invisible paper trail would continue to tell the story of value imperfectly. The value chain would still be hard to simplify.

Marta closed her notebook and looked out the window. The city lights reflected off the snow, each one a point of illumination in a complex network.

Value, she thought, was like that. Created everywhere, owned nowhere, taxed somewhere in between.

And VAT law, for all its ambition, was still learning how to follow it.

3.8 THE JUDGMENT

The decision was announced plainly.

As always, the Court of Justice does not mention the human conflict that led to the case. It does not talk about audits or negotiations, not to mention the frustration of the parties. The Court focuses on the legal system. The case is not seen as a story but as a problem of structure. It is about how the VAT system should work when modern business practices pull it apart.

The reference had been made by a national court confronted with a case that resisted classification under the ordinary categories of EU VAT law. A non-EU supplier had contracted to deliver and install complex equipment at a customer's premises within the European Union, issuing a single bundled invoice for a fully operational system. The goods were imported into the Member State and installation was carried out locally through a subsidiary acting under the supplier's direction. While import VAT was paid at the border by the customer acting as declarant, the supplier itself was not registered for VAT in the Member State. When the tax authorities examined the transaction, the difficulty lay not in the payment of import VAT as such, but in determining whether and when the supplier had carried out a domestic taxable supply of goods with installation under Article 36 of the Directive, who was liable to account for VAT on that supply, and how that domestic chargeability interacted, if at all, with the prior importation of the goods. It was that misalignment between the legal characterization of the supplier's transaction and the existing VAT paid at importation that prompted the national court to seek guidance from the Court of Justice.

The national court did not ask the Court of Justice to resolve the dispute. It asked the Court to say what the law meant.

The Questions Referred

The referring court sought guidance on a limited set of interrelated questions concerning the moment at which a supply of goods occurs for VAT purposes, the chargeability of VAT where acceptance is deferred, the legal relationship between import VAT and domestic VAT, and the conditions under which neutrality may operate where enforcement against a non-established supplier is impaired.

More specifically, the Court was asked whether Article 14(1) of Directive 2006/112/EC must be interpreted as meaning that a supply of goods takes place at the moment when goods are physically delivered and installed, notwithstanding that ownership and the right to dispose of the goods as owner remain contractually with the supplier until acceptance. It was also asked whether Articles 63 and 66 preclude a Member State from treating VAT as chargeable before such acceptance, and whether VAT paid on importation may be regarded as VAT "due or paid" for the purposes of Articles 167 and 168 where, at the time of import, no domestic supply of goods has yet occurred. Finally, the referring court sought clarification as to whether the principle of fiscal neutrality may override the structural requirements of chargeability and taxable transactions where VAT cannot effectively be enforced against a non-established supplier.

The referring court further asked whether, in circumstances such as those at issue in the main proceedings, the performance of installation activities in a Member State by a subsidiary of a non-EU supplier, acting under that supplier's instructions and using its own personnel and infrastructure, could, in principle, be capable of giving rise to a fixed establishment of that supplier for VAT purposes, within the meaning of Articles 44 and 192a of Directive 2006/112/EC.

The Court noted at the outset that these questions were closely connected and concerned the fundamental architecture of the common system of VAT. While the referring court did not ask the Court to determine whether, on the facts of the main proceedings, the supplier had a fixed establishment in the Member State concerned, it noted that the interpretation of Articles 14, 36, 44, 63 and 192a of the Directive would necessarily shape the legal conditions under which such an establishment, and the related obligation to register for VAT, might arise under national law.

Preliminary Observations

The Court began by recalling that VAT is a general tax on consumption, designed to be neutral as regards the burden of taxation on taxable persons engaged in economic activities. However, that neutrality is ensured not by dispensing with the structural requirements of the tax, but by applying them consistently. Neutrality does not exist independently of legality. It follows from the correct application of the rules governing taxable transactions, chargeability, and deduction.

The Court further recalled that the concepts used in the Directive constitute autonomous concepts of EU law which must be interpreted uniformly, having regard to the context in which they occur and the objectives pursued by the legislation. It is not sufficient that VAT has been paid. It must also be legally due in respect of a taxable transaction.

Against that background, the Court turned first to the concept of a "supply of goods" within the meaning of Article 14(1) of the Directive.

The Supply of Goods and the Transfer of the Right to Dispose

Article 14(1) defines a supply of goods as the transfer of the right to dispose of tangible property as owner. As the Court has consistently held since its judgment in *Safe* (C-320/88), that concept does not refer to the transfer of ownership in accordance with the formal requirements of national civil law but covers any transfer of tangible property whereby one party is authorized to dispose of it as if it were the owner. A contractual clause deferring ownership until formal acceptance cannot, in itself, determine the moment at which a supply is deemed to take place for VAT purposes.

The Court reiterated that, in determining whether such a transfer has occurred, it is necessary to examine all the circumstances of the case, in particular whether the transferee has obtained the power to dispose of the goods and to bear the risks associated with them.

In the present case, the goods in question have been physically delivered to the customer's premises, installed, and made operational. They were capable of being used for the purposes for which they were intended and, in practice, were integrated into the customer's production environment. Those elements, the Court observed, strongly suggested that the customer had acquired the factual ability to dispose of the goods.

The existence of a contractual clause retaining ownership with the supplier pending formal acceptance could not, in itself, preclude such a finding. While contractual provisions are relevant in assessing the allocation of rights and obligations between the parties, they cannot be decisive for the purposes of VAT where they do not reflect the economic and commercial reality of the transaction. Such contractual arrangements may be relevant, but they are not decisive, when they do not reflect the economic and commercial reality of the transaction.

The Court distinguished this situation from that examined in *Budimex* (C-224/18), where the completion of the service was genuinely dependent on formal acceptance and where, until that acceptance, the works could not be regarded as complete. In *Budimex*, acceptance corresponded to the substantive completion of the service; it was not merely a procedural step.

By contrast, where the goods have already been delivered, installed, and made operational, acceptance clauses may serve functions related to quality control, final payment, or risk management, but they do not necessarily correspond to the moment at which the customer acquires the right to dispose of the goods as owner for VAT purposes.

Accordingly, the Court held that Article 14(1) must be interpreted as meaning that a supply of goods may be regarded as having occurred at the moment when goods are physically delivered and installed, even where ownership is contractually retained, provided that the customer has in fact acquired the power to dispose of the goods as owner. It is for the referring court to assess whether those conditions are met in the circumstances of the main proceedings.

Chargeability and the Tax Point

The Court next addressed the question of chargeability. Under Article 63 of the Directive, the chargeable event occurs and VAT becomes chargeable when the goods are delivered or the services are performed. Article 66 allows Member States, in certain circumstances, to derogate from that rule, but such derogations must be interpreted strictly.

While Article 66 allows Member States to defer VAT chargeability in certain circumstances, the Court emphasizes that such derogations are strictly interpreted and cannot override the factual occurrence of the supply. Thus, even where contracts defer acceptance, the taxable event and the potential chargeability of domestic VAT occur when goods are delivered, installed, and usable by the customer.

The referring court had asked whether VAT could be regarded as chargeable before acceptance where acceptance was contractually defined as the moment of completion.

The Court reaffirmed that the imposition of VAT is fundamentally dependent on the occurrence of the taxable transaction. Where a supply of goods has occurred within the meaning of Article 14, VAT becomes chargeable at that moment, unless a specific derogation applies.

As the Court had already held that a supply of goods may occur prior to formal acceptance, it followed that VAT may become chargeable at that earlier moment. Contractual provisions deferring acceptance cannot, by themselves, postpone the chargeability of VAT where they do not reflect the actual state of performance. It is not sufficient that contractual terms exist. The tax point must be determined by reference to objective circumstances, not by reference to private arrangements.

In this respect, the Court referred to its judgment in *FGSZ* (C-507/18), in which it held that subsequent adjustments or formal acts cannot alter the moment at which the taxable event occurred. The tax point must be determined by reference to objective circumstances, not by reference to private arrangements capable of varying from one transaction to another.

Import VAT and Domestic VAT

The Court subsequently examined the relationship between import VAT and domestic VAT. According to Article 2(1)(d) of the Directive, the importation of goods is considered a taxable transaction that is separate from any subsequent supply of those goods within the territory of a Member State. Articles 30 and 70 specify that import VAT becomes chargeable at the time when customs duties become chargeable.

The Court recalled that import VAT serves a specific function within the VAT system. It ensures that goods imported from third countries are taxed in a manner equivalent to goods supplied within the European Union. That function requires import VAT to be treated as a taxable event separate from any domestic supply.

The fact that the customs value of imported goods may include elements relating to services to be performed after importation does not alter that legal separation. Nor does the payment of import VAT imply that VAT has been paid in respect of a subsequent domestic supply. VAT paid on importation cannot, as such, be regarded as deductible in respect of a domestic supply that has not yet occurred, and payment alone does not confer a right to deduction.

Accordingly, the Court held that VAT paid on importation cannot be regarded as VAT "due or paid" in respect of a domestic supply of goods which has not yet occurred within the meaning of Articles 2 and 14 of the Directive.

Fixed Establishment

The Court further observed that the interpretation of Article 36 of Directive 2006/112/EC, which governs supplies of goods with installation or assembly, formed an essential part of the legal framework within which the questions referred must be assessed.

Under Article 36, where goods are supplied with installation, the place of supply is deemed to be the place where the installation is carried out, irrespective of whether the supplier is established in that Member State. That provision ensures that the Member State in which the goods become usable and economically operative is entitled to tax the supply, without requiring the supplier to have a fixed establishment in that territory.

In the present case, the installation activities performed by the subsidiary were decisive in rendering the goods functional and integrating them into the customer's production environment. Those activities were therefore capable of bringing the transaction within the scope of Article 36, subject to the referring court's assessment of whether a single composite supply of goods with installation existed.

Against that background, the Court emphasized that the existence of such a composite supply, localized pursuant to Article 36, does not, of itself, imply that the supplier has a fixed establishment in the Member State concerned. The objectives pursued by Article 36 would be undermined if the localization of a supply of goods with installation were to entail, as a matter of course, the attribution of the installer's resources to the supplier for all VAT purposes.

The Court reiterated that a fixed establishment requires that the taxable person have, in the Member State concerned, a sufficient degree of permanence and a suitable structure enabling it to receive and use services for the purposes of its own economic activity. The mere performance of installation services by a subsidiary, even where those services are essential to the supply of goods and carried out under the supplier's instructions, does not necessarily satisfy that criterion.

To hold otherwise would risk conflating two distinct mechanisms established by the VAT Directive, namely the determination of the place of supply under Article 36 and the attribution of a taxable presence under Articles 44 and 192a. Such an approach would extend the concept of a fixed establishment beyond its intended purpose and make the difference between territoriality and establishment unclear.

Accordingly, while the circumstances of the main proceedings may support the application of Article 36, they do not, in themselves, establish that the subsidiary constituted a fixed establishment of the parent capable of receiving services within the meaning of Article 44 of the Directive. It remains for the referring court to determine whether the subsidiary's resources were placed at the disposal of the parent in a manner exceeding what is required for the performance of installation activities forming part of a composite supply of goods.

The Right to Deduct

The Court then examined the implications of those findings for the right to deduct. Under Articles 167 and 168 of Directive 2006/112/EC, the right to deduct arises when the deductible tax becomes chargeable and may be exercised only in respect of VAT due or paid in relation to taxable transactions carried out by the taxable person.

The Court reiterated that the right to deduct is an integral part of the VAT system and is intended to ensure fiscal neutrality. However, that right presupposes that the VAT in question is legally chargeable and that it is borne by the taxable person in the context of their own economic activity. The mere payment of VAT, in the absence of a taxable transaction giving rise to a right of deduction, is not sufficient.

In that regard, the Court referred to its judgment in *Weindel Logistik Service* (C-621/19), in which it held that import VAT is deductible only where the imported goods are used by the taxable person for the purposes of their taxable output transactions, and where a direct and immediate link exists between the importation and those transactions. The designation of a person as importer of record, or the fact that import VAT has been paid at customs, cannot of itself establish such a link.

The Court further recalled its settled case law, including *Reemtsma* (C-35/05) and *Danfoss* (C-94/10), according to which VAT paid in circumstances that do not correspond to a taxable transaction does not confer a right to deduct. It is not sufficient for the VAT to have been paid; it must also relate to a transaction that has actually taken place and is chargeable.

In the present case, the referring court had identified a situation in which import VAT was paid at a time when, according to the Court's interpretation, the right to dispose of the goods as owner had not yet arisen and no domestic supply of goods had yet occurred within the meaning of Article 14 of the Directive. In such circumstances, the Court held that the payment of import VAT cannot, by itself, give rise to a right to deduct in respect of a domestic taxable supply that is deemed to occur only at a later stage.

Neutrality and Enforcement

Finally, the Court addressed the question whether the principle of fiscal neutrality requires the right to deduct to be granted where VAT cannot effectively be enforced against the supplier, in particular where the supplier is not established in the European Union.

The Court acknowledged that such situations may give rise to economic hardship and may undermine the neutrality of the tax in practice. The Court nevertheless observed that the common system of VAT is not designed to guarantee that tax will always be neutral in its economic effects in every individual case. Where the allocation of VAT burdens results from the application of objective rules governing taxable transactions, place of supply and chargeability, any resulting imbalance cannot, as such, be regarded as contrary to the principle of fiscal neutrality. That principle ensures equality of treatment between comparable taxable transactions, but it does not operate to redistribute tax burdens arising from the lawful application of those rules. However, it reiterated that neutrality cannot justify departing from the structural requirements of the VAT system.

The Court recalled that enforcement difficulties cannot alter the definition of taxable transactions or the conditions for deduction. To hold otherwise would risk transforming the VAT system into one dependent on administrative convenience rather than legal coherence.

The Court therefore held that the principle of fiscal neutrality does not require a Member State to grant the right to deduct VAT solely on the ground that VAT cannot be effectively recovered from a non-established supplier.

Conclusion

In answering the questions referred, the Court clarified that VAT must follow the objective reality of transactions, not the contractual or accounting choices of the parties. Acceptance clauses may be relevant where they correspond to the substantive completion of a transaction, but they cannot postpone the existence of a supply where the goods have already been delivered and made available for use. Import VAT and domestic VAT are legally distinct taxable events, and the right to deduct arises only in respect of VAT legally due.

The judgment did not resolve the national dispute. It could not. But it restored the internal logic of the VAT system by reaffirming that neutrality flows from legality, not from administrative accommodation.

What the judgment ultimately made clear was not the party at fault, but where the cost of coherence would fall. VAT neutrality survived as a principle, but not as a guarantee of comfort. Import VAT paid too early could not be transformed into a right to deduct simply because someone, somewhere, had borne the burden. And domestic VAT, once legally due, could not be ignored just because collecting it is difficult. For Nano Source, the structural strategy it had previously employed, comprising delayed acceptance, offshore establishment, and functional performance through a subsidiary, proved ineffective in protecting it from Polish VAT once the equipment had been delivered, installed, and made available to the customer. For SilPol, it meant that VAT neutrality would be restored only prospectively, through legal deduction methods, not retroactively by changing tax already paid. The system remained neutral in theory, yet unforgiving in practice. And that, the Court seemed to say, was not a defect but rather the cost of maintaining coherence.

For Marta, reading the judgment in her office days later, the meaning was unmistakable. The Court had not chosen neutrality over structure, nor structure over neutrality. It had chosen coherence.

And coherence, she knew, has consequences.

The Court had spoken without witnesses, without testimony, without narrative. It had spoken in abstractions, principles, and definitions. That was its role.

What remained, the human cost, the allocation of loss, the discomfort of a system that can be correct without being kind, would now return to the national stage.

That, she reflected, was where the law ended.

And where its silence began.

PART IV - THE BORDERLESS FUTURE

VAT in the age of algorithms, AI, and real-time data

4.1 THE ALGORITHMIC TAX AUTHORITY

The more Marta reflected on it, the clearer it became that automation had not simply accelerated administration. It had subtly altered the hierarchy of norms. In the classical model, legislation defined obligations, administrative practice implemented them, and courts corrected excesses. In the new model, systems implemented obligations first, and the law struggled to catch up. What had once been interpretation had become configuration.

Two governance logics help explain this transformation. The first is the so-called "Brussels effect". The idea that EU regulatory standards become global standards because market actors adopt them across jurisdictions to avoid fragmentation. The second and more recent perspective is experimentalist governance, under which regulators design frameworks that evolve through monitoring, feedback, and iterative revision rather than formal substantive rules.

Under the EU's VAT in the Digital Age (ViDA[3]) reform, real-time reporting, structured invoices, and automated cross-checks were introduced to promote trust, not to limit it. They are expected to become structural components of compliance. This does not simply accelerate enforcement, but it also redistributes where enforcement is exercised. While ViDA seeks harmonization through common digital infrastructures, its effectiveness depends on how Member States implement and revise those infrastructures over time.

Decisions on the right to deduct, refund releases, and others that were once taken by auditors post-transaction audit now occur at the moment transactions enter their digital reporting infrastructures.

But infrastructures designed to build trust can also restrict it. As administrations accumulated transaction data, they began setting plausibility thresholds, determining which patterns could be accepted automatically and which required review. These thresholds were rarely doctrinal. They were shaped by operational experience, but above all by political pressure to reduce the VAT gap. This pressure transformed fraud exposure and audit constraints into specific system design choices.

In policy language, this resembled what governance scholars call experimentalist administration. Systems were adjusted iteratively through monitoring and feedback rather than formal rulemaking.

---

[3] The "VAT in the Digital Age" package, adopted in March 2025, marks a significant update of the EU's VAT rules. It responds to the way business and tax administration have increasingly moved into digital spaces. The reform introduces new digital reporting requirements, revises how VAT applies to platform-based activities, and aims to make cross-border VAT compliance across the EU easier.

Yet from the taxpayer's perspective, the effect was simpler and more troubling. Decisions once grounded in legal reasoning were now triggered by system-generated suspicion, often without explanation.

She saw this most clearly in disputes where taxpayers argued that a transaction was economically real but technically misclassified, or that a deduction was denied not because VAT was not due, but because a field had been completed incorrectly or too late. In such cases, the administration no longer argued substance against substance. It argued system logic. The question was no longer whether VAT neutrality had been breached, but whether the system had been followed.

This inversion troubled her deeply.

Neutrality was never supposed to depend on software behaving properly. Time and again, the Court had said that the right to deduct was not a procedural privilege but a core feature of the VAT system itself. The idea is that taxes should not burden businesses doing their job. Formalities had their place, but they were not meant to take over the main purpose. This is only acceptable if it is necessary to stop misuse or to protect the collection. What troubled Marta was that automation appeared to be reversing that logic. It wasn't happening through big arguments or changes in beliefs. Instead, it was happening gradually, with small decisions and actions that people didn't notice until it was too late.

Marta recalled a recent case in which deduction had been denied because the supplier's invoice, though reflecting a genuine supply, had not been cleared through the national platform within the statutory time frame. The delay was marginal, the tax had been paid, the supply undisputed. In earlier years, such a case would have been resolved through proportionality analysis. Now, the denial was automatic.

The system had no discretion, and the administration claimed none either.

Discretion, it seemed, had been outsourced to code.

This raised a profound constitutional question within the European Union's legal order. Where, exactly, did administrative discretion now reside? If decisions were produced by automated processes, who bore responsibility for their consequences? The official who relied on the system? The legislature that mandated it? The designers who coded it? Or the taxpayer who failed to adapt perfectly to its logic?

The Court had not yet fully articulated an answer. But Marta sensed that the issue would not remain dormant for long. As automation deepened, disputes would increasingly concern not the interpretation of VAT directives, but the legality of administrative architectures themselves. Whether systems respected proportionality. Whether they allowed for correction. Whether they preserved access to rights.

And whether they could be challenged at all.

The automated administrator, by its nature, resisted narrative. It did not explain itself but produced outputs. A rejection notice did not reason in the traditional sense. It referenced a rule, a validation error, or a missing element. The taxpayer was left to infer the legal logic behind the technical message. In practice, this often meant hiring consultants fluent not only in VAT law, but in system manuals and implementation guides.

Law had acquired a new dialect.

The one that worried Marta most was not technical but about knowledge. It was about what the system could actually know, what information counted as proof, and who was assumed to be telling the truth. It was about who was expected to provide evidence and who was trusted automatically without question.

In the classical VAT system, the burden of proof followed a familiar path.

The taxpayer declared transactions, claimed deductions, and retained documentation.

The tax authority audited selectively, questioned inconsistencies, and, if it suspected irregularity, bore the burden of demonstrating that a declared transaction did not reflect economic reality or that an abuse of rights had occurred. This allocation was not accidental. It flowed from the structure of VAT as a self-assessed tax balanced by the principle of neutrality and safeguarded by proportionality.

Automation changed that rhythm over time.

In a real-time, system-validated environment, the declaration no longer merely asserted compliance, but it appeared to confirm it. Once an invoice passed clearance, once it was validated by the platform, once it received a system-generated identifier, the transaction acquired a semblance of correctness. It became data that the administration itself had accepted, processed, and stored. In practical terms, the system treated it as true.

For example, a property developer had created a subsidiary to provide management services for one of its buildings. The subsidiary invoiced the parent company for these services, charging VAT that was correctly applied and paid. Under EU VAT law, these services constituted a taxable supply, so the invoices were formally legitimate. Economically, however, the subsidiary performed little real work. Its main purpose was solely to convert an otherwise exempt lease activity into a VAT advantage for the parent company. Tax authorities knew the company existed and held a VAT ID, but they could not see, in real time, that the structure was designed solely to produce a tax advantage. Automation cleared each invoice because form alone was correct, leaving the underlying abuse invisible unless a human auditor later investigated.

And unless something later "flagged" an anomaly or a statistical deviation, the transaction remained untouched.

On its face, this seemed efficient and nothing to worry about. But Marta saw the doctrinal shift hiding beneath the surface. The system no longer asked the taxpayer to prove that the transaction was genuine.

It assumed genuineness by default. The burden subtly moved. It was no longer on the taxpayer to demonstrate substance, but on the administration, or rather, on the system to detect its absence.

This inversion sat uneasily with the doctrine of abuse of rights as developed by the Court of Justice.

In *Halifax*, the Court had articulated a two-part test that was as elegant as it was demanding. First, the transactions must result in a tax advantage contrary to the purpose of the VAT legislation. Second, it must be apparent from objective factors that the essential aim of the transactions was to obtain that tax advantage. Abuse, importantly, was never something the law assumed. It had to be established, concretely by the tax authorities, on the basis of objective facts. It was a conclusion, not a default.

But automation risked weakening this logic.

In a system that treated compliance as presumed unless a deviation appeared, abuse stopped being the result of a comprehensive legal assessment. It became an anomaly. A response to patterns and thresholds. The inquiry subtly shifted. Rather than inquiring whether a transaction was abusive based on its intended purpose and economic substance, the system evaluated whether it deviated enough from the anticipated framework to justify scrutiny.

Marta realized how profound this change was. Abuse of rights was never meant to be statistical. It was contextual, intentional, and factual. It meant looking beyond the surface to ask why a business was organized a certain way, how it actually functioned day to day, and what the real goal of that setup was. Algorithms operated differently. They were very good at noticing unusual activity or repeated behaviors. What they could not do was grasp intention or purpose. They could flag anomalies, but they could not explain why someone acted the way they did.

She realized the risk was not that abuse would go unnoticed.

In many respects, automated systems made detection easier and faster. The real risk lay elsewhere. That the legal meaning of abuse would begin to bend, imperceptibly, toward the logic of the tools used to detect it.

Under the classical approach, a structure could be abusive precisely because it was singular and carefully constructed to look ordinary. Its uniqueness was often its disguise. In an automated environment, that same uniqueness might serve as protection rather than evidence. Transactions that conformed neatly to prescribed formats, respected timing rules, populated the correct fields, and moved through systems without friction could escape scrutiny even where their sole rationale was the production of a tax advantage.

Once again, form threatened to overtake substance. Not this time through strict legal formalism, but through the authority of infrastructure itself. Marta thought of the Court's insistence, repeated across decades of case law, that VAT rights could not be denied solely on the basis of formal irregularities if substantive conditions were met. The inverse principle was equally true, though less frequently articulated. Substantive abuse could not be legitimized by perfect formal compliance. Abuse doctrine existed precisely to prevent the system from being exploited by arrangements that respected the letter while violating the spirit.

Automation blurred that distinction. When the system itself validated the form, the temptation was to treat validation as substance. The administration, increasingly reliant on system outputs, might hesitate to question what it had already accepted. The psychological shift was subtle but powerful. The system had spoken.

This created a paradox in litigation. If an automated system accepted a transaction, and later the administration alleged abuse, who bore the burden of proof? The taxpayer could plausibly argue that it had relied in good faith on system validation. The administration, in turn, might argue that validation was purely formal and could not prevent abuse. The Court would then be asked to adjudicate not only on abuse, but on the legal significance of automation itself.

Marta anticipated the emergence of such disputes and arguments. Taxpayers would invoke legitimate expectations, arguing that system clearance created a presumption of legality. Authorities would likely respond that no system can bypass meaningful review. Courts would then have to decide whether the use of automation actually changes how evidence should be evaluated.

And underlying all of this was a deeper concern. Automation risked normalizing a reversal of the burden of proof without explicit legal basis.

In abuse cases, the burden traditionally lay with the tax authority to establish objective factors indicating abuse. But if systems filtered transactions in advance, leaving only flagged cases for scrutiny, then the absence of a flag might be treated *de facto* as evidence of legitimacy. The burden shifted silently, not by law but by architecture.

This was particularly troubling in cross-border contexts where the same information carried different implications. Automated systems were national. They reflected national data sets, national risk models, national priorities. A transaction perfectly ordinary in one Member State might appear significant in another, or vice versa. Abuse doctrine, however, was EU law. It required coherence across borders.

Marta worried that automation would fragment abuse analysis, not through divergent legal standards, but through divergent detection thresholds. What triggered suspicion in one system might pass unnoticed in another. Abuse would become, in part, a function of system design.

The Court had always resisted such fragmentation. In cases like *Part Service, Weald Leasing,* and *RBS Deutschland,* it emphasized that abuse analysis required a comprehensive view of the transaction and its economic context. Individual features could not be isolated and treated as determinative.

However, automated systems tend to separate transactions into smaller components at the detection stage, despite the Court's earlier refusal to view them in isolation. They rely on identifiable criteria and treat them as enough to trigger a legal conclusion and related consequences.

Intent posed another difficulty. Abuse doctrine focused on the essential aim of obtaining a tax advantage. Intent was inferred from facts, but it was still a human concept. Systems could identify that a structure produced a tax advantage but they could not assess whether that advantage was essential or incidental. They could not weigh commercial justification against tax optimization.

Marta saw the danger of a new impoverished version of abuse emerging. It was simpler and lacked detail, focusing only on breaking patterns.

In such a model, abuse would be what the system detected, and legitimacy would be what it failed to see.

Yet she also saw another, equally troubling possibility. If systems assumed correctness unless transactions were flagged, then abuse might flourish precisely where it was most sophisticated. Those with the resources to design transactions that mirrored statistical norms could exploit the blind spots of automation. Abuse would not disappear. It would evolve.

This raised a final, uncomfortable question. Was the "algorithmic tax authority" compatible with the Court's insistence that abuse of rights be exceptional, carefully reasoned, and narrowly applied?

Marta suspected that compatibility was possible but not automatic. It required conscious legal framing. Systems needed to be treated as tools, not decision-makers. Validation could not be equated with legality. Absence of a flag could not be equated with absence of abuse. And crucially, the burden of proof could not be allowed to drift without judicial acknowledgment.

She imagined a future judgment in which the Court would be forced to articulate these boundaries. It would likely reaffirm that automated validation did not create substantive rights, nor did it extinguish the administration's obligation to prove abuse. It might emphasize that reliance on systems could inform legitimate expectations only within strict limits. It would probably insist that abuse analysis remain grounded in objective assessment of economic reality, not in system outputs.

But until such guidance emerged, the risk of inefficient disputes remained.

Automation did not stop the abuse of rights. It changed the way we identify and argue these abuses. And unless the law consciously adapted, automation risked recalibrating the burden of proof and the balance between taxpayer and state.

As Marta reflected on this, she understood that the most dangerous feature of automation was its apparent neutrality. Systems did not argue. They did not justify. They did not explain. They simply operated. And in doing so, they could shift foundational legal principles without ever naming them.

That, she reflected, was where vigilance mattered most. The real risk did not lie with obvious fraud or deliberate evasion, but with the gradual reshaping of legal doctrine through technical design choices. The concept of abuse of rights initially emerged as a countermeasure to rigid formalism. In a context increasingly dominated by automation, it requires renewed protection. This protection must extend to the unexamined assumptions built into software.

In automated compliance systems, transactions are treated as unproblematic only so long as they conform to the system's predefined logic. Deviation itself becomes grounds for suspicion. And when that happens, it is not the authority but the taxpayer who must once again prove correctness.

Marta had seen it already. A Polish manufacturer acquires a large industrial machine from abroad, the kind of purchase that rarely attracts attention in the traditional audit cycle. The machine arrives. It is installed. Engineers sign off on its functionality. Production begins. The supply chain moves on. From the perspective of economic reality, the transaction is complete and unquestionable. Yet the decisive moment no longer occurs on the factory floor. It occurs inside the system.

The electronic invoice passes through the national platform without resistance. The XML structure is flawless. The VAT identification numbers match. The reverse-charge mechanism is correctly indicated. To the machine, the transaction looks fine. And yet, somewhere deeper in the architecture, the supplier's profile triggers a silent recalibration. The foreign seller is new to the market. Its transaction history is thin. Its statistical footprint does not yet resemble that of an established trading partner. No rule has been broken, but a threshold has been crossed.

Nothing happens immediately. There is no rejection, no warning, no decision. The invoice remains valid. The VAT return is filed. The deduction is claimed. And then, without explanation, the refund does not arrive. The system does not say no, but it simply hesitates. Weeks later, a notification appears, generated not by an inspector but by a risk engine. The deduction is under verification. Documentation is required.

The burden has already shifted. The company is asked to produce the contract, delivery records, installation protocols, acceptance reports, proof of payment, and sometimes even photographs of the machine in operation. Not because abuse has been identified, but because the system has not been convinced. Formal compliance has become provisional. Economic reality must now be demonstrated, piece by piece, not to rebut an accusation, but to satisfy an algorithmic doubt.

Marta recognized the doctrinal dissonance immediately. The abuse of rights doctrine was never meant to function this way. In cases like *Halifax*, the Court insisted that abuse must be proven, not presumed. That artificiality must be demonstrated through objective factors. That intent cannot be inferred merely from structure. Yet here, without invoking the doctrine by name, the system was applying its logic by default. Suspicion had become ambient. Neutrality, conditional.

The machine did not ask whether the transaction was artificial. It asked whether it looked familiar. And unfamiliarity in a data-driven environment had become its own kind of risk. The consequence was not a finding of abuse, but a structural shift where unfamiliar transactions were scrutinized and burdened without ever being formally classified as abusive. A procedural inversion in which lawful economic activity was temporarily treated as suspect, pending documentary justification.

This was not fraud detection. It was trust management, delegated to code. And Marta understood that once this logic took root, distinguishing between protecting the VAT system and subtly altering its principles would become increasingly difficult. The law still spoke of abuse as an exception. But the system, by the way it was built, started to act as if every transaction might be abusive unless the taxpayer could later show that it was not.

That lack of visibility was hardly a coincidence. These systems were built with efficiency in mind, not transparency. Their internal reasoning was usually hard to understand, not because of deliberate secrecy but because it was often too complicated, and often it involved claims of intellectual property. Even when documentation was available, it rarely addressed the underlying value judgments. It described the mechanics of the system, but not the reasons those particular choices had been made. The danger, Marta thought, was not that automation would become oppressive. It was that it would become unquestioned.

She remembered how, in courts without witnesses, when testimony is absent, documents alone take a decisive evidentiary role, and carry more weight that they would if they were coupled with oral evidence as well. Automation pushed this further. In that shift, documents themselves were being replaced by validated data objects that had already been checked before anyone ever saw them. The further the process moved away from lived reality, the more difficult it was to bring in the surrounding context.

Even so, context still had to be accounted for.

Consider again the cross-border installation cases that had animated earlier chapters. Whether a supply of goods with installation occurred, whether the place of supply shifted, whether a fixed establishment existed… these were questions that depended on facts. Who did the work? Where? Under whose control? With what permanence? None of these questions could be answered by an invoice alone. And yet, the invoice now drove the system.

Marta saw the risk clearly. If the system treated the invoice as truth, then the legal analysis risked becoming circular. The invoice said the supply was X, therefore the supply was X, therefore the VAT treatment followed. Substance disappeared behind declaration.

This was not merely an administrative concern. It struck at the heart of the EU's legal coherence. The VAT system depended on consistent interpretation across Member States. If each Member State embeds its own assumptions into its automated systems, then divergence will re-emerge not through legislation, but through system architecture, even if those systems are technically interoperable. Harmonization on paper could coexist with fragmentation in practice.

The ViDA initiative promised interoperability, but Marta knew that interoperability was not the same as uniformity of meaning. Systems could talk to each other while still speaking slightly different languages. A supply classified one way in one system might be treated differently in another, not because the law differed, but because the validation logic did.

In that environment, the Court's role would become both more important and more difficult. It would not be asked only to interpret legal concepts, but also to consider whether those concepts were being respected in the way administrative systems were built and used. At times, the Court would have to face a difficult question. A refusal produced by an algorithm might itself conflict with the basic principles of VAT.

Signs of this issue had already begun to appear in practice in Italy, through the use of the SDI system and its automated controls on deduction. Several years after SDI became fully operational, Italian tax authorities began experimenting with automated pre-filled VAT returns and automated consistency checks.

The system compared incoming and outgoing invoices in real time. Where an incoming invoice appeared in SDI, but the corresponding outgoing VAT reporting by the supplier showed anomalies, late filing, incorrect codes, or technical rejections, the system automatically flagged the customer's deduction as "high risk." In some cases, refunds were frozen or delayed without any human assessment of the underlying transaction.

One illustrative scenario, discussed informally among practitioners before ever reaching a courtroom, involved a mid-sized Italian manufacturer that had purchased specialized machinery from a domestic supplier. The machinery was delivered, installed, tested, and used in production. The invoices were properly issued through SDI, cleared by the system, and paid in full. Months later, the supplier became subject to a tax audit unrelated to that transaction and was found to have made errors in its VAT reporting for a different period. The automated risk engine retroactively reclassified the supplier as "non-reliable" for several months.

Nothing indicated that the machinery transaction was fictitious or abusive but the system automatically blocked the manufacturer's input VAT deduction. The reasoning followed purely a set of automated rules. A mismatch existed between the supplier risk profile and the deduction claim. No inspector reviewed the delivery notes, installation protocols, or production logs. No one assessed whether the supplier's unrelated compliance failures had any bearing on the reality of the supply. The denial came from the system.

When the manufacturer objected, the administration's initial response was revealing. It did not argue abuse, nor did it allege fraud. It argued that the automated system had detected a risk and that, pending resolution, deduction could not be allowed. In effect, the algorithm's suspicion displaced the legal requirement to demonstrate objective factors indicating abuse or the non-existence of the supply.

Had such a case reached the Court of Justice, the questions would have been unavoidable. Could a right to deduct, described repeatedly by the Court as a fundamental component of VAT neutrality, be restricted by a purely automated inference, absent any finding that substantive conditions were not met? Could an algorithmic risk score replace the evidentiary burden traditionally borne by the tax authority? And more fundamentally, could administrative convenience justify a system in which legality was presumed false unless a machine decided otherwise?

The Court's existing jurisprudence offers clues to how it might respond. In cases such as *Mahagében and Dávid* (Case C-80/11), the Court held that tax authorities may not deny deduction solely because of irregularities on the supplier's side, unless they establish, on the basis of objective evidence, that the taxable person knew or should have known of fraud. An automatic denial based on supplier risk measures would not align well with that principle. The system would be acting where the Court has insisted on individualized assessment.

What made the example unsettling was not that automation made a mistake, errors are familiar to law, but that it made the mistake silently, without explanation. There was no articulated legal test, no proportionality analysis, no weighing of neutrality against enforcement. The denial was not justified. It was "generated".

In such circumstances, the Court would no longer be reviewing a tax assessment in the classical sense. It would be reviewing the architecture of administration itself. It would have to ask whether a Member State, by embedding certain assumptions into code, had effectively rewritten VAT law without legislative debate or judicial scrutiny. It would have to determine whether an algorithm could be treated as a neutral tool, or whether it constituted an administrative act subject to the same legal constraints as any human decision-maker.

The real-life lesson from SDI was therefore not about technology failing, but about the law stepping back. When decisions emerge from systems rather than officials, the locus of legality shifts upstream, into design choices that are rarely transparent and almost never litigated directly. The Court, if confronted with such a case, would be forced to reassert a foundational truth.

The truth that VAT principles, neutrality, proportionality, and legal certainty bind not only tax inspectors and legislators, but also the machines through which the tax system now speaks.

In that sense, the algorithmic denial would not merely be a technical malfunction. It would be a constitutional moment for VAT law, testing whether the EU's legal order could still recognize, challenge, and correct decisions when those decisions no longer looked like decisions at all, but like outputs.

Marta suspected that when such a case finally arrived, the Court would resist framing it as a technological issue. It would return, as it always did, to first principles. Was there a taxable supply? Was VAT due? Was deduction justified? Had fraud occurred? Were formal requirements proportionate to their aims?

But even if the Court answered those questions, implementation would remain uncertain. A judgment could declare a principle, but changing a system was not as simple as amending a practice. Code had inertia. It resisted nuance.

This was where Marta saw the greatest risk. That legal correction would lag behind administrative automation, creating periods where rights existed in theory but were systematically frustrated in practice. The automated administrator could comply with the letter of the law while undermining its spirit, not because of bad intentions, but through the rigidity of the code.

And yet, she also saw the opposite effect. Automation made patterns visible that had never been visible before. Carousel fraud, missing trader schemes, and artificial chains, these had thrived on opacity and delay. Real-time reporting disrupted them fundamentally. The system was not the enemy of justice, but it served as an imperfect ally.

The challenge, Marta concluded, was not to resist automation, but to civilize it.

That required a deliberate effort to include legal rules in the system design from the start, not as an afterthought. To ensure that systems allowed for correction, explanation, and proportionality.

To preserve human review where substance was at stake. To accept that not every legal question could be resolved at the moment of the transaction.

As she prepared to leave for the evening, Marta thought again of the phrase that had haunted her since the beginning of this transformation. The taxman becomes a node in your IT system. It was meant as reassurance, a promise of integration. But she now understood it differently.

When the taxman becomes a node, the law risks becoming a protocol.

The task ahead for administrators, legislators, and judges alike was to ensure that behind the protocols, the law remained recognizable. That neutrality remained more than a balance of inputs and outputs. That substance retained meaning beyond what could be declared in a structured field.

Only then could the automated taxman be more than a machine that executed rules. Only then could it serve the deeper purpose of the VAT system. To tax economic reality fairly, consistently, and humanely, even in a world increasingly governed by code.

Marta stepped into the cold evening air, the city lights reflecting off wet pavement like scattered data points. Tomorrow, there would be more files, more logs, more validated truths. But for now, she allowed herself a final thought, one that felt less like analysis and more like resolve.

Automation may administer the law, but it must never be allowed to replace judgment. As long as value is created by people, the law must remain capable of seeing them, even when the system cannot.

With that, she walked on, carrying with her the understanding that the future of borders, neutrality, and justice would not be decided by machines alone, but by how firmly humans insisted on remaining present within them.

4.2 TWO IMAGES OF THE SAME TRANSACTION

Marta did not notice the mirror at first.

It appeared slowly, not as something she could see, but as something she felt. Rules that once seemed purely domestic were now shaped by decisions made elsewhere, through foreign systems and foreign ways of understanding business. As Poland's VAT administration became more automated, her work felt less national and more global. She began to see that the system was not just examining transactions at home. It was constantly comparing itself to other countries, and recognizing its own reflection in them.

Each invoice that passed through KSeF[4] carried with it more than structured data. It carried the imprint of another legal culture. Another accounting logic. Another understanding of when value was created, when risk transferred, when a transaction became real. The system treated these invoices as statements of objective truth. Marta knew better. They reflected a particular way of seeing the transaction, not the full reality behind it.

In the past, paper audits made borders obvious. Customs stamps, different languages, handwritten signatures, and courier envelopes all clearly showed how separated countries were. In the new world, borders became almost invisible. The digital invoice looked the same whether it came from Warsaw or Brussels. But even if the format was identical, the rules and expectations behind it were not.

She had seen it clearly in the Nano Source case. From the perspective of the Polish VAT system, the transaction asked a set of simple questions: where did the supply take place? Who performed it? Who bore the tax? From the perspective of the U.S. parent company, the same transaction was not a series of taxable events but a single commercial arc.

---

[4] "Krajowy System e-Faktur" is Poland's national electronic invoicing platform, through which invoices are issued in a structured format and validated by the tax administration before becoming legally effective.

Designed, approved, invoiced, and recognized according to internal milestones that made perfect sense within their own framework.

Neither side was acting dishonestly. Neither was careless. They were simply speaking different languages.

Marta realized this was the real problem of the global mirror. Automated tax systems could see everything on an invoice, but seeing was not the same as understanding. The authorities could see the amount, the date, and the parties involved. What they could not see was how that transaction was understood in another country, or how it actually worked in day-to-day business there.

VAT, for all its technical complexity, had always been deceptively simple at heart. It was a way of mapping human activity. Where people worked, where goods moved, where services were performed, where consumption finally occurred. The rules only made sense when traced back to those movements. Automation had not changed this. It had only added more layers of data on top of the same basic picture.

And yet, as Marta compared systems across borders, she saw that the same map was being drawn again and again, independently, in country after country. Sometimes it was called VAT. Sometimes GST. Sometimes something else entirely. The details changed, with different names, rates, and exceptions, but the basic structure of the system stayed the same everywhere.

Value was taxed in stages. Businesses were meant to remain neutral. Consumption was the final reference point. Transparency through the chain was the ideal. Even countries that did not call it VAT started using the same approach in practice, using digital platforms and reporting tools to collect tax at the time of each transaction instead of relying on trust between parties.

Marta realized, as she watched the city wake below her from a conference window, that VAT had grown into more than just a European tax. It had become a shared way of seeing economic reality. Not by treaty. Not by global agreement. But by necessity.

Global commerce had forced convergence where politics had not.

The mirror, however, did not reflect harmony. It reflected tension.

European VAT law was functional and precise about presence and performance. Many non-EU systems were contractual and centralized. Where the European VAT asked where work was done, other systems often asked when revenue was recognized. Where VAT law focused on physical or human presence, other systems focused on corporate decision-making or internal acceptance protocols. The distinction seemed small at first, almost just a matter of words, but in reality it went to the very heart of how different countries saw economic activity.

Marta had encountered this divergence countless times, though rarely had it been articulated so clearly. In the European VAT tradition, taxation followed activity. It followed workers, production lines, construction sites, and engineers installing equipment where the work physically took place. A service was not just a line in an accounting system or a number on a screen. It was something real, carried out somewhere by someone. The law insisted on finding that place, even when it was inconvenient or when the contract suggested it should be counted somewhere else.

But outside the VAT world, particularly in jurisdictions shaped by corporate income tax logic rather than consumption tax, reality was often defined differently. There, the decisive moment was not performance, but recognition. Not where value was physically created, but when it was turned into revenue. The supply existed, legally and economically, when it met internal criteria, such as being approved by headquarters, passing a milestone, or being recorded in the company's general ledger.

Marta remembered a case involving a multinational engineering firm headquartered in North America, supplying turnkey ind.ustrial equipment to several European plants. From the European customer's perspective, the transaction unfolded in fragments.

The machinery arrived in crates, engineers appeared on site weeks later, installation took months, testing dragged on, and only at the very end did the system become operational. From a VAT perspective, these fragments mattered. They defined whether there was a single composite supply or multiple supplies, whether installation was ancillary or dominant, and whether the place of supply shifted from export to domestic performance.

From the supplier's internal perspective, however, none of this fragmentation truly existed. The project lived as a single line in the enterprise resource planning system. Revenue was not recognized when engineers bolted machines to concrete floors, but when the customer issued a formal acceptance certificate, and headquarters approved the milestone. Until that point, the work was considered 'in progress' and did not show up as actual income in the company's accounts.

When the invoice was finally issued, it reflected that internal logic. A single document. A single date. A single value. Perfectly consistent with international accounting standards. Perfectly opaque to VAT law.

The tension was not accidental. Accounting systems were designed to answer different questions. They asked when income could be booked, when risk had sufficiently passed to justify recognition, when performance obligations under contracts were deemed satisfied. VAT law, by contrast, asked where the activity physically unfolded and who actually carried it out. The two systems intersected, but they were not aligned.

This divergence was even more obvious in industries focused on services. Marta thought of a global consulting firm where teams frequently crossed borders. Consultants flew from London to Warsaw, from Berlin to Madrid, delivering advice, designing systems, training staff. Internally, the firm treated these activities as centrally coordinated services rendered by the headquarters entity. Time sheets were coded to projects, but invoices were issued from a single jurisdiction, often months after the work was completed, once internal approvals were finalized.

From a VAT perspective, however, the services had been performed in specific Member States, by identifiable individuals, on identifiable dates. The factual reality might have supported something more territorially embedded. The place of supply rules pointed insistently toward those locations. Yet the invoice, when it eventually appeared, spoke only of a global service delivered from abroad. The algorithm saw a foreign invoice, a reverse charge, a clean deduction. The law, if asked to look deeper, would see dozens of local presences that never surfaced in the data.

Even more revealing were cases involving digital or hybrid supplies. Marta once examined a software implementation project sold by a U.S. technology company to a European manufacturer. The contract described the supply as a license coupled with "remote support and configuration." In practice, however, teams of specialists spent weeks on the customer's premises, configuring systems, integrating machinery, training operators, solving unforeseen problems that no remote connection could address.

Internally, the supplier treated these on-site activities as incidental. The real value, in its view, lay in the software itself, developed and owned abroad. Revenue recognition followed the logic of licensing. Once the software was deployed and acceptance confirmed, revenue was booked. The physical presence of engineers was merely a cost center, not a value driver.

VAT law disagreed. The law was indifferent to where the intellectual property had been conceived. It asked instead where the customer obtained the use and benefit of the service, where the functionality was made operational, where the human effort materialized into something usable. From that angle, the engineers on the factory floor mattered more than the software architects thousands of kilometers away.

This was not a question of bad faith. The supplier was not attempting to avoid tax. It was simply operating according to a different mindset, one that measured value at headquarters rather than where the work was actually done on the ground.

Marta saw the same divergence in manufacturing. In some global supply chains, goods were physically produced, assembled, and tested in one country, but ownership and decision-making resided elsewhere. Components might be shipped into a Member State, assembled by a local workforce, and shipped out again, all under toll manufacturing arrangements. For corporate tax purposes, the value was often attributed to the principal abroad. For VAT purposes, the local transformation could not be ignored.

Where VAT law focused on physical presence, other systems focused on control. Who decided what to produce? Who bore commercial risk? Who owned the inventory on the balance sheet? These questions mattered deeply in transfer pricing and corporate taxation. VAT asked what happened here?

Internal acceptance protocols illustrated this most clearly. Many multinational groups operated under strict internal governance rules. No revenue could be recognized, no invoice issued, until headquarters approved delivery. Acceptance was not merely the customer's signature; it was a multi-layered internal process involving legal, technical, and financial sign-offs.

From the company's perspective, the supply did not exist until that internal moment. From the VAT perspective, the supply might have existed weeks or months earlier, when machines were installed, services rendered, or goods made available to the customer. The law cared little for internal hierarchies. It cared about economic reality as experienced externally.

Automation intensified this divergence. Systems recorded what they were designed to record. An ERP system captured delivery dates and invoice issuance. An e-invoicing platform validated structure and timing. Neither captured the messy, human reality of work performed across borders before it was formally recorded.

This was why Marta had learned not to confuse data with the truth. The global system showed not reality itself, but each system's own version of it. Accounting showed what managers controlled.

VAT law reflected functional presence. Automation, if not handled carefully, tended to favor the accounting view simply because it was easier to program.

The challenge was not to choose one perspective over the other, but to understand that they answered different questions, and that conflict arose when one was mistaken for the whole truth. VAT law did not deny the legitimacy of revenue recognition rules. It simply refused to let them redefine where and how value had actually been created.

In this gap between recognition and performance, between control and presence, between abstract acceptance and concrete activity, Marta saw the core friction of modern taxation. Global businesses operated seamlessly across borders, guided by centralized logic. VAT systems, even automated ones, remained stubbornly territorial, insisting that economic life still happened somewhere.

And perhaps, she reflected, this insistence might not be a flaw at all, but a protection. It reminded everyone that behind every reported number were real people, real places, and real actions that no internal system or automated process could ever fully capture.

Automation made these differences seem smaller than they really were. An invoice that passed validation looked compliant everywhere. The real risk was assuming that this order, which looked fine on the outside, meant everything underneath was actually aligned.

The invoice travelled easily across borders but not its interpretation. Administrations receiving identical structured data still assessed its credibility through domestic risk assessment frameworks. Some systems released refunds automatically when transactional chains were properly aligned. Others paused, requesting supplementary documentation that another jurisdiction never considered necessary.

Standardized data reduced informational gaps, but it did not remove the need for interpretation.

Different documentation and verification practices across administrations, and fraud histories influenced how authorities responded to the same digital information.

This complicated the expectation that regulatory harmonization produces behavioral uniformity. In VAT administration, convergence was emerging less through substantive alignment than through procedural observation. Authorities observed each other's clearance systems and detection outcomes, borrowing operational practices while preserving doctrinal autonomy.

Marta had learned that algorithms are excellent at enforcing sameness. They are poor at interpreting differences. When foreign transactions deviated from domestic patterns, systems did not ask why. They flagged risk. Difference itself became suspicious, not because it was abusive, but because it was unfamiliar.

This was not about anyone trying to cheat the system. It was built into the design. An algorithm trained to expect domestic patterns would inevitably treat foreign ways of doing business as anomalies.

Marta realized that these rigid expectations had broader consequences. Small or non-EU businesses faced higher barriers simply to be treated like everyone else. The costs of registration, reporting, and adapting to local rules could discourage cross-border trade. The pursuit of uniformity risked favoring those already inside the system.

The global mirror thus distorted as much as it revealed. It made the world legible to the state, but only in its own terms. When understanding was lacking, the responsibility shifted in the background to those who were easiest to reach.

Usually, that meant the customer.

As tax enforcement becomes more automated, the automation could one day penalize legitimate transactions simply because they looked foreign or unfamiliar, before any human had a chance to review them. This was a world in which structure could be more important than substance, and where the law's focus on intent and economic reality might easily change to follow the logic of code.

Marta had seen the pattern repeat. A foreign supplier failed to register. Or registered too late. Or misunderstood local obligations. The invoice existed. The system recorded it. The tax, however, was not properly charged. Neutrality fractured, not in principle, but in practice. And when the system corrected itself, it corrected downward, onto the domestic, compliant, visible party.

The customer became the shock absorber, assuming responsibilities that once rested with the supplier's jurisdiction.

This was where the mirror became uncomfortable to look into. VAT neutrality promised that businesses would not bear the burden of tax. Yet neutrality depended increasingly on the coherence of actors beyond the system's effective reach. Where that coherence failed, neutrality became aspirational rather than real.

The Court, Marta knew, was acutely aware of this tension. Its judgments spoke the language of principle. Neutrality, proportionality, abuse of rights… But they were rendered in a world where enforcement realities pressed constantly against doctrinal purity. The Court could insist that deduction not be denied lightly, that abuse be proven, that form yield to substance. But it could not rewrite the fact that most compliance was now filtered through automated systems long before a judge ever saw a case.

VAT was moving faster than courts could decide cases. It was more global than the laws themselves. It was guided more by algorithms than by human judgment.

And yet, for all this, Marta did not see the global mirror as a failure.

She saw it as a warning.

A warning that law, once encoded, risks mistaking visibility for truth. That global convergence can produce coherence without understanding.

That neutrality, if enforced mechanically, can become something fragile and unfair. The Court of Justice has encountered this issue repeatedly. It happens when VAT is paid and intended to be neutral, but is denied by law because one condition is not met.

One of the clearest illustrations is *Reemtsma Cigarettenfabriken* (C-35/05). There, a German company paid VAT charged incorrectly by an Italian supplier on services that should have been reverse-charged. The VAT was paid in full, the services were genuine, and the economic burden was undeniably borne. Yet the Italian tax authorities refused the refund claim because the VAT had not been "legally due." Neutrality, applied strictly, would have left the taxpayer permanently out of pocket despite the absence of fraud or abuse. The Court intervened only partially. It confirmed that deduction was impossible, but required Member States to provide some alternative mechanism for recovery. Neutrality survived but only because the Court acknowledged that strict formal rules would otherwise produce an unjust result.

A similar weakness appears in *Ecotrade* (C-95/07 and C-96/07). The taxpayer misclassified intra-Community transport services under the reverse charge mechanism after invoices described the supplies as "chartering of the vessel" or "shipping" and in some cases omitted VAT or referred to exemption. As a result, the transactions were recorded only in the purchase register and not in the register of issued invoices. The Italian tax authority subsequently denied the right to deduct on the basis of these formal accounting defects and the expiry of a two-year national time limit for exercising deduction. Although the Court of Justice of the European Union accepted that Member States may impose reasonable limitation periods, it rejected the complete denial of deduction where the substantive conditions were fulfilled, and no tax loss had occurred.

Yet the Court has not always softened the edge. In *Vădan* (C-664/16), the taxpayer could not produce invoices at all and attempted to rely on alternative evidence. The Court accepted that neutrality does not require deduction where the taxpayer cannot demonstrate that VAT was actually due and paid in respect of specific supplies. In this case, neutrality gave way to legal rules, even though the economic activity itself was real.

Taken together, these examples expose the underlying tension. Neutrality is not an automatic guarantee of fairness. When enforced without regard to context, who paid, who bore the burden, whether public revenue was lost, it can become a system that is internally consistent yet externally unjust. The Court's jurisprudence does not deny neutrality. It tempers its application to ensure that the principle does not override the factual substance of transactions.

At the same time, it was also a warning that VAT, precisely because of its global spread, carried within it a rare opportunity to become not just a tax, but a shared economic language. One capable of translating between systems instead of forcing them all to look the same.

Later, sitting and looking out over the city, Marta thought that perhaps VAT had never truly belonged to any one country. It had always lived in between. Between suppliers and customers, between jurisdictions, between form and substance. Automation had not changed that. It had merely made the in-between visible.

The global mirror was not something to escape. It was something to learn how to look at.

And if the future of VAT was indeed global, then its survival would depend not on stronger algorithms alone, but on the humility to recognize that every system sees the world from somewhere and that behind every line of data lies a human movement no mirror can fully capture.

4.3 THE LIMITS OF VAT NEUTRALITY IN PRACTICE

Neutrality had once seemed like the most modest of principles. It arrived early in the architecture of VAT, framed not as a moral ambition but as a technical necessity. A way to ensure that tax did not accumulate invisibly as goods and services passed through the chain of production. Businesses would charge VAT, deduct VAT, and pass the burden onward until it reached its final place in consumption. The system was meant to work predictably, ensuring that VAT flowed through businesses without creating extra costs or unfair advantages, and that the tax ultimately landed only on the final consumer.

Yet neutrality did not remain modest. Over time, as VAT spread across borders, it became something more powerful. It grew into a firm legal principle, almost like a constitutional rule, used not just to organize the tax but to protect businesses' rights and freedom to operate fairly. In judgments, legal opinions, and national implementations, neutrality became a standard that people followed almost automatically. VAT must never distort the market, must never discriminate, and must never interfere with genuine economic activity.

And still, the cases kept coming.

They came not as challenges to neutrality, but as proof of its limits. Each case revealed the same tension, from a distinct perspective, that neutrality, when applied mechanically, could produce outcomes that seemed profoundly non-neutral in human terms. VAT paid but non-deductible because the trader "should have known" of fraud. VAT wrongly charged had to be reclaimed from the supplier rather than the State. The right to deduct was refused due to non-compliance with formal requirements. The customer paid VAT that was not legally due. The system, in its effort to be impartial, sometimes became indifferent.

Marta had noticed this change years before automation and global data flows made it obvious. It appeared in the margins of court decisions, in the careful wording of legal opinions, and in the Court's repeated reminder that neutrality, the idea that VAT should not create extra costs for businesses, was important but not unlimited. It kept showing up again and again. Businesses could only rely on neutrality if certain legal rules were fully met. Marta realized that these rules were increasingly hard to follow in real life, especially for companies trading across borders. Even when VAT was correctly calculated and invoices were accurate, the law sometimes denied rights such as deductions if the exact conditions were not met. Neutrality existed in principle, but in practice it never stood alone. It was always followed by a condition.

What was happening was not that neutrality was disappearing. It was transforming. A new kind of neutrality was taking shape, less neat and more complicated, influenced by gaps in enforcement and the new realities of global trade. Neutrality was no longer just about whether businesses could deduct the right amount of VAT. It became a question of who carried the economic risk, who could exercise the right of deduction or obtain repayment, and whose transactions satisfied the formal conditions. Who the system could see, and who it could not.

What Marta observed was not the disappearance of neutrality, but its division into two distinct ways of assessing transactions. One administrative logic relied on scalable indicators such as algorithmic risk scores. The other still depended on contextual substantiation involving contracts, business purpose, and commercial explanation.

Both claimed adherence to the same doctrinal principle. Yet they assessed credibility differently. Automated plausibility privileged conformity with predefined risk patterns. Traditional review required concrete documentation and a credible commercial explanation.

In practice, limited administrative resources meant that one approach could be scaled easily, while the other required time and individual attention. As transaction volumes multiplied and audit personnel remained finite, administrations increasingly relied on system-based filtering to determine which cases merited human attention.

The principle of neutrality thus remained doctrinally intact while its operational gatekeeping shifted toward automated triage.

In the traditional VAT system, neutrality was based on the idea that the system generally worked as expected. Suppliers were identifiable. Customers were established. Transactions occurred within jurisdictions capable of enforcement. Errors could be corrected. VAT unduly charged could be refunded. The chain, if disrupted, could be repaired.

But today's VAT system operates in a world that is no longer balanced. This imbalance is not abstract. It shows up every day in global supply chains, online services, remote work, and the creation of value that no longer depends on physical location. Suppliers increasingly operate from outside the European Union, not as an exception but as a norm. Digital platforms stand between buyer and seller, orchestrating transactions without ever becoming suppliers themselves. Algorithms generate invoices and reports with perfect formal compliance, yet without any comprehension of what had actually occurred. Import VAT is paid by entities that never supplied anything, while domestic VAT became legally due from actors the system could not meaningfully reach. Neutrality, in this world, did not disappear but it fractured.

Consider first the simplest illustration. A non-EU supplier selling goods into the European Union via an online marketplace. The goods are manufactured in Asia, marketed through a global platform headquartered in the United States, shipped via a logistics provider registered in yet another jurisdiction, and delivered to an EU consumer or business. VAT law, in response, assigns collection obligations to marketplaces, introduces deemed supplier rules, and expands IOSS[5] and OSS regimes.

These measures are designed to restore neutrality by ensuring that VAT is

[5] The Import One Stop Shop (IOSS) is an EU VAT scheme that facilitates the declaration and payment of VAT on distance sales of imported goods with a value not exceeding EUR 150, allowing VAT to be collected at the point of sale and reported through a single monthly return.

collected once, at the correct point, without disadvantaging EU suppliers.

However, neutrality in this context is no longer balanced. It has become a way to make up for what the system cannot control. The rules cannot reach everyone equally, so the responsibility falls on those who are visible, registered, and technologically integrated. Neutrality still exists, but it depends on bending the rules around what the authorities can actually enforce.

This bending becomes far more visible and far more fragile in the world of influencers.

The influencer economy is built almost entirely on non-monetary value exchange. A fashion brand sends clothing to a content creator in exchange for visibility. A cosmetics company provides free products, travel, or exclusive experiences in return for posts, stories, or videos. A technology firm lends devices for 'review purposes', fully aware that the review itself is the consideration. Payment may be hybrid, deferred, contingent, or entirely absent in cash terms. Yet value clearly moves. Consumption occurs. Economic activity exists.

From a VAT point of view, these influencer arrangements are not strange exceptions. They are classic examples of barter deals, where value is exchanged without straightforward cash payments. The influencer provides advertising by posting content, promoting the brand, or creating videos. In return, the brand gives something of value, such as clothing, makeup, gadgets, travel, or special experiences. Under standard VAT rules, each side is seen as making a taxable supply. That means VAT should be applied both to what the influencer provides and what the brand provides. The value used for VAT is not the cash exchanged, but the fair market value of what each side receives. Tax experts and accounting guides treat these in-kind arrangements the same way they treat any other non-cash exchange. Both sides must record the supplies and calculate VAT based on the open market value of what they get.

But neutrality breaks down as soon as geography comes into play. Influencer activity often crosses borders, which creates familiar VAT problems about where the service is supplied, who must charge the tax, and how neutrality can be maintained. Rules about the location of the supplier, where the customer is, and which countries require registration or have thresholds make compliance complicated. For influencers who are not paid in cash, these rules can be especially confusing, and mistakes can easily happen. Even though EU and national governments have introduced new rules to make cross-border digital services easier to track and tax, many practical problems remain. The system can struggle to see who should pay, how to enforce the rules fairly, and how to make sure the tax burden does not fall unfairly on one side. The influencer may be based in Spain, posting content viewed all over the world. The brand may be established in Korea, shipping products from a warehouse in Germany, and invoiced by a logistics company in the Netherlands. The platform facilitating the interaction, such as Instagram, TikTok, or YouTube, is neither buyer nor seller, it is just the stage. Sometimes, no traditional invoice is issued. Sometimes, no cash changes hands. Sometimes payments are made in cryptocurrency, adding another layer of complexity because the system struggles to trace who received what and when.

In these cases, no VAT is charged, no VAT is deducted, and the rules that normally protect neutrality are difficult to apply.

Formally, the system sees little.

Substantively, VAT has failed to attach to real value creation and real consumption.

If neutrality were applied strictly, the influencer should account for output VAT on advertising services supplied to a non-EU customer, likely zero-rated or outside scope depending on place-of-supply rules, while simultaneously paying VAT on the goods received as consideration. The brand, conversely, should account for VAT on the supply of goods, possibly as a deemed supply or self-supply. In practice, neither happens.

Why? Because tax authorities do not have visibility or enforcement capacity on both sides of the transaction.

Today, the influencer is human and visible but often unaware, informal, or economically marginal relative to the administrative burden. The brand is economically powerful but legally distant. The platform is central to the exchange, and while they historically bore little direct VAT liability, EU law increasingly treats them as deemed suppliers so to capture VAT on transactions that otherwise bypass traditional invoices and cash flows. The VAT system, built to track invoices and cash payments, still struggles to recognize value when it moves through attention, posts, likes, and other non-cash exchanges.

Neutrality does not break down because the law is confusing. It breaks down because the idea of neutrality assumes that everyone can be seen by the system and that the rules can be enforced equally for all. In reality, some actors are easy to track and regulate, while others operate across borders or in informal ways. When some actors are visible and others are not, and some transactions can be enforced while others cannot, VAT neutrality fails to protect all participants equally.

The same distortion appears in cross-border digital services. Take a freelance graphic designer in Portugal who works through a global online marketplace and serves clients around the world. The platform handles payments, sets the rules, controls how the service is delivered, and may even influence prices. Even so, it claims it is only an intermediary. Under current VAT rules, that claim is often accepted unless the platform is legally treated as part of the supply. As a result, the designer is responsible for charging and paying VAT. Although the platform controls the transaction and takes a significant share of the money, VAT law largely ignores that reality. The platform's role in shaping, profiting from, and scaling the business is not reflected in how VAT is charged or collected, so the tax system continues to treat the individual freelancer as the main value creator, even though most economic power and profit sit with the platform.

Neutrality survives formally, but not economically.

The problem grows even more when algorithms take over. Automated invoicing systems create documents using rules set in advance, such as the location of an IP address, the declared residence, the billing address, or whether a VAT number is valid. These proxies stand in for reality. When the data matches the actual work, everything works smoothly, and neutrality is maintained. But when the data does not reflect reality, the system produces distortions without anyone noticing.

A content creator may register as established in one Member State while performing services physically in another. An algorithm assigns a place of supply based on registration data, not lived reality. VAT is charged, deducted, or reported accordingly. No one intervenes because nothing flags as incorrect. The result is that neutrality exists only on paper, following procedures, rather than being substantive, reflecting the true economic activity.

The influencer economy makes this problem very obvious. Value is created where the content is actually made, where the influencer has built their reputation, and where their audience trusts and engages with them. VAT, however, follows registration, contracts drafted by brands, or platform terms governed by foreign law. The disconnect is not accidental. It is structural.

Another illustration comes from giveaways.

Influencers routinely organize giveaways of products provided by brands.

From a VAT perspective, these are supplies without consideration, or deemed supplies, depending on context. The brand transfers goods for promotional purposes.

The influencer distributes them. Who is the supplier? Who is the consumer? Who owes VAT, and where?

In practice, VAT is rarely accounted for. The goods cross borders under low-value thresholds. Customs declarations may undervalue them.

VAT is not charged at import. No domestic supply is declared. Yet consumption occurs, and competitive neutrality is affected. A domestic retailer selling the same product must charge VAT, but an influencer's giveaway effectively bypasses the system.

Neutrality in this context translates into real competitive advantages or disadvantages. Businesses operating through traditional channels bear tax burdens that platform-mediated, influencer-driven models eventually escape. What was meant to keep all business models on equal footing now risks giving an unfair advantage to those who operate through platforms and influencers.

What unites these examples is not innovation, but structural repetition. The same pattern appears wherever value becomes intangible, global, and platform-mediated. The VAT system continues to rely on visibility, registration, and traceable supply chains. But the contemporary economy increasingly relies on attention, data, influence, and hybrid forms of compensation. The neutrality principle is put under pressure by the tension between these two realities.

The Court of Justice has not yet spoken directly about influencers. But its existing jurisprudence already hint at the issue. In cases on barter, on advertising services, on composite supplies, on economic reality, the Court insists that VAT attaches to what is actually supplied, not how it is labelled. At the same time, it refuses to invent enforcement mechanisms where the Directive provides none.

The result is a neutrality that knows what should happen, but often cannot make it happen.

This is the basic imbalance built into today's VAT system. Neutrality is not the same as equality. The rules try not to favor one type of business over another, but that does not mean every company pays the same amount of tax or faces the same obligations. Instead, neutrality is more like a goal we aim for, shaped by the scope of the rules, the design of technological systems, and the allocation of VAT responsibility within the supply structure. The system focuses on keeping transactions orderly and consistent rather than on treating every business exactly the same. Structure and coherence take priority over true equality, and some actors like cross-border platforms and influencer-driven models, can end up better protected or advantaged simply because of how the system is designed.

And yet this is not a failure of VAT on its own. It reflects a global economy that has moved faster than the laws designed to govern it. Influencers, platforms, digital exchanges, and automated systems are not exceptions. They are signs showing where value is being created today. They point to the need for the tax system to catch up, adapt to new realities, or face the risk of distortions that cannot be ignored.

In this sense, neutrality has not disappeared, but now it helps us see problems. It acts like a spotlight that shows where the system struggles. It is meant to protect businesses from bearing the burden of VAT, but when it does not work as intended, it reveals underlying structural limits. It reveals areas where economic activity has shifted faster than the law, where new business models, cross-border arrangements, or digital exchanges are creating value that existing rules do not fully recognize. Failures of neutrality make visible the places where the tax system must adapt.

That, Marta would say, is where the real work begins.

In *Reemtsma*, neutrality did not lead to deduction, but to the obligation of Member States to provide alternative remedies. In *Ecotrade*, neutrality overrode procedural time limits but not substantive proof. In *Vădan*, neutrality stopped where evidence disappeared. In *Senatex*, the Court allowed invoices to be corrected retroactively to preserve neutrality, but only because the underlying transaction was certain. In *Mahagében* and *Tóth*, neutrality was protected from fraud, but not from negligence.

The pattern was unmistakable. Neutrality was no longer a blunt entitlement.

It was conditional, contextual, and negotiated.

This was the first doctrinal recalibration. Deduction was no longer guaranteed simply by virtue of paying VAT.

The second recalibration came with enforcement.

VAT had always relied on a simple premise. The person liable for tax is identifiable and subject to the jurisdiction imposing it. Article 193 of the Directive states this plainly. The supplier is liable. All other mechanisms, such as reverse charge, joint liability, and special schemes, are exceptions implemented to ensure tax collectability in instances where the standard model proves inadequate.

But what happens when failure becomes structural rather than exceptional?

The Court faced this issue indirectly, under circumstances that made enforcement against the supplier ineffective in situations where the supplier was difficult to identify, unable to refund VAT, or legally incapable of fulfilling VAT obligations. Again and again, the judges repeated the same principle. The impossibility of enforcement against the supplier cannot, by itself, justify shifting the burden onto the customer in a way that undermines neutrality. And yet, in practice, that was often precisely what happened.

A domestic customer paid VAT charged incorrectly by a foreign supplier. Deduction was denied because the VAT was not legally due. Recovery from the supplier was impossible. The tax authority had collected revenue but disclaimed responsibility. Neutrality existed in theory, but not in effect.

The Court's response was cautious, limiting itself to interpreting the Directive rather than rewriting it. It declined to create automatic rights where the law did not provide them.

Instead, it suggested remedies, such as refund actions, civil claims, and administrative corrections, knowing full well that these were often illusory in cross-border contexts.

This was the second recalibration.

Neutrality continued to frame the system, but in practice it could not always be secured, particularly in cross-border contexts where enforcement was difficult.

And then came automation.

Real-time reporting systems promised neutrality through precision. If every invoice was captured, validated, and cross-checked, neutrality would be preserved by design. Errors would be caught early. Fraud would be flagged instantly. Deduction would flow smoothly because the system itself would confirm entitlement.

But automation changed the evidentiary hierarchy. Invoices ceased being just records of what happened and started being treated as proof that the transaction really existed. If the system accepted the invoice, the transaction existed. At least for procedural purposes. If the system rejected it, the transaction was suspect, regardless of reality.

Neutrality shifted again. It became procedural.

In this environment, the right to deduct increasingly depended not on economic participation but on digital conformity. A taxpayer who had genuinely received services could be denied a deduction because an XML schema was wrong. A supplier who had completed work may be removed from the platform due to the expiration of their account. Historically focused on value creation, VAT law now primarily emphasized data integrity.

The Court had not yet fully confronted this version of neutrality, but the trajectory was clear. As compliance became automated, neutrality would be enforced *ex ante* by systems rather than *ex post* by judges. The danger was not over-enforcement, but under-recognition.

The risk that real economic activity would fall through the cracks of formal logic.

This led Marta to a realization that unsettled her more than any single case.

Neutrality had been designed to protect businesses from tax becoming a cost.

But in the modern system, neutrality increasingly protected the system from businesses. It ensured coherence and enforceability, albeit occasionally at the cost of neutrality in individual instances.

This was not cynicism. It was structural.

VAT was never designed to decide what is fair or unfair. Its purpose was simply to track and collect tax on goods and services. When the system worked as intended, small mistakes or unusual cases could be ignored. But as trade across borders grew more complex, those small exceptions added up. They were no longer marginal problems. They became recurring patterns.

The concept of neutrality has evolved from simply making sure that no business pays more VAT than it should. Today, it also involves deciding where a tax loss should be recognized when the system does not treat both sides of a transaction equally. Should the loss fall on the supplier who cannot be enforced? On the customer who cannot deduct? On the Member State that collected the wrong tax? Or on the system itself, through refunds that disrupt public revenue planning?

The Court had never answered this explicitly. Instead, it distributed the burden case by case, principle by principle, always insisting that neutrality must be preserved but never defining what preservation meant in a world where deduction and remittance could not be aligned on both sides of the supply chain.

This ambiguity was not accidental. It was the price of survival.

A rigid neutrality would have broken the system. An absolute neutrality would have invited abuse. A purely formal neutrality without real action would be meaningless. The Court chose a fragile equilibrium with neutrality serving as a direction, not a fixed destination.

In this equilibrium, neutrality does not guarantee deduction. It guarantees only that denial of deduction must be justified by something more than administrative convenience. It must be grounded in law, evidence, and proportionality.

This is why the Court repeatedly insists on the distinction between substantive and formal conditions. Substantive conditions go to the heart of the taxable event. Was there a supply, by a taxable person, used for taxable activities? Formal conditions serve as proof. When formalities become more important than substance, neutrality intervenes. But when the substance, the existence of a genuine taxable supply, cannot be demonstrated, neutrality cannot justify a deduction.

This is not an inconsistency. It is triage.

The new neutrality thus operates less like a rule and more like an evaluative framework. It forces the Court to ask, in each case, what would distort the system more, allowing deduction here, or denying it? Which outcome preserves the internal logic of VAT as a tax on consumption, rather than as a sanction on error?

In some cases, the answer favors the taxpayer. In others, it favors coherence of the system.

What has changed is that neutrality is no longer presumed. It must be argued, demonstrated, and contextualized. It lives not in Articles alone, but in the reasoning that connects them.

For Marta, this realization was sobering but clarifying. The neutrality she had learned as a young lawyer was clean and balanced. It belonged to a simpler era. The neutrality she now enforced was messier, burdened by global trade, digital systems, and jurisdictional limits.

It required judgment.

And judgment, she knew, could not be automated.

The new neutrality was not weaker than the old one. It was heavier. It carried the weight of a world where value moved faster than law, where systems saw invoices but not people, where VAT could be paid without being due and due without being paid.

In that world, neutrality was no longer the absence of distortion. It was the management of unavoidable distortion.

That, Marta understood, was the true evolution.

Neutrality had not failed. It had grown up.

4.4 WHEN SUBSTANCE BECOMES FICTION

The international view made it clear how things were connecting, but it also revealed a problem. Many people believed that once economic reality was identified, it would solve everything. Across jurisdictions, across systems, across courts, substance had become the universal solvent. Where form misled, substance corrected. Where contracts obscured, substance clarified. Where taxpayers planned, substance judged. It was elegant but increasingly unquestioned.

Yet Marta began to sense that something essential was being lost.

Substance, she realized, was no longer descriptive. It started as a way to describe what really happened, but now, it was slowly turning into a way to judge what should count and what should not. It had become interpretative. And then, imperceptibly, evaluative.

In its early doctrinal life, substance-over-form functioned as a limitation on legal formalism. It prevented taxpayers from hiding behind artificial structures. It reminded courts that law existed to regulate real economic life, not paper fictions. In VAT, this had been a revolution. The tax followed economic reality, not contractual choreography. It meant that tax was based on what actually happened in the real economy, not just on how transactions were written down on paper.

But looking at the bigger picture told a different story. Substance was no longer invoked only to dismantle false ideas. It was increasingly used to step in when the law was unclear, to correct outcomes that felt wrong, and to fill gaps created by global trade, the digital economy, and inconsistent enforcement.

The danger was not that substance replaced form. The danger was that the substance began to replace limits. In cases involving complex group structures, for example, transactions that met the wording of the VAT Directive and reflected real activity were later reread as a single artificial arrangement once a tax advantage became visible. What had originally been a series of lawful choices was reconstructed as a plan whose purpose was assumed from its outcome.

In case after case, across Member States and beyond, courts and administrations reached instinctively for "economic reality" as the decisive criterion. What was really happening? Who truly bore the risk? Where was the value actually created? These questions sounded factual, even neutral. But they were not answered prospectively. They were reconstructed retrospectively, through the lens of outcomes already known.

This was the first shift as substance started to reach back in time and reinterpret past transactions.

Instead of asking what economic reality the parties faced when they acted, tax authorities increasingly asked what reality 'must have existed' to justify the result now visible. Transactions were reread not as open-ended commercial acts, but as steps in a narrative whose ending was already written. Once tax loss appeared, substance aligned itself accordingly.

Intent followed the same path. In VAT law, what a person thinks or intends is not supposed to matter. The law looks at what actually happened, not at hidden motives. This is important because tax should be applied based on facts, not guesses about people's minds. The Court has said this many times. In abuse cases, it requires objective elements, things that can be seen and checked, rather than assumptions about intent.

But in practice, something changed.

Instead of first asking what the law allows, tax authorities began to look first at the result. If a transaction led to a tax advantage, that advantage itself started to look like proof of intent. The structure was treated as suspicious because of what it produced.

If the transaction could be explained by business reasons, those reasons were sometimes treated with doubt.

If it could not be easily explained, it was called artificial. In both cases, the outcome came first, and intent was read backwards from it.

This meant that intent was no longer proved.

It was assumed.

What was meant to describe the reality began to create a story about reality, instead of observing it.

Marta saw this most clearly in complex supply chains. In global arrangements involving multiple entities, shared functions, and distributed risk, substance analysis demanded a single "real" supplier, a single "real" decision-maker, a single source of value. But modern commerce did not offer such clarity. It offered coordination, not hierarchy. It offered networks, not centers.

The law, uncomfortable with plurality, collapsed complexity into singularity. It selected one entity as "the one that really mattered," not because business reality demanded it, but because VAT logic required it. Neutrality, enforceability, and fiscal coherence all depended on finding someone to hold.

And so substance became selective.

This selectivity was rarely acknowledged. Courts spoke of "the overall assessment," of "all relevant circumstances," of "economic and commercial reality." Yet the choice of which circumstances mattered was already guided by what the system needed. Substance analysis gravitated toward the actor with presence, assets, or solvency. It aligned itself with enforceability while claiming to reflect reality.

The global mirror made this pattern unmistakable. In jurisdiction after jurisdiction, substance tended to focus on whoever was closest, easiest to reach, or most powerful, rather than on the full reality of the transaction. Where non-EU suppliers stood beyond reach, substance located itself in EU-based intermediaries. Where platforms disclaimed responsibility, substance found decision-making elsewhere. Where individuals lacked documentation, substance attributed knowledge.

This was not bad faith. It was a necessity. But necessity, Marta knew, was the most dangerous justification in law.

The problem became even more serious with digitization. Algorithms could not understand substance, so they relied on proxies. Location was reduced to an IP address. Control was reduced to terms of service. Value creation was reduced to the movement of data. Once these shortcuts were encoded into systems, they became fixed. Real economic substance was no longer examined but simply taken for granted. The system appeared to work until it did not, and when it failed, the response was not to question the proxy but to increase suspicion.

The proxies were never presented as truth. They were presented as indicators, as scalable approximations of economic reality designed for systems that processed millions of transactions. Timestamp integrity, platform identifiers, and supply-chain continuity each became a signal through which substance could be inferred without reconstructing the underlying commercial story.

Administrations refined these indicators continuously, adjusting their weight as fraud patterns evolved. Governance scholars would describe this as iterative calibration. An experimental effort to align proxies more closely with underlying reality. Yet calibration required knowledge of error. How often were compliant taxpayers flagged, and how often fraudulent chains passed undetected?

Here the system encountered an institutional paradox. Tax administrations, bound by fiscal secrecy rules and anti-fraud confidentiality obligations, disclosed little about the performance metrics of their risk engines. The indicators evolved, but those subject to them had little visibility into how accurate they were.

Errors, once imaginable, turned into remote possibilities. Taxpayers found themselves needing to counter not just a presumption, but an entire narrative.

Here, substance crossed another threshold. It began to function as a moral filter.

In abuse cases, the language slowly changed. Structures were no longer described as simply artificial but as aggressive. Planning was no longer seen as efficient but as suspicious. Neutrality was no longer treated as something to maintain but as something that had to be defended against manipulation. The Court, careful in its phrasing, nonetheless allowed an atmosphere to develop in which substance was associated with honesty, while form was potentially misleading, masking the transaction's real purpose.

This moralization did not announce itself. It seeped in through adjectives, through tone, through the framing of facts. A transaction "lacked economic justification." An arrangement "served no purpose other than." A structure "could not reasonably be explained."

Reasonableness became the turning point. But whose reasoning prevails?

In a global economy, ideas of what is reasonable were no longer the same everywhere. What looked artificial in one country could be perfectly normal in another. What a court viewed as tax driven might be seen by an industry as standard market practice. Yet substance analysis rarely stopped to question the assumptions it was built on. It treated local intuition as if it were universal.

This was the real mistake of substance. Not that it was wrong, but that it forgot it depended on context.

Marta did not reject *Halifax*. She respected it. The doctrine had saved VAT from collapse. Without abuse control, neutrality would have been weaponized. But *Halifax* emerged in a world characterized by identifiable actors, straightforward transactions, and clear advantages.

It operated under the assumption that economic realities could be understood without the need to reconstruct motives or reduce multiple realities into a singular one.

The world reflected in the global mirror was different.

Influencers, platforms, data brokers, logistics integrators, algorithmic pricing engines… these actors did not fit neatly into substance categories forged in an industrial economy. Their value creation was relational and dispersed. Asking where substance lay was no longer a factual inquiry but an interpretive act.

And interpretation, once out of bounds, became fiction.

Courts, confronted with unfamiliar business models, often defaulted to analogies and comparisons to understand them. An influencer was treated as an advertiser. A platform as an intermediary. A data transfer as a service. Each analogy brought with it inherited substance criteria. But the fit was imperfect. Something always escaped.

VAT law had encountered this discomfort before.

When the European Community first attempted to tax cross-border supplies of goods within what would become the Single Market, it faced a reality that did not yet exist in legal terms. Goods moving freely across internal borders without customs controls. The Sixth Directive was drafted in a world where borders still mattered administratively, even as political ambition sought to dissolve them. The result was a conceptual compromise. Transitional arrangements that treated intra-Community supplies as exempt exports paired with taxable acquisitions, while formally preserving the destination principle.

On paper, the system worked. In practice, it encountered challenges immediately.

Economic reality moved faster than legal imagination. Goods circulated continuously, supply chains fragmented, ownership transferred without physical movement, and logistics models evolved that no longer aligned with customs-era assumptions. Courts, tax authorities, and taxpayers reached instinctively for analogies. An intra-Community supply was treated like an export. An acquisition was treated like an import. Warehouses were treated as borders. None of these analogies was wrong, but none of them was fully right either.

What followed was not doctrinal clarity, but decades of interpretive patchwork.

From the early 1990s onward, the Court of Justice was repeatedly asked to locate the "place" of a supply of goods in arrangements that bore little resemblance to the linear producer-to-consumer model the Directive presupposed. Call-off stock, chain transactions, triangulations, and consignment stock arrangements each forced the Court to decide which link in a commercial sequence mattered most. Each judgment clarified one configuration while destabilizing another.

The problem was not judicial inconsistency. It was a structural mismatch.

Goods had become mobile in ways the law had not anticipated. Control, risk, and ownership no longer aligned neatly. VAT law, committed to taxing consumption at destination, had no choice but to approximate reality through legal constructs, fictions that were tolerated because they worked well enough. Neutrality was preserved, but only at the cost of increasing complexity.

It took nearly thirty years for that instability to be acknowledged openly.

The destination principle for goods was never abandoned, but its operationalization was repeatedly deferred, adjusted, and supplemented. The definitive system promised in the 1990s never arrived. Instead, rules meant to be temporary became permanent. Compliance burdens shifted onto taxpayers. Fraud exploited the gaps. Courts refined concepts incrementally, but the underlying tension remained unresolved.

Only recently with the ViDA proposals has the EU tried to realign legal structure with economic reality.

It has done this by accepting tools it once resisted, such as real-time reporting, rules that treat platforms as suppliers, and the idea that tax systems must follow the flow of data as well as the physical movement. Even now, the solution is prospective, technological, and administrative rather than purely doctrinal.

The lesson is sobering.

When VAT law meets a new way of doing business that it does not yet fully understand or even have words for, it does not fix the problem right away. Instead, the system adapts slowly. It tries to fit the new activity into old legal categories, even when the comparison is not perfect. It relies on broad ideas like economic reality to keep things working for the time being. Only later, once the new business model becomes familiar, does the law settle into clearer rules and a more stable balance.

Today, with online platforms, social media influencers, businesses making money from data, and algorithms acting as middlemen, we are seeing exactly this same pattern in action.

An influencer is treated as an advertiser because advertising is the closest available category but the influencer is also a distributor, a brand, a media channel, and sometimes the product itself. A platform is treated as an intermediary because the law needs a familiar category yet platforms increasingly shape pricing, access, and consumption in ways that resemble neither agent nor principal. Data transfers are treated as services because the law needs to classify them, but the real value comes not from doing the work itself, but from collecting, reusing, and analyzing the information.

Just as with intra-Community goods movements in the 1990s, these comparisons work in practice, but they are not perfect and can let problems slip through.

And just as before, courts respond by refining substance, asking who really controls, who really benefits, who really decides. Over time, these questions accumulate into doctrine.

But until the law is rewritten to reflect the new economic grammar, substance analysis carries a disproportionate burden. It fills gaps. It smooths outcomes. It compensates for conceptual delay.

History suggests that resolution will come, but not anytime soon.

The destination principle for goods took decades to make the rule that goods should be taxed where they are consumed actually work in practice, and even today it is not fully complete. In the meantime, courts will keep drawing comparisons, tax authorities will keep guessing how the rules apply, and businesses will keep working in a world where the law is always a step behind new ways of doing business.

What looks like confusion in the law is not a failure. It is a delay.

But delays have consequences. And until the next structural reform arrives, substance will continue to do work it was never meant to do. Not because it is wrong, but because the law has not yet learned how to speak the language of the economy it seeks to tax.

When things did not go as planned, especially when VAT was not collected as expected, changes were made to reinforce the system. When enforcement fell short, the concept of substance was applied more broadly. When neutrality broke down, substance was used to fix the problem.

The law became reactive.

Marta understood the danger. The rule of substance-over-form, which was meant to protect against manipulation, could instead be used to reshape reality. It could treat past actions differently to make current outcomes seem correct.

It could force order where there was none and penalize new or unusual business practices simply for not looking like the old, familiar ways.

Worst of all, it could do so while speaking the language of reality.

The global mirror made this obvious. Different countries, using the same VAT rules, came to similar decisions by relying on similar interpretations of substance even when their markets were very different. Repeating the same approach built confidence. Seeing the same conclusions again and again made them seem legitimate. Over time, this way of interpreting substance became accepted as the standard.

The growing focus on substance put this principle at risk. By bringing judgment back into the analysis, it reopened distinctions that VAT was meant to eliminate.

Marta wondered whether the system had confused clarity with truth.

Substance was appealing because it promised certainty. It seemed to offer a way to make complex situations easier to understand. But in trying to simplify, it could also oversimplify. The global economy did not have just one form of substance. It had many layers. It did not have a single reality. Different people, places, and systems experienced it in different ways.

Law, she understood, could decide which perspective to follow. But it should not act as if its choice was the only possible one. The problem with substance was not doctrinal. It was about knowledge. The issue was what the law could actually see and measure. Courts did not misunderstand the law, nor did they apply the wrong principles. Rules like substance-over-form, economic reality, abuse of rights, and neutrality were mostly solid. The real mistake was assuming that the law could fully capture and judge the complex realities of economic life, where value, risk, and activity often unfolded in ways that were hidden or distributed across borders.

Doctrine answers how a legal system should reason once the relevant facts are known. The real question is how those facts are discovered in the first place. What evidence is visible, what signals are trusted, and what reality is assumed to be legible. The error of substance, therefore, was not a failure of legal reasoning, but a failure of perception.

For decades, VAT law operated on an implicit assumption that economic reality could be reconstructed through documents, contracts, invoices, and organizational charts. If one could identify who signed, who invoiced, who bore contractual risk, and who employed staff, one could determine where value was created and who should bear the tax. Substance was treated as something hidden behind form, but nonetheless discoverable through diligent investigation.

That assumption held true, more or less, in an economy where value creation was tangible, and localized. Goods were manufactured somewhere, transported somewhere else, installed or sold somewhere else again. Services were performed by identifiable people, at identifiable locations, during identifiable periods of time. Even when taxpayers attempted to manipulate form, the underlying activity usually left traces. Time sheets, shipping records, site visits, machinery, employees…

The comforting idea in that world was that substance existed on its own regardless of what papers or contracts said, and the job of the law was simply to see past the formalities and get to the real economic facts.

What changed was not the doctrine but the nature of economic reality itself.

In the platform economy, the influencer economy, the data economy, and algorithmically mediated markets, value is no longer created in places where the law instinctively looks. It does not necessarily coincide with physical presence, human labor in a single jurisdiction, or bilateral exchanges of goods or services. Value may arise from visibility rather than production, from access rather than ownership, from data aggregation rather than performance, from network effects rather than effort.

In such an environment asking where the substance is becomes a very different kind of question. It is no longer just hidden behind paperwork. It is spread out across people and places and often hard to pin down.

The law still asks questions that made sense in an older economy, such as who did the work, where, who controlled the resources, and who took the risk.

Courts answer those questions faithfully, using the best doctrinal tools available. But the answers increasingly depend on proxies, contracts, invoices, and corporate structures, because the actual economic processes do not map cleanly onto legal categories. Substance is often assumed rather than clearly seen because the law insists that it must exist somewhere, even when it is spread across people, platforms, and borders.

This is where the error about what the law can actually know emerges.

When a court attributes substance to a specific company or place, it is not always pointing to where the economic value really arose. It is pointing to where the law can recognize that value using the evidence that is available. That assignment can make sense, be fair, and follow the rules and still be incomplete or somewhat artificial. For example, treating an influencer's activity as an advertising service supplied from their place of residence is doctrinally logical. Treating a platform as an intermediary rather than a principal may be contractually accurate. Treating data provision as a taxable service supplied where the provider is established may follow the Directive. None of these choices is doctrinally wrong.

But they rely on a simplified assumption that value is created in a single place, can be assigned to one party, and can follow a clear order that the law can interpret. A substance based approach asks not just who receives payment, but where the real economic value is created, who bears the risks, and who performs the activities that make the transaction valuable.

The "error of substance" does not arise from courts prioritizing form over substance. It comes from focusing on the substance itself when that substance can only be seen through forms. Because the law cannot directly see the real economic activity, substance is often reconstructed from what can be observed.

In other words, substance becomes a legal story built from available evidence rather than a true reflection of how value was actually created.

This explains why modern VAT rulings often seem correct but also feel a bit forced. The reasoning is careful, the principles well-founded, the outcome defensible, and yet the reader senses that the law is resolving disputes by forcing new realities into old conceptual frames.

In that sense, substance has not failed the law. The law has reached the limits of what it can know.

The gap in what can be known grows even bigger when automated systems are used. When these systems assume everything is correct unless something looks wrong, the law can see even less of what is actually happening. What is not recorded in the data is not just missing, it is invisible. Substance is no longer something a court might overlook. It is something the system was never built to observe.

Thus, the deepest tension in contemporary VAT law is not between form and substance, but between knowable reality and lived economic reality. The doctrine remains intact, but the world it seeks to describe has changed shape. VAT fails because the economic model itself has become unobservable. Transactions, digital flows, and automated exchanges happen in ways the law cannot detect. Value is created, shifted, and extracted in invisible layers. The nominal "supplier" may receive nothing, while algorithms route revenue, risk, and benefit across jurisdictions in milliseconds.

Seen this way, the error of substance is not a mistake to be corrected by sharper reasoning alone. It is a signal that VAT law, like all law, depends on assumptions about how the world can be known and that those assumptions are now under strain.

This does not render substance obsolete. It is structurally inaccessible.

And this fragility, rather than doctrinal confusion, is what defines the current moment in the evolution of VAT.

It lay in the belief that reality is singular, observable, and aligned with legal outcomes. Once this belief became common, fewer checks remained, responsibility was passed on, and ideas stopped being questioned.

But economic reality and legal reality drifted apart. Automated systems enforced the letter of law without apprehending its purpose. The VAT net became perforated, with entire streams of value flowing where it cannot be observed, reported, or taxed. The illusion persisted that all activity is accounted for, while in reality, the economy escaped the law entirely.

Taxpayers were asked not only to comply, but to conform to structures that matched the system's preferred narrative.

This was where neutrality began to change character.

No longer merely a principle of equal treatment, it became a principle of acceptable reality. Those whose business models aligned with established substance paradigms passed easily. Those who did not faced friction, scrutiny, and mistrust.

Innovation became risk.

As Marta closed her notes, she did not feel alarmed but aware of her responsibility. The global mirror had revealed both the strength and the weakness of VAT's logic. Substance was indispensable to understanding and applying the law. But if it was relied on without care, it could become nothing more than accepted stories rather than a true reflection of economic reality.

The task ahead was not to discard substance, but to guide it carefully, to keep it humble, to understand its limits, and to make it a tool for interpreting reality rather than rewriting it. Only by doing this, she thought, could neutrality endure. Only then could the system show the world as it truly was, instead of the world the law wanted it to be.

4.5 BORDERS AFTER GEOGRAPHY

Marta had spent most of her career believing that borders were facts. This was not about abstractions or stories. Borders were real. They were lines on maps, made tangible by checkpoints, by different languages, by legal systems, and by the persistent force of sovereignty. Goods crossed it. People crossed it. Sometimes, services crossed it in an unclear way, and the only evidence they left was paperwork meant to explain their path. But tax law followed.

Her daily work showed that this belief was no longer true.

What unsettled her was not that borders were weakening. It was that they were no longer where the law insisted on looking for them. The physical frontier, the place where a truck stopped, a container was opened, a stamp applied, still existed, but it no longer did the work it once did. Borders had not disappeared. They had simply shifted to new places. They no longer sat at roads, ports, or checkpoints, but in data flows, digital platforms, contracts, and systems that determined where value was created and where tax was expected to be paid.

The migration was not dramatic. There were no declarations, no treaty amendments announcing the end of geography. Instead, borders were included in systems, fields, databases, validation rules, and reporting obligations. They reappeared not as fences, but as conditions. Not as walls, but as mechanisms.

Fiscal sovereignty had not receded but it had been reframed. Member States retained authority over rates, exemptions, and domestic audit doctrine. What changed was the informational environment within which those sovereign powers operated.

Digital reporting regimes now consolidated and expanded through initiatives such as VAT in the Digital Age, rendered cross-border transactions visible in ways previously unattainable. Administrations could observe supply chains beyond their territorial reach even while taxing rights remained nationally bounded.

This, however, did not produce a Brussels effect in the classical sense.

EU VAT rules were not extending outward to reshape global tax systems. Instead, a shared reporting and enforcement infrastructure was consolidating inward by integrating transactional visibility while leaving substantive fiscal choices politically and legally decentralized. This was not the future. It was already the present.

The first sign had come years earlier, within the European Union, when customs clearance ceased to be the decisive moment for VAT in cross-border trade. Import VAT was once the gatekeeper of fiscal sovereignty. A charge levied precisely because a good had crossed a physical boundary. The logic was intuitive. The state exercised its taxing power at the moment the goods entered the country. The border was the tax point.

But that logic fractured the moment supply chains stopped aligning with entry points.

High-value goods began arriving long before ownership transferred. Equipment crossed borders only to be stored, installed, adjusted, tested, and sometimes even rejected. The related services travelled with the goods and were closely connected to them, even though the law still treated them as separate transactions.

Use and consumption no longer happened at the moment of import and often not in the country where the goods first arrived. VAT rules adjusted to this reality, and the old idea of the border as a clear physical dividing line gradually lost its role.

Then came digital reporting.

At first, it seemed procedural. A way to reduce fraud. A way to speed up audits. A way to replace paper with machine-readable formats. But as platforms like

SDI[6], KSeF[7], SAF-T[8], SII[9], and their counterparts proliferated, something more profound occurred. States stopped needing to see goods cross borders. They only needed to see transactions appear in systems.

A supply that was never declared electronically might as well not exist. A supply declared incorrectly might exist in the wrong jurisdiction. The border was no longer something you crossed on the ground, but something you encountered when information was submitted, or not, inside an administrative system.

Marta began to understand that jurisdiction was no longer enforced at the frontier, but inside the transaction itself.

Every e-invoice contained a set of jurisdictional claims. A place of supply, VAT rate, customer status, reverse-charge flag, currency, and time stamp. Each claim was a miniature border assertion. The system did not ask where the truck went. It asked where the invoice said the supply belonged.

And increasingly, the system believed the invoice.

This shift turned long-standing legal thinking upside down. In the past, borders were seen as fixed facts that transactions had to follow. Now it was the transaction itself that determined where the border mattered. Jurisdiction no longer flowed from physical location, but from how an activity was described and recorded.

A supply classified as domestic became domestically taxable even if every physical element of performance occurred elsewhere.

---

[6] Italy's centralized electronic invoicing platform through which VAT invoices must be transmitted, validated, and exchanged with the tax authorities in near real time.
[7] Poland's national electronic invoicing system that requires structured VAT invoices to be issued and received through a government-run platform, enabling continuous transaction monitoring.
[8] An OECD developed standard for the electronic exchange of accounting and tax data between businesses and tax authorities, adopted in various forms by multiple countries to facilitate audits.
[9] Spain's real-time VAT reporting system requiring large taxpayers to submit detailed invoice data to the tax authorities shortly after issuance or receipt.

A supply classified as cross-border triggered reporting obligations and reverse-charge mechanisms, even if no border was ever crossed by a person or object. The legal border was no longer tied to geography. It moved according to tax rules and administrative classifications, not mountains, rivers, roads, or checkpoints.

This was most visible in services, where geography had always been fragile. Services such as consulting, licensing, advertising, platform access, and cloud computing have historically resisted geographical boundaries. That was not new. What changed was that goods began to follow the same path. When installation, setup, software, and customer services combined into one business, the traditional idea of location became unclear.

The question, then, was unavoidable. Where did the border actually lie?

Marta discovered the answer not in the literal interpretation of the law, but in its practical application. Borders appeared wherever a problem had to be corrected. When reported information no longer matched what was really happening, an authority stepped in and claimed responsibility. Borders were no longer drawn on maps. They emerged wherever the law could be enforced. If not, then the border effectively does not exist in practice.

A company might be physically present in a state and yet invisible to its tax system. Another might have no people, no assets, no premises, and yet be fully legible, taxable, and auditable through its data footprint. Presence was no longer about being physically there. It was informational. That tension was not entirely ignored at the international level, but it was addressed in a different tax universe. Over the past decade, the OECD devoted enormous intellectual and political capital to the problem of non-physical presence in corporate income tax, most visibly through the BEPS Project and later the Two-Pillar solution. Concepts such as "significant economic presence," "value creation," and "user participation" were developed precisely to deal with companies that could extract profits from a jurisdiction without people, assets, or brick-and-mortar establishments.

In that discussion, the presence of users, data, and digital activity began to replace territorial connections.

VAT never entirely followed that route, not because the idea lacked appeal, but because its architecture would not allow it. VAT does not tax profits, but transactions. It does not ask where value accrues to shareholders, but where value is consumed. As a result, VAT law continued to rely on formal connecting factors, place of supply rules, customer status, and reverse charge mechanisms, rather than developing a standalone doctrine of digital or informational presence. Where corporate tax sought new nexus rules, VAT largely doubled down on enforcement tools. Registration obligations, platform liability, e-invoicing, and real-time reporting.

The consequence is a conceptual imbalance. Corporate tax now openly accepts that a business can be present in a country without any physical footprint, for example, through data, users, or digital activity. VAT, by contrast, often collects tax in similar situations without ever clearly saying that such a presence exists. Instead, being visible in data systems becomes a practical stand-in for legal presence, not because the law clearly defines it that way, but because tax authorities need something they can see and act on. VAT did not formally rethink what presence means.

It simply adapted its rules around whatever form of presence administration could detect and enforce.

This reconfiguration created a gradual but profound imbalance. Large, systemically integrated businesses became very visible. Their transactions went into national databases. They were checked and analyzed. Smaller or less integrated actors, by contrast, could remain partially opaque not by hiding, but by falling below the thresholds of attention.

Borders, in other words, now followed data density.

This was not a conspiracy, nor a deliberate policy choice. It happened naturally as a result of how automated tax systems work. These systems can only respond to the information they are given, and they handle best the transactions that are standardized, organized, and occur in large numbers. Jurisdiction attached itself to those flows.

For Marta, this raised a deeply uncomfortable question about whether sovereignty was being exercised equally or selectively.

The old idea of a border assumed that everyone crossing it would be treated the same under the law. A truck entering a country faced the same rules no matter what it carried. Borders based on data work very differently. They only "activate" when certain patterns, unusual signals, or risks are detected. This means that two transactions can be the same in economic terms. Yet they may be treated very differently, depending on how they are recorded, reported, or shown in digital systems.

The border had become conditional.

This conditional logic was especially clear in how VAT registration worked. Legal concepts like establishment, fixed establishment, and place of supply set out which businesses had to register in which country and for which transactions.

In practice, however, registration followed a simpler question.

Could the authorities actually enforce the rules if the business was not registered?

This was not cynicism. It was administrative realism.

When a non-resident supplier made supplies that were legally domestic but practically unenforceable, the system faced a dilemma. Enforcing registration could be doctrinally correct and operationally futile. Allowing reverse charge preserved collection but distorted legal coherence. Neither solution was clean.

Borders, here, did not disappear. They fragmented.

The law insisted on one border. The system enforced another.

The result was a layered jurisdiction encompassing legal, administrative, and practical dimensions. The border existed in all three, but not in the same place.

Marta saw this fragmentation play out repeatedly. In assessments that recognized domestic supplies but relied on customers for collection. In court decisions that affirmed doctrinal purity while tolerating enforcement gaps. In guidance notes that spoke of neutrality while structuring obligations around compliance feasibility.

None of this was accidental. It was the law adapting under pressure.

The most revealing moment came when Marta realized that customs authorities and tax authorities were no longer co-located in logic, even when they shared buildings. Customs still focused on controlling physical goods at the border. Tax focused on making sure transactions were properly recorded and reported. Their borders overlapped less and less.

A container could clear customs flawlessly and still generate no VAT event. An entirely virtual supply could generate a tax liability instantly, even though nothing physically moved. The border was no longer a shared institutional experience. It existed for specific purposes, depending on what the authorities were trying to control.

This had consequences beyond administration. It reshaped legal imagination.

If borders were no longer primarily territorial, then jurisdiction itself was no longer linked to land. The connection was no longer territorial but relational, formed through links between supplier and customer, between declared data and underlying transactions, and between administrative systems and economic actors.

VAT, more than any other tax, exposed this shift because it sits where trade, consumption, and information meet. It could collect tax on transactions even when nothing physically moved and on value even when the supplier was not physically present.

It enforced neutrality through traceability rather than proximity.

In that sense, VAT became the first tax that could work easily in a world where geography mattered less than data and connections.

But comfort did not mean clarity.

The legal framework continued to employ terms such as "place of supply," "place of consumption," and "place of establishment." Yet these places increasingly functioned as legal coordinates rather than physical locations. They were points in a conceptual map, not dots on the earth.

That level of abstraction was not without consequences. As borders became less clear, it became harder to solve the conflicts around them. While a taxpayer may challenge the geographical location where a service was rendered, contesting the system-designated location of a transaction proves to be considerably more difficult. That location is no longer determined by people and places, but by legal rules built into databases, VAT identification numbers, and automated reporting systems.

Marta worried about this to some extent. Not because she doubted the legitimacy of automated administration, but because she understood its authority. Systems, once operational, develop their own rules. What they recognize becomes real. What they do not, disappears.

Borders were no longer set at customs checkpoints or debated in legal disputes over physical frontiers. They were embedded in schemas, APIs, validation rules, and reporting obligations. They were decided by architecture.

And architecture, once built, resists scrutiny.

Yet Marta did not see this as a tragedy. She saw it as a responsibility.

If borders had moved, then legal thought had to follow. Courts could no longer reason as if territorial presence were the primary organizing principle. Legislators could no longer assume that sovereignty expressed itself at entry points.

Neutrality could no longer be defended without considering that comparable transactions could be taxed differently.

The challenge was not to restore geography, but to understand what had replaced it.

Borders, she concluded, had become events rather than lines. They appeared during data validation, when a transaction was recorded, or when a liability became real. They existed as much in time as in space. Sometimes a border was crossed not by stepping over it, but simply by saying it was crossed.

This realization reframed everything that followed.

The question was no longer whether borders would survive globalization. They already had, by changing from physical lines on a map to place-of-supply rules, reverse-charge mechanisms, OSS reporting, and deemed-supplier provisions.

The real question was whether the law could learn to see them.

And whether justice could still be done in a world where the VAT border is no longer a physical customs frontier, but a legal determination embedded in reporting systems and place-of-supply rules.

4.6 TAXING WHAT COMPANIES DO, NOT WHERE THEY ARE

In any legal system, borders have a clear role. They delineate the jurisdictional authority and allocate risk. In public law, borders are meant to determine which sovereign may legislate, administer, and enforce. In tax law, they perform an even more fundamental role. They show which country has the right to tax and when. Without borders, taxes would feel unclear and unpredictable to most people.

VAT has always depended on this promise of territorial clarity. It was designed to operate within bounded markets, administered by national authorities, and coordinated through relatively simple rules of allocation. As long as economic activity remained closely tied to physical presence, territorial criteria worked well enough. They were imperfect, but they aligned sufficiently with economic reality to sustain legitimacy and administrability.

What has changed is not that borders matter less in law, but that they matter less in deciding the result. Borders are still clearly written into laws and court decisions. They continue to structure competence and procedure. Yet increasingly, they no longer settle the outcome of VAT analysis. They frame the inquiry without resolving it. The decisive work has begun to migrate elsewhere.

This migration has not been the result of a single reform or conceptual rupture. It has occurred gradually over time as more exceptions, detailed rules, and methods of interpretation have been introduced. VAT has not abandoned territory. It has simply grown beyond it.

What changed was what the system now looks at first when making decisions. In the past, territory was the main reference point. Where territory once defined allocation, function now intervenes. VAT analysis increasingly turns on how a transaction operates, where value is realized, and which legal fiction the system is prepared to sustain. Use, access, control, and substance matter not because lawmakers formally chose them, but because borders alone stopped being a reliable way to decide who should tax what.

Determining that function increasingly depended on infrastructures shaped jointly by regulators and technologists. Platforms classified supplies in real time. Reporting systems translated place-of-supply rules into structured data fields. Jurisdiction was no longer inferred solely through legal interpretation but built into the design of the systems themselves.

The shift did not eliminate interpretive disputes, but it moved them earlier into coding choices and reporting classifications. Legal judgment became embedded in administrative and technological architectures shaped jointly by legal and software engineering expertise.

This shift is often described as technical, even inevitable. But it is neither. It reflects a deeper institutional problem in which the way law is organized by country no longer matches how modern economic activity actually works.

For much of its history, VAT could rely on territory because economic value cooperated. Goods were made in identifiable places, shipped across visible national borders, and used mostly within one country. Services were usually provided locally and depended on where the seller or the customer was located. In that context, borders functioned as reliable proxies. They did not capture economic reality perfectly, but they captured it well enough.

Even then, territory was never more than an instrument. It simplified complexity by translating economic activity into jurisdictional categories. It worked not because it was conceptually pure, but because reality tolerated the simplification. As long as value waited for borders, borders could decide.

That tolerance has eroded. More and more transactions now take place across several countries, over long periods of time, and through complex business networks that are hard to separate. Services are performed but not consumed locally. Control is exercised remotely. Goods are delivered but not accepted. Components may be dispatched from several Member States, consolidated in transit for invoicing purposes, stored and reconfigured in another country, and only finally assembled at the customer's premises elsewhere.

At no point does the economic process coincide exactly with a single place of supply or a single taxable moment.

VAT doctrine has responded pragmatically. Composite supplies absorb fragmentation. Fixed establishment doctrines stretch to capture economic presence without physical permanence. Place-of-supply rules multiply and specialize. None of these moves abolishes territory. Each compensates for its insufficiency.

What we see now is a tax system that still talks about borders but no longer depends on them to reach decisions. When borders no longer clearly show who is responsible, VAT looks instead at how a transaction actually works.

The closest historical parallel lies outside tax law. Intellectual property law encountered the problem of mobile, non-localized value much earlier. Creative works and inventions have always resisted territorial confinement. A work may be created in one country, exploited in another, and consumed globally without ever crossing a border in a traditional sense.

Intellectual property law confronted this reality in the late nineteenth century. With the Paris Convention of 1883 and the Berne Convention of 1886, states accepted that protection of inventive and creative value required coordinated recognition across borders. Over time, this coordination deepened. By the end of the twentieth century, intellectual property had developed a dense multilateral architecture capable of managing cross-border exploitation and enforcement conflict.

How and when value is recognized across borders changes the rules of the game. When VAT emerged as a general consumption tax in the mid-twentieth century, intellectual property law had already spent decades experimenting with international coordination. By the time VAT harmonization became a serious project in the European Union, intellectual property law had already accepted binding multilateral obligations as a condition of coherence.

The adoption of the TRIPS Agreement marked an important change.

Intellectual property rules were no longer based only on countries recognizing each other's systems, but became binding obligations that could be enforced internationally. Minimum standards became conditions of participation in the global trading system, backed by the possibility of trade retaliation. Sovereignty was not abandoned, but it was disciplined externally.

VAT has never taken this step, and the reason is structural rather than accidental. VAT is not merely a regulatory framework. It is a central instrument of fiscal policy. Decisions about VAT rates, exemptions, thresholds, and how tax is collected directly affect government income, prices paid by consumers, and how money is redistributed within a country. They are politically visible and democratically sensitive.

Unlike intellectual property rules, which affect government finances only indirectly, VAT rules immediately change how much money the state collects. If countries agreed to binding international VAT rules, they would limit their own freedom to decide tax rates, exemptions, and enforcement. Governments have consistently been unwilling to give up that level of democratic control over public revenue. The absence of a global VAT treaty framework is therefore not a failure of ambition. It reflects the political limit of how much coordination is possible in consumption taxes. That limit becomes clear when we consider what a VAT treaty would actually require.

Agreement on tax rates would affect how money is shared within each country. Agreement on what is taxed and what is exempt would influence social policy, industrial choices, and the cost of living. An agreement on enforcement responsibilities would redistribute administrative burdens and risks between tax authorities. Dispute resolution mechanisms would require acceptance of decisions made outside the country on important tax matters.

These are not technical disagreements. They are distributive conflicts. They produce winners and losers within and between states. It is precisely such conflicts that governments have been unwilling to externalize.

Instead of binding treaties, VAT coordination has grown through non-binding guidance, cooperation between tax authorities, and regional alignment. The OECD's International VAT and GST Guidelines exemplify this approach. They explain in detail how taxing rights should be divided in cross-border transactions, especially for services and digital supplies. They encourage convergence without imposing obligation.

This non-binding character is not a transitional compromise. It reflects a stable equilibrium. Soft law allows states to coordinate without surrendering ultimate authority. It enables convergence while preserving reversibility. In this sense, OECD guidance represents not a step toward binding international VAT law, but the maximum level of coordination that VAT can tolerate without undermining fiscal sovereignty.

Within the European Union, coordination has gone further, but only within a bounded political space. Harmonization has been achieved through directives, administrative cooperation, and judicial interpretation. Even here, however, agreement has been possible only because fiscal authority ultimately remains national. Outside the European Union, coordination relies almost entirely on voluntary alignment.

As VAT analysis moves away from territory and shifts toward function, this institutional structure becomes increasingly pressured. Functional criteria now decide outcomes with growing frequency. Yet the authority behind these criteria is diffuse. Legislatures endorse them indirectly. Courts refine them incrementally. Administrations apply them pragmatically. No single institution claims responsibility for the overall architecture.

The result is not the disappearance of borders, but their transformation. Borders no longer determine outcomes by themselves. They operate as reference points for applying place-of-supply rules, reverse-charge mechanisms, intra-Community acquisitions, and reporting obligations.

Responsibility is reconstructed after the fact, through audit, interpretation, and dispute, rather than being fixed in advance by the location of the warehouse, shipment, or customer.

Formal legal approval is no longer the main source of authority. Instead, the system relies on informal power. Experts agree on common approaches, tax authorities trust each other's practices, and officials coordinate their work in technical ways. This allows the system to operate without clearly stating who has the final right to decide. This arrangement is effective, but fragile. It depends on continued cooperation, not on clear and enforceable rules. It produces outcomes without clearly identifying who authorized the criteria that produced them.

VAT thus finds itself in a distinctive position. Like intellectual property law, it must follow value rather than territory. Unlike intellectual property law, it cannot support that shift with a binding international authority. Function emerges as a solution to a practical problem, not as a legitimized principle.

Function does not replace territory as a legal concept.

It replaces it as a decision-maker. When borders no longer allocate responsibility convincingly, function intervenes. But this still leaves uncertainty about who has the final authority.

This displacement of territory by function exposes a deeper tension at the heart of modern VAT design. If it is no longer possible to determine with certainty where consumption takes place, and taxing rights must instead be assigned through legal mechanisms such as administrative proxies, deemed-consumption rules, platform liability regimes, or market-access nexus criteria, the traditional link between destination and consumption begins to break down. VAT continues to target final consumer spending, but it now often determines where that consumption is taxed through legal and administrative criteria instead of by locating it within a territorially bounded sovereign space. Although the tax base is preserved, the traditional assumption that consumption happens in a clearly identifiable place, and that this place determines the taxing state, is increasingly giving way to rules that depend on practical enforceability, economic connection, and a business's participation in a domestic consumer market. In these conditions, the question can no longer be avoided, because if consumption is inferred, or fractionally attributed through functional criteria rather than observed territorially, in what sense does VAT remain a tax on consumption at all?

VAT is conventionally described as a consumption tax because it is designed to burden final consumption within the boundaries of a particular jurisdiction. Consumption is presumed to take place somewhere, and that place determines the taxing right of a sovereign authority. The destination principle, in this sense, is not merely an economic rule. It is a constitutional assumption. It links the economic effect of the tax to the authority of a specific territory.

Yet VAT case law increasingly demonstrates that this link no longer performs its allocating role reliably. Where territorial criteria fail to capture economic reality, courts and administrations turn instead to functional indicators. In disputes concerning complex or digitally mediated transactions, the decisive question is often no longer where an activity is formally located, but where it is effectively used or exploited.

This development is visible, for example, in cases concerning fixed establishments. In *Berkholz* and later in *DFDS*, the Court of Justice acknowledged that physical presence alone does not determine where a supply is taxed. What matters is whether a structure allows a business to carry out supplies in a sufficiently stable and autonomous manner. The emphasis shifts from formal establishment to functional capacity. The border is drawn not at the place of incorporation or registration, but at the point where economic activity is effectively organized and accessed.

The same logic appears more explicitly in later case law. In *Welmory*, the Court confronted a platform-based business model in which economic activity was distributed across several jurisdictions. Rather than locating consumption territorially, the Court focused on where the platform's services were actually used and where economic reality unfolded. The analysis did not deny the relevance of location, but it refused to let location decide the outcome on its own.

More recently, in *Dong Yang*, the Court rejected the idea that a subsidiary's mere presence automatically creates a fixed establishment for its parent. Instead, it required an assessment of whether the parent had access to human and technical resources enabling it to receive and use services. The decisive criterion was not legal form or territorial presence, but functional access and economic integration.

The reliance on functional criteria is not confined to fixed-establishment doctrine. It appears across distinct areas of VAT case law wherever territorial rules fail to allocate taxing relevance convincingly. In use-and-enjoyment cases, the Court has accepted that formal place-of-supply rules may be displaced when they fail to reflect where services are actually exploited, allowing taxing rights to follow economic use rather than contractual or geographic location. A similar logic emerges in disputes concerning electronically supplied, broadcasting, and telecommunications services, where consumption is treated not as a territorially situated event but as a pattern of access and utilization that may span several jurisdictions simultaneously. The same functional reasoning can be observed in relation to goods, particularly in cases involving installation or assembly supplies, where physical movement alone is not decisive, and taxation is instead tied to the place where goods become operational and acquire economic relevance. Even in chain transactions, traditionally regarded as the most territorial domain of VAT, the allocation of taxing rights increasingly depends on economic control and the functional role of transport within the transaction rather than on the mere crossing of borders.

Taken together, the case law demonstrates that VAT now assigns taxing relevance through functional indicators of use, access, and economic role rather than by physical location, challenging the traditional notion of consumption-based taxation.

In such cases, VAT continues to burden use in an economic sense, but it ceases to operate as a consumption tax in the traditional public-law sense. Consumption is no longer located and taxed by a single sovereign. It is attributed, sometimes indirectly and sometimes fractionally, through criteria that reflect functional dependence rather than territorial attachment. VAT increasingly depends on functional roles rather than territorial location, particularly when the consumer cannot be precisely identified. In practice, digital platforms such as Netflix, Spotify, or OnlyFans face operational challenges in verifying users' locations, applying the correct VAT rates across multiple jurisdictions, and ensuring timely reporting and remittance. Decentralized NFT marketplaces face even greater challenges, as purchasers are often anonymous or pseudonymous, making it extremely difficult to determine which jurisdiction has taxing rights and to collect VAT reliably from each user.

This transformation does not convert VAT into an income tax, nor does it dissolve its neutrality logic. What it alters is the constitutional link between taxation and territory. VAT increasingly relies on an implicit claim that states may tax economic use that matters to them, even when that use cannot be clearly located. That claim is rarely articulated, yet it underpins a growing body of case law.

VAT therefore continues to describe itself as a consumption tax, even as the concept of consumption it relies on becomes more abstract and less territorial. The persistence of that language masks a shift in how taxing rights are justified. Consumption remains the economic reference point, but territory no longer performs the decisional work it once did.

This transformation does not signal failure. VAT continues to function, and in many respects it functions remarkably well. But it does so by relying on criteria that operate in the shadow of formal sovereignty. Borders persist, but they are increasingly negotiable. They are redrawn through interpretation rather than imposed through geography.

In moving from territory to function, VAT does not abandon its foundations.

It exposes their limits. And in doing so, it shifts the responsibility for deciding taxing rights to courts and tax authorities, because borders alone can no longer determine where VAT should apply.

4.7 HOW INTERPRETATION CREATES THE FUTURE VAT SYSTEM

By the time a court is asked to decide the case, the shift has already taken place. VAT no longer relies on territory as a stable point of reference. It continues to speak in territorial terms, but it no longer trusts them to do the decisive work. Borders still appear in the law, in directives, and in case law, yet they increasingly function as starting points rather than conclusions. What matters is no longer where something is located, but how it operates, where value is realized, and which legal fiction the system is prepared to sustain.

This transformation does not look so dramatic. It emerges over time through a series of adjustments that appear technical when taken in isolation. Place-of-supply rules are refined. Concepts such as fixed establishment and economic presence are stretched. Composite supplies absorb transactions that once would have been split. None of this abolishes territory. Instead, it renders territory provisional.

At this stage, the resemblance with intellectual property law becomes difficult to ignore. In both fields, territorial attachment has given way to the focus on economic reality, not because legislators abandoned geography, but because geography ceased to organize economic reality in a meaningful way. In intellectual property law, this shift was acknowledged early and institutionalized through international coordination. In VAT, it occurs more hesitantly, from administrative practice and judicial interpretation.

What distinguishes VAT is not the presence of functional reasoning, but the absence of a single authority that defines it. Economic reality decides outcomes, but their legitimacy is often discussed indirectly or by implication. The functional criteria appear as pragmatic tools designed to make the system work. Judgment is still exercised, but it is less clear who is responsible for the underlying criteria and on what basis.

It is in that space that the problem of judgment arises.

When borders no longer determine outcomes, decisions must still be made.

Someone must decide which facts count, which relationships matter, and which version of economic reality the law will recognize. That decision is no longer grounded in territory. It is established by judgment.

The Nano Source case did not present itself as a challenge to VAT doctrine. On the surface, it appeared as a familiar configuration. Equipment manufactured outside the Union, imported into a Member State, installed on site, and contractually accepted only after successful testing. None of these elements was unusual. Each had been addressed, in one form or another, by existing rules and case law.

What made the case difficult was not complexity, but alignment. The transaction unfolded over time. Value emerged gradually, through design, delivery, installation, calibration, and eventual acceptance. Risk shifted in stages. Control was exercised remotely, then locally, then jointly. At no single moment did the transaction come in a way that allowed VAT law to attach itself without remainder.

From the perspective of the business, the project was coherent. Nano Source managed the process centrally. Technical decisions were coordinated across jurisdictions. Local presence existed to make the system function, not to fragment it. The equipment was not simply delivered. It was made operational. Until acceptance, it remained, in a meaningful sense, incomplete.

From the perspective of VAT law, coherence was harder to maintain. Importation triggered a taxable event. Installation suggested a supply of services performed domestically. Customer paid the import VAT. Contractual acceptance deferred transfer of ownership. Each legal qualification captured part of the reality while distorting another. The law could not observe the transaction as a whole without abandoning the categories through which it normally operated.

When the file reached Marta's desk, it did not announce its difficulty. It became problematic only as she began to reconstruct it.

Each attempt to stabilize the transaction required a choice. Treating the installation as ancillary preserved economic unity, but weakened territorial attachment. Treating it as a separate supply respected location, but fractured the transaction. Allowing deduction of import VAT maintained neutrality, but loosened the link between tax and supply. Denying it preserved structure, but imposed costs that appeared disconnected from any abuse.

None of these outcomes could be dismissed as legally indefensible. Each could be justified by reference to doctrine. Each, however, drew the border in a different place.

Marta was not confronted with a gap in the law. She was confronted with an excess of legal possibilities. The problem was not that the law failed to provide an answer, but that it provided several, none of which could be applied without suppressing part of the economic reality. The task was not to discover the correct rule, but to decide which fiction the system could sustain.

The assessment that followed reflected that limitation. It did not accuse the company of manipulation or intent. It did not invoke abuse. Instead, it reconstructed the transaction through the lens of enforceability. Installation was treated as decisive. Import VAT was separated from domestic taxation. The assessment acknowledged that this solution was imperfect, but it was one that the system could administer.

For Nano Source, the assessment felt disproportionate. From their perspective, VAT had detached itself from economic substance. From Marta's perspective, substance had become unmanageable. The case made clear that she could not treat the transaction as one legally coherent supply without disturbing the territorial logic of VAT. Judgment did not resolve the tension. It located it.

Once the dispute headed toward litigation, it took on a different shape. The detailed story of the project slowly disappeared, replaced by simplified questions that could be formally referred. In the end, only abstract ideas like neutrality, deduction, and classification remained.

The case stopped being a concrete file and turned into a system problem.

Yet the border had already been drawn. Not at the customs post. Not at the place of installation. But at the moment judgment decided which version of the transaction the law would recognize.

That border was invisible.

It existed only in the reasoning that justified the assessment.

At the heart of the difficulty lay a concept that was meant to resolve uncertainty, not create it. The notion of substance has long functioned as a corrective in VAT law. It allowed authorities and courts to look past formal arrangements and to align taxation with the underlying economic reality. When transactions were fragmented artificially, substance promised reintegration. When legal form distorted value, substance helped restore the tax treatment that reflects the actual economic activity.

In the Nano Source case, the substance no longer performed that stabilizing function. Instead of describing reality, it began to produce it. The assessment did not uncover an underlying economic truth waiting to be revealed. It constructed a version of the transaction that could be taxed. Other versions were possible, but they were rendered legally irrelevant by the choice that had already been made.

This was not an error in application. It was a limit of how the case could be understood. Substance could only operate by selecting certain facts as decisive and treating others as peripheral. Installation mattered. Sequencing mattered. Contractual acceptance mattered. But they could not all matter equally. The moment substance was applied, multiple possible readings collapsed into a single narrative shaped by VAT rules.

What disappeared in this process was uncertainty. The transaction had developed over time, with changing risks and shared responsibility. Different outcomes were possible at different moments.

Substance analysis fixed the story at one point in time and treated the final result as if it had been unavoidable. Once open choices were later presented as facts.

The arguments faded into the background, hidden behind the doctrine used to justify the decision.

This transformation carried normative consequences. Once substance is treated as reality rather than as choice, deviation becomes suspect. What does not fit the selected narrative appears artificial, even when it reflects genuine commercial practice. No one says "abuse", but the suggestion is there. The system becomes less tolerant of complexity, not because complexity is fraudulent, but because it is difficult to administer.

Marta sensed this shift without immediately naming it. The file did not suggest wrongdoing. It revealed complexity. Too many connections, too many stages, too many points at which value might plausibly be said to arise. Substance simplified this complexity, but it did so by deciding in advance what the system was prepared to see.

In this sense, the doctrine of substance became the point at which decisive choices were made, though those choices were not openly acknowledged as such. Borders were no longer defined at customs posts or by formal place-of-supply rules. They were drawn when the law decided which elements of a transaction were legally relevant and which could be set aside. The border appeared to follow from the facts, as if it had always been there.

This inversion was subtle but significant. Substance was no longer a tool for uncovering the full economic reality of a transaction. It became a means of stabilizing the system by narrowing the range of facts that were treated as relevant. The law did not fail to capture the transaction fully. It chose not to.

The pressure to make the doctrine of substance more predictable did not arise in isolation. It was reinforced by the increasing use of automated systems in VAT administration. These systems promised consistency, efficiency, and neutrality.

They validated invoices, matched declarations, and detected irregularities. They reduced discretion by narrowing the range of acceptable outcomes.

In practice, automation did not remove judgment. It displaced it.

Decisions that had once been made explicitly were embedded in design choices, thresholds, and classification rules. Validation came to resemble legality, not because the two were equivalent, but because validation was what the system could observe.

This shift altered the distribution of responsibility. Errors became harder to identify once they were expressed as system outputs. The burden of proof moved to the taxpayer, who now had to explain why a validated result was nevertheless incorrect. Abuse doctrine, designed to capture intentional distortion, risked being repurposed to address what systems could not accommodate.

In the Nano Source case, the result was shaped less by legal theory than by administrative necessity. The assessment had to lead to a clear, enforceable VAT outcome. Registering Nano Source in Poland and taxing a domestic composite supply provided that clarity. Alternative interpretations, even if economically coherent, would have been more difficult to manage within the VAT system.

Marta understood the implication clearly. If systems came to define what counted as normal, deviation would increasingly be interpreted as risk. Judgment would survive only at the margins, invoked to correct anomalies rather than to shape outcomes. The law would continue to speak in the language of neutrality, even as neutrality acquired a different meaning.

What was at stake was not the replacement of human decision makers, but the transformation of their role. Officials no longer determined where the legal border should be drawn. Instead, they were asked to confirm and defend boundaries that had already been produced by automated systems. The order of events is crucial.

When human review comes only after automated validation, its ability to question or reshape the outcome is significantly reduced.

This did not make automation incompatible with VAT law. But it made its limits visible. Systems could administer rules. They could not determine which interpretation of a complex transaction should prevail when more than one is plausible.

That decision remained irreducibly human, even as the conditions under which it was exercised became less visible.

If judgment had moved into systems, governance had to follow it there. Override mechanisms, audit trails, explainability requirements became the new points at which accountability could be exercised. They determined whether automated suspicion could be contested, whether risk classifications could be interrogated, and whether narrative explanation still had procedural entry points.

In experimentalist terms, such safeguards formed the feedback loops through which administrative infrastructures could remain revisable rather than rigid. Without such safeguards, administrative systems risked becoming opaque decision-makers of fiscal credibility, setting unseen thresholds beyond which suspicion could no longer be meaningfully challenged.

Here, too, the border was invisible. It did not separate jurisdictions. It separated what could be decided from what would no longer be questioned. Once crossed, it disappeared from view.

Marta understood then that the transformation she was witnessing did not belong to one reform or one jurisdiction. Across administrations, enforcement was being re-engineered through infrastructures designed to process uncertainty at scale. Systems learned, recalibrated, and borrowed design features from one another.

Convergence did not occur through formal alignment of legal doctrines, but through practical experimentation with administrative procedures and technological systems. States retained their sovereignty, yet in practice, they began operating within shared frameworks of data exchange, monitoring, and risk assessment.

Borders remained, but they now marked differences in calibration rather than differences in law.

Conclusion

VAT is routinely presented as a neutral, technical system, one that applies fixed rules to known facts and produces outcomes that look unavoidable. That has long been the source of its strength. Because it appears impersonal, it draws little political attention. Where a matter is labelled technical, it is handed to experts rather than argued in public; and because VAT is taken to be neutral, it crosses borders without ever confronting the governments or interests sitting behind them.

Neutral, technical, impersonal. That is the official story.

It is not the whole one. Neutrality is not the absence of judgment; it is judgment exercised while the choices behind it are kept out of view. Throughout this book, VAT has done more than observe economic reality. It has shaped the legal version of that reality, deciding what counts as a supply, when value arises, who is liable, and who may shelter behind the system's protections. These are not technical settings. They are judgments, and they have always been judgments, a long-standing feature of VAT law rather than a recent intrusion.

What has changed is not the presence of judgment, but where it is exercised and how the control it carries is expressed.

In the past, national borders did much of this work. A good crossing a border made a legal transaction; a service performed in a jurisdiction fell under that jurisdiction's law. Geography did the work that doctrine now has to do by other means.

That is no longer the environment in which VAT operates.

Contemporary transactions unfold over time and across multiple legal and operational layers, and they rarely sit still long enough to fit a single category. Value develops incrementally, across several parties, and may only become legible once the arrangement has run its course. Control can transfer before ownership does; use can occur before formal acceptance; risk is distributed in ways no single invoice was built to capture.

Borders still exist. They no longer sit where the law places them. They emerge, instead, through the process of interpretation itself, in the decision over which facts receive legal recognition and which are quietly set aside, in whether installation is treated as essential or incidental, in the moment economic control is judged to have passed, and in the assumptions compliance systems make, often invisibly, about what a "normal" transaction looks like.

These are not lines that can be drawn on a map. They sit where certainty ends and guesswork begins; between facts a system can process and facts that will not fit one; at the boundary between what the law demands an answer to and what it has learned to tolerate not knowing. They are difficult to identify not for want of importance but because they never take the form of an explicit rule. They emerge, instead, gradually, from the everyday interpretive choices judges and regulators make. Technology and automation do not change this logic. They extend it.

As earlier chapters have shown, the rise of digital enforcement has reshaped VAT by assessing compliance in real time and reallocating responsibility among participants. Technology speeds up detection. It also shifts the burden of proof.

Previously, a tax authority had to identify a problem and explain its suspicion before the taxpayer was asked to answer. The taxpayer could then reply, question the evidence, and offer a different account of the facts. A decision followed only once both sides had been heard.

Automation alters that structure.

Systems built to apply legal rules end up doing something more consequential: they embed assumptions about what looks plausible, which risks deserve a flag, and how much evidence is enough, recalibrating over time in response to detected fraud, resource constraints, and the political pressure to protect revenue. Governance scholars call this experimentalist administration, where enforcement evolves through continuous monitoring rather than through legislative change. For a taxpayer, however, that evolution is not iteration.

It is opacity. Proof burdens shift quietly, redesigned inside a compliance system rather than debated inside a parliament.

What remains insufficiently examined is what this recalibration does to neutrality, and whether continuous anti-fraud enforcement is gradually moving the evidentiary balance away from the taxpayer and toward the state. Increasingly, taxpayers receive a conclusion without ever being shown the evidence behind it.

A transaction is flagged. The agency blocks the refund and opens an audit. The reasoning behind the flag is rarely disclosed, the model treated as proprietary, too complex to explain, or simply beside the legal point. The taxpayer is given the outcome, not the reasoning, and by the time it arrives, the burden of proof has already changed hands.

The taxpayer must now show that the transaction is real, that its structure matches economic fact, and that the paperwork holds up, all without being told precisely what triggered the authority's doubt in the first place.

This is not an accidental side effect of technology. It is a structural consequence.

While fraud once had to be proven the old way, fact by fact, document by document, increasingly it is inferred from pattern and number. A transaction looks risky. That, on its own, is treated as enough. Rather than explain its doubt, the authority asks the taxpayer to dissolve it, treating its own suspicion as the default and converting the taxpayer's task from supplying evidence to offering reassurance. The taxpayer supplies documents and explanations not to answer a specific accusation but to address a concern that may never be fully articulated. What now matters is not whether the authority can prove fraud, but whether the taxpayer can talk the system back into treating the transaction as normal.

Automation, in this way, has built a new kind of border. On one side sit the tools tax authorities use, and the data those tools can read and compare. On the other sits the taxpayer's lived reality, its operational limits, its timing mismatches, its human error, its transactions that make perfect commercial sense and still look irregular once reduced to data. Crossing that border requires translation. The two sides no longer share a language.

Judgment has not disappeared from this process. It has simply moved.

It now happens earlier, and elsewhere. Legal interpretation is translated into executable form inside validation protocols, risk thresholds, and reporting schemas, the systems that decide which transactions look credible, which look irregular, and which never reach a human being at all. These infrastructures do not develop in isolation, for tax administrations watch one another's reporting frameworks, clearance systems, and fraud-detection results, borrowing selectively while keeping their own doctrine intact. Convergence, today, proceeds procedurally rather than doctrinally; it is built on shared visibility, not shared interpretation.

The border, once purely territorial, is now partly infrastructural, drawn by how a system has been calibrated to recognize economic reality. That calibration begins long before any particular taxpayer or transaction is examined, in the moment authorities decide how the software should behave, what counts as normal, where the warning line sits, and which pattern is allowed to trigger concern. People make these design choices. Automated systems then embed them, without further scrutiny, and by the time a real case arrives, the choice has already been made; there is little room left to question it individually.

This matters because it becomes harder to see who is actually responsible. When something goes wrong, it is filed as a technical glitch rather than recognized for what it actually is, namely the outcome of a human judgment about what to monitor and what to ignore. For businesses and individuals, the result is a strange kind of system, one that claims to be neutral while quietly redefining what neutrality means.

None of this means VAT is failing, or that the answer lies in a retreat to strict territorial certainty. While the system continues to function, and in many respects functions well, enabling cross-border trade at a scale unimaginable when it was first designed, it does so using borders that no longer match their own legal definitions. In practice, those borders now depend on whether a transaction can be read by a digital infrastructure, formatted as standard data, and processed automatically, rather than on the underlying economic activity itself.

The most important borders today run between the data a machine can verify and the facts that require a contextualized, human reading. Set the version of a transaction that survives legal reconstruction next to the version that actually happened, and they are not the same transaction.

This book has tried, briefly, to make the invisible visible. By following a single transaction from invoice to audit, from shipment to installation, from accounting logic to legal reasoning, it has shown that VAT is not a static code to be looked up and applied. It is an ongoing interpretive practice, carried out by inspectors, CFOs, tax practitioners, and judges, all working under time pressure, with incomplete information, inside institutions that enable their judgment as much as they constrain it.

VAT does not merely apply to economic life. It actively shapes the reality it claims only to record.

As commerce grows more digital and less attached to physical presence, the tension at VAT's heart will only intensify. The system, eventually, will face a choice, between continuing to mask its boundaries behind administrative outcomes and admitting that those boundaries are made through interpretation and ought to be opened to explanation and challenge.

The transformation traced in these pages was never confined to a single reform or a single jurisdiction. Tax authorities across Europe have been overhauling enforcement, building systems to manage uncertainty at scale, imposing digital reporting obligations, holding platforms liable, exchanging data in real time, all of it producing a shared procedural environment even where fiscal sovereignty remains formally intact. Although the pattern echoes earlier waves of regulatory diffusion, it did not produce a classical Brussels effect; EU tax rules have not spread the way product standards once did.

What has emerged instead is a distinct kind of governance. Administrations run parallel experiments, watch one another's results, recalibrate, and gradually align their operational practices, even without ever harmonizing their legal interpretations. These adaptive infrastructures now shape compliance directly, as algorithmic assessment determines neutrality through plausibility judgments, automated audits assert evidentiary rights without fully disclosing the reasoning behind them, and fiscal authorities keep control even as data and decisions cross borders and pool information from multiple jurisdictions. The law itself is now experienced through infrastructure, and its governance lives in that infrastructure's design and operational choices, whether or not anyone outside the system ever sees them.

For now, the system holds. Invoices keep circulating. Deductions keep being claimed. Transactions keep being validated in milliseconds, and within that framework, decisions keep being made about which facts are acceptable and which version of events the law will recognize as valid, decisions essential to keeping the system running, even when nobody outside it is shown the reasoning.

This, in the end, is where VAT actually functions.

Not at the border. At the moment a determination is made about what shall count.

A. EU LEGISLATION

Treaties

Consolidated Version of the Treaty on the Functioning of the European Union [2012] OJ C326/47 (TFEU)

Treaty establishing the European Economic Community (signed 25 March 1957, entered into force 1 January 1958) 298 UNTS 11 (Treaty of Rome)

Directives

Council Directive 67/227/EEC of 11 April 1967 on the harmonisation of legislation of Member States concerning turnover taxes (First VAT Directive) [1967] OJ 71/1301

Council Directive 67/228/EEC of 11 April 1967 on the harmonisation of legislation of Member States concerning turnover taxes – Structure and procedures for application of the common system of value added tax (Second VAT Directive) [1967] OJ 71/1303

Council Directive 77/388/EEC of 17 May 1977 on the harmonisation of the laws of the Member States relating to turnover taxes – Common system of value added tax: uniform basis of assessment (Sixth VAT Directive) [1977] OJ L145/1

Council Directive 91/680/EEC of 16 December 1991 supplementing the common system of value added tax and amending Directive 77/388/EEC with a view to the abolition of fiscal frontiers [1991] OJ L376/1

Council Directive 2006/112/EC of 28 November 2006 on the common system of value added tax [2006] OJ L347/1

Council Directive 2008/8/EC of 12 February 2008 amending Directive 2006/112/EC as regards the place of supply of services [2008] OJ L44/11

Council Directive (EU) 2017/2455 of 5 December 2017 amending Directive 2006/112/EC and Directive 2009/132/EC as regards certain value added tax obligations for supplies of services and distance sales of goods [2017] OJ L348/7

Regulations

Commission Regulation (EEC) No 2454/93 of 2 July 1993 laying down provisions for the implementation of Council Regulation (EEC) No 2913/92 establishing the Community Customs Code [1993] OJ L253/1

Council Implementing Regulation (EU) No 282/2011 of 15 March 2011 laying down implementing measures for Directive 2006/112/EC on the common system of value added tax [2011] OJ L77/1

Council Regulation (EEC) No 2913/92 of 12 October 1992 establishing the Community Customs Code [1992] OJ L302/1

Council Regulation (EU) 2017/2454 of 5 December 2017 amending Regulation (EU) No 904/2010 on administrative cooperation and combating fraud in the field of value added tax [2017] OJ L348/1

Regulation (EU) No 952/2013 of the European Parliament and of the Council of 9 October 2013 laying down the Union Customs Code (recast) [2013] OJ L269/1

Commission Proposals and Communications

European Commission, 'A Common System of VAT: A Programme for the Single Market' (Communication) COM(96) 328 final

European Commission, 'Completing the Internal Market: White Paper from the Commission to the European Council' (Communication) COM(85) 310 final

European Commission, 'VAT in the Digital Age' (Proposal) COM(2022) 701 final

B. CASES

Court of Justice of the European Union

Aktiebolaget NN v Skatteverket (Case C-111/05) [2007] ECLI:EU:C:2007:195

Apothekerkammer des Saarlandes and Others v Saarland and Ministerium für Justiz, Gesundheit und Soziales (Case C-171/07) [2009] ECLI:EU:C:2009:316

Apple and Pear Development Council v Commissioners of Customs and Excise (Case 102/86) [1988] ECR 1443

Berkholz v Finanzamt Hamburg-Mitte-Altstadt (Case 168/84) [1985] ECR 2251

Bockemühl v Finanzamt Gummersbach (Case C-90/91) [1992] ECLI:EU:C:1992:353

Budimex SA v Dyrektor Izby Skarbowej w Katowicach (Case C-224/11) [2013] ECLI:EU:C:2013:174

Budimex SA v Dyrektor Izby Skarbowej w Łodzi (Case C-224/18) [2019] ECLI:EU:C:2019:1070

Cabot Plastics Belgium NV v État belge (Case C-232/22) [2023] ECLI:EU:C:2023:920

Card Protection Plan Ltd v Commissioners of Customs and Excise (Case C-349/96) [1999] ECLI:EU:C:1999:93

Coöperatieve Aardappelenbewaarplaats GA v Hoofdproductschap voor Akkerbouwprodukten (Case 154/80) [1981] ECR 445

Danfoss A/S and AstraZeneca A/S v Skatteministeriet (Case C-94/10) [2011] ECLI:EU:C:2011:674

Dávid v Nemzeti Adó- és Vámhivatal Észak-alföldi Regionális Adó Főigazgatósága (Case C-18/13) [2014] ECLI:EU:C:2014:299

DFDS A/S v Skatteministeriet (Case C-260/95) [1997] ECLI:EU:C:1997:77

Dong Yang Electronics sp. z o.o. v Dyrektor Izby Administracji Skarbowej w Łodzi (Case C-547/18) [2020] ECLI:EU:C:2020:350

DSV Road A/S v Skatteministeriet (Case C-187/14) [2015] ECLI:EU:C:2015:636

Dun & Bradstreet Austria (Case C-203/22) [2025] , ECLI:EU:C:2025:117

Ecotrade SpA v Agenzia delle Entrate – Ufficio di Genova 3 (Joined Cases C-95/07 and C-96/07) [2008] ECLI:EU:C:2008:267

Evita-K EOOD v Direktor na Direktsia 'Obzhalvane i upravlenie na izpalnenieto' – Varna pri Tsentralno upravlenie na Natsionalnata agentsia za prihodite (Case C-78/12) [2013] ECLI:EU:C:2013:486

Fenix International Ltd v Commissioners for Her Majesty's Revenue and Customs (Case C-695/20) EU:C:2023:127

FGSZ Szállítói Zrt v Nemzeti Adó- és Vámhivatal Fellebbviteli Igazgatósága (Case C-507/18) [2020] ECLI:EU:C:2020:372

Finančné riaditeľstvo Slovenskej republiky v Weindel Logistik Service SR spol. s r.o (Case C-621/19) [2021] ECLI:EU:C:2020:814

Finanzamt Wilmersdorf v Gerhard Becker (Case C-104/12) [2013] ECLI:EU:C:2013:99

Fonderie Officine Riunite (FOR) SpA v Amministrazione delle Finanze dello Stato (Case 266/81) [1982] ECR 3693

Halifax plc, Leeds Permanent Development Services Ltd and County Wide Property Investments Ltd v Commissioners of Customs and Excise (Case C-255/02) [2006] ECLI:EU:C:2006:121

Hamamatsu Photonics Deutschland GmbH v Hauptzollamt München (Case C-529/16) [2017] ECLI:EU:C:2017:984

Hong-Kong Trade Development Council v Staatssecretaris van Financiën (Case C-89/81) [1982] ECR 1277

Idexx Laboratories Italia Srl v Agenzia delle Entrate (Case C-590/13) [2015] ECLI:EU:C:2015:429

Italmoda SrL v Agenzia delle Entrate (Case C-131/13) [2014] ECLI:EU:C:2014:2455

Kennemer Golf & Country Club v Staatssecretaris van Financiën (Case C-174/00) [2002] ECLI:EU:C:2002:200

Kollroß v Finanzamt Linz (Case C-660/16) [2018] ECLI:EU:C:2018:372

Levob Verzekeringen BV and OV Bank NV v Staatssecretaris van Financiën (Case C-41/04) [2005] ECLI:EU:C:2005:649

Mahagében kft v Nemzeti Adó- és Vámhivatal Dél-dunántúli Regionális Adó Főigazgatósága (Case C-80/11) [2012] ECLI:EU:C:2012:373

Marks & Spencer plc v Commissioners of Customs and Excise (Case C-62/00) [2002] ECLI:EU:C:2002:435

Newey v Commissioners for Her Majesty's Revenue and Customs (Case C-653/11) [2013] ECLI:EU:C:2013:409

Part Service Srl v Ministero dell'Economia e delle Finanze and Agenzia delle Entrate (Case C-425/06) [2008] ECLI:EU:C:2008:108

RBS Deutschland Holdings GmbH v Finanzamt für Großunternehmen in Hamburg (Case C-277/09) [2010] ECLI:EU:C:2010:810

Reemtsma Cigarettenfabriken GmbH v Ministero delle Finanze (Case C-35/05) [2007] ECLI:EU:C:2007:167

Senatex GmbH v Finanzamt Hannover-Nord (Case C-518/14) [2016] ECLI:EU:C:2016:691

Shipping and Forwarding Enterprise Safe BV v Staatssecretaris van Financiën (Case C-320/88) [1990] ECR I-285

Skatteministeriet v Henriksen (Case C-173/88) [1989] ECR 2763
Skandia America Corp. (USA), filial Sverige v Skatteverket (Case C-7/13) [2014] ECLI:EU:C:2014:2225
Titanium Ltd v Skatteverket (Case C-931/19) [2021] ECLI:EU:C:2021:446
Tolsma v Inspecteur der Omzetbelasting Leeuwarden (Case C-16/93) [1994] ECLI:EU:C:1994:80
Vădan v Agenţia Naţională de Administrare Fiscală – Direcţia Generală de Soluţionare a Contestaţiilor (Case C-664/16) [2018] ECLI:EU:C:2018:933
VSTR v Staatssecretaris van Financiën (Case C-587/10) [2012] ECLI:EU:C:2012:592
Weald Leasing Ltd v Commissioners for Her Majesty's Revenue and Customs (Case C-103/09) [2010] ECLI:EU:C:2010:804
Welmory sp. z o.o. v Dyrektor Izby Skarbowej w Gdańsku (Case C-605/12) [2014] ECLI:EU:C:2014:2298
Wirtl v Finanzamt Landshut (Case C-661/16) [2018] ECLI:EU:C:2018:372

C. ADVOCATE GENERAL OPINIONS

Opinion of AG Léger in *Aktiebolaget NN v Skatteverket* (Case C-111/05) [2007] ECLI:EU:C:2007:195
Opinion of AG Jacobs in *Kennemer Golf* (Case C-174/00) [2002] ECLI:EU:C:2001:288
Opinion of AG Kokott in *Budimex* (Case C-224/11) [2012] ECLI:EU:C:2012:695
Opinion of AG Kokott in *Dong Yang Electronics* (Case C-547/18) [2019] ECLI:EU:C:2019:1073
Opinion of AG Poiares Maduro in *Halifax* (Case C-255/02) [2005] ECLI:EU:C:2005:200
Opinion of AG Warner in *Coöperatieve Aardappelenbewaarplaats GA* (Case 154/80) [1981] ECR 445

D. INTERNATIONAL INSTRUMENTS

Treaties and Conventions

Agreement on Trade-Related Aspects of Intellectual Property Rights (adopted 15 April 1994, entered into force 1 January 1995) 1869 UNTS 299 (TRIPS Agreement)

Berne Convention for the Protection of Literary and Artistic Works (adopted 9 September 1886, as revised) 1161 UNTS 3

Marrakesh Agreement Establishing the World Trade Organization (adopted 15 April 1994, entered into force 1 January 1995) 1867 UNTS 3

Paris Convention for the Protection of Industrial Property (adopted 20 March 1883, as revised) 828 UNTS 305

United Nations Convention on Contracts for the International Sale of Goods (adopted 11 April 1980, entered into force 1 January 1988) 1489 UNTS 3 (CISG)

Vienna Convention on the Law of Treaties (adopted 23 May 1969, entered into force 27 January 1980) 1155 UNTS 331

WIPO Copyright Treaty (adopted 20 December 1996, entered into force 6 March 2002) 2186 UNTS 121

WIPO Performances and Phonograms Treaty (adopted 20 December 1996, entered into force 20 May 2002) 2186 UNTS 203

WTO Agreements

WTO Agreement on Implementation of Article VII of the General Agreement on Tariffs and Trade 1994 (Customs Valuation Agreement) https://www.wto.org/english/docs_e/legal_e/20-val_e.htm

E. NATIONAL LEGISLATION

Poland

Act of 29 August 1997 – Tax Ordinance (*Ustawa z dnia 29 sierpnia 1997 r. Ordynacja podatkowa*) (consolidated text, Journal of Laws 2023, item 2383)

Act of 10 September 1999 – Fiscal Penal Code (*Ustawa z dnia 10 września 1999 r. Kodeks karny skarbowy*) (consolidated text, Journal of Laws 2023, item 654)

Act of 11 March 2004 on Tax on Goods and Services (*Ustawa z dnia 11 marca 2004 r. o podatku od towarów i usług*) (consolidated text, Journal of Laws 2024, item 361)

F. ACCOUNTING STANDARDS

Financial Accounting Standards Board, *Accounting Standards Codification Topic 606: Revenue from Contracts with Customers* (ASC 606) (effective 2018)

Financial Accounting Standards Board, *Accounting Standards Codification Topic 606-10-25-30: Revenue Recognition – Transfer of Control* (ASC 606-10-25-30)

International Financial Reporting Standards Foundation, *IFRS 15: Revenue from Contracts with Customers* (effective 2018)

G. OECD MATERIALS

OECD, *BEPS Actions* (OECD Publishing 2015)

OECD, *Consumption Tax Trends 2020: VAT/GST and Excise Rates, Trends and Policy Issues* (OECD Publishing 2020)

OECD, *International VAT/GST Guidelines* (OECD Publishing 2017)

OECD, *Mechanisms for the Effective Collection of VAT/GST Where the Supplier Is Not Located in the Jurisdiction of Taxation* (OECD Publishing 2017)

OECD, *Revenue Statistics 2023* (OECD Publishing 2023)

OECD, *Tax Challenges Arising from Digitalisation – Interim Report 2018* (OECD Publishing 2018)

OECD/G20, *Two-Pillar Solution to Address the Tax Challenges Arising from the Digitalisation of the Economy* (OECD Publishing 2021)

H. NATIONAL ADMINISTRATIVE MATERIALS

Italy

Agenzia delle Entrate, *Sistema di Interscambio (SDI)* https://www.agenziaentrate.gov.it/portale/web/guest/schede/comunicazioni/fatture-e-corrispettivi

Poland

Ministry of Finance (Poland), *National e-Invoicing System (KSeF)* https://www.gov.pl/web/kas/krajowy-system-e-faktur

Spain

Agencia Tributaria, *Suministro Inmediato de Información (SII)* https://sede.agenciatributaria.gob.es/Sede/en_gb/iva/suministro-inmediato-informacion.html?

I. EU COMMISSION DOCUMENTS AND REPORTS

European Commission, *Customs Valuation Compendium* (2021) https://taxation-customs.ec.europa.eu/customs-4/customs-procedures-import-and-export-0/customs-valuation_en

European Commission, *Study and Reports on the VAT Gap in the EU-28 Member States: 2021 Final Report* (TAXUD/2015/CC/131, September 2021)

European Commission, *VAT Aspects of Cross-Border E-Commerce – Options for Modernisation: Final Report* (2016)

European Court of Auditors, *Special Report No 24/2015: Tackling Intra-Community VAT Fraud: More Action Needed* (2015)

J. INTERNATIONAL ORGANIZATIONS

IMF, *Current Challenges in Revenue Mobilization: Improving Tax Compliance* (IMF Policy Paper, 2015)

World Bank, *Digital Dividends: World Development Report 2016* (World Bank 2016)

K. SECONDARY SOURCES

Books and Monographs

Abbott FM, Cottier T and Gurry F, *International Intellectual Property in an Integrated World Economy* (4th edn, Wolters Kluwer 2019)

Berr CJ and Trémeau H, *Le droit douanier: Communautaire et national* (7th edn, Economica 2006)

Bird RM and Gendron P-P, *The VAT in Developing and Transitional Countries* (Cambridge University Press 2007)

de la Feria R and Vogenauer S (eds), *Prohibition of Abuse of Law: A New General Principle of EU Law?* (Hart Publishing 2011)

de la Feria R, *The EU VAT System and the Internal Market* (IBFD 2009)

Ebrill L, Keen M, Bodin J-P and Summers V, *The Modern VAT* (IMF 2001)

Englisch J (ed), *VAT in an EU and International Perspective: Essays in Honour of Han Kogels* (IBFD 2011)

Gervais DJ, *The TRIPS Agreement: Drafting History and Analysis* (5th edn, Sweet & Maxwell 2021)

James K, *The Rise of the Value-Added Tax* (Cambridge University Press 2015)

Kollmann J, *Taxable Supplies and Their Consideration in European VAT: With Selected Examples of the Digital Economy* (2019).

Lamensch M, *European Value Added Tax in the Digital Era* (IBFD).

Lauré M, *La taxe sur la valeur ajoutée* (Librairie du Recueil Sirey 1953)

Lyons T, *EC Customs Law* (2nd edn, Oxford University Press 2018)

Merkx M, *Establishment in European VAT* (Kluwer Law International 2013)

Ricketson S and Ginsburg JC, *International Copyright and Neighbouring Rights: The Berne Convention and Beyond* (2nd edn, Oxford University Press 2006)

Schenk A and Oldman O, *Value Added Tax: A Comparative Approach* (2nd edn, Cambridge University Press 2007)

Schenk A, Thuronyi V and Cui W, *Value Added Tax: A Comparative Approach* (2nd edn, Cambridge University Press 2015)

Terra B and Kajus J, *A Guide to the European VAT Directives* (IBFD 2022)

Thuronyi V (ed), *Tax Law Design and Drafting* (vol 1, IMF 1996)

van Doesum AJ, van Kesteren HWM and van Norden GJ, *Fundamentals of EU VAT Law* (Kluwer Law International 2016)

Wattel PJ and Marres O, *European Tax Law* (7th edn, Kluwer Law International 2020)

Xu Y (ed), *VAT in the Digital Era* (Oxford University Press 2023).

Journal Articles and Book Chapters

'Digital Services Taxes and the Limits of the OECD's Pillar One Blueprint' (2021) 30 EC Tax Review 4

'Tax Fraud and the Rule of Law' (2020) 76 Bulletin for International Taxation 340

'The Concept of "Economic Activity" in VAT' (2011) 20 EC Tax Review 276

'The Concept of Abuse of Law in European VAT' in R de la Feria and S Vogenauer (eds), *Prohibition of Abuse of Law: A New General Principle of EU Law?* (Hart Publishing 2011)

'The Right to Deduct VAT on the Acquisition of a Building before Its Intended Use: Conclusions from Recent ECJ Case Law' (2013) 22 EC Tax Review 19

'The Rise and Fall of the Gross Turnover Tax' (2013) 20 International Tax and Public Finance 1261

Abidin C, 'Mapping Internet Celebrity on TikTok: Exploring Attention Economies and Visibility Labours' (2020) 12 Cultural Science Journal 77

Ainsworth RT and Todorov G, 'Stopping VAT Fraud with Distributed Ledgers – A Romanian Roadmap' (2018) Boston University School of Law, Law and Economics Research Paper No 18-05

Allen C, 'The Evaluation of VAT/GST in OECD Countries in Electronic Commerce' (2025) 36(4) *International VAT Monitor.*

Amand C, 'Single versus Multiple Supplies: Where to Draw the Line?' (2016) 25 EC Tax Review 242

Avi-Yonah RS and Fishbien N, 'The Digital Consumption Tax' *Tax Journal.*

Bal A, 'The Sky is the Limit: The Emerging Taxation of the Digital Economy' (2020) 48 Intertax 584

Becker J and Englisch J, 'EU Digital Services Tax: A Populist and Flawed Proposal' (2018) SSRN Working Paper

Cnossen S, 'Mobilizing VAT Revenues in African Countries' (2020) 27 International Tax and Public Finance 1077

Cockfield AJ, 'Transforming the Internet into a Taxable Forum: A Case Study in E-Commerce Taxation' (2001) 85 Minnesota Law Review 1171

Crum B, 'The EU AI Act: Between the Brussels Effect and Experimentalist Governance' (2025) *Internet Policy Review.*

Cui W, 'The Superiority of the Digital Services Tax over "Significant Digital Presence" Proposals' (2019) 72 National Tax Journal 839

de Carvalho Uhdre D, 'Digital Reality, Indirect Taxation and International Trends' (2025) 3(1) *Brazilian Journal of Law, Technology and Innovation* 117.

de la Feria R, 'Prohibition of Abuse of (Community) Law: The Creation of a New General Principle of EC Law through Tax' (2008) 45 Common Market Law Review 395

De Simone L and Olbert M, 'How Do Multinational Companies Respond to Destination-Based Consumption Taxes?' (Working Paper).

De Veirman M, Cauberghe V and Hudders L, 'Marketing through Instagram Influencers: The Impact of Number of Followers and Product Divergence on Brand Attitude' (2017) 36 International Journal of Advertising 798

Ebrill L and others, 'The Allure of the Value-Added Tax' (2002) 39 Finance & Development 44

Echevarría Zubeldia G, 'Is VAT an Alien Concept to Influencers?' (2023) 34(5) *International VAT Monitor* (IBFD)

Englisch J, 'Abuse of Law and Fiscal Neutrality in VAT' in R de la Feria and S Vogenauer (eds), *Prohibition of Abuse of Law: A New General Principle of EU Law?* (Hart Publishing 2011)

Fridensköld E, 'VAT and the Internet: The Application of Consumption Taxes to E-Commerce Transactions' (2004) *Information & Communications Technology Law.*

Gadžo S, 'The Market as a Tax Nexus: The Old, the New and the Unknown' in *Innovation and Taxation* (2022) ch 2.

Garkushenko ON and Thiel M, 'VAT in Conditions of Transition to the Digital Economy: Lessons for Ukraine' (2018) 4(84) *Economy of Industry* 42.

Genschel P and Schwarz P, 'Tax Competition: A Literature Review' (2011) 9 Socio-Economic Review 339

Hellerstein W, 'Jurisdiction to Tax in the Digital Economy: Permanent and Other Establishments' (2014) 68 Bulletin for International Taxation 346

Hinnekens L, 'Challenges of Applying VAT and Income Tax Territoriality Concepts and Rules to International Electronic Commerce'.

Hongler P and Pistone P, 'Blueprints for a New PE Nexus to Tax Business Income in the Era of the Digital Economy' (2015) IBFD White Papers

Hudders L and others, 'The Commercialization of Social Media Stars: A Literature Review and Conceptual Framework on the Strategic Use of Social Media Influencers' (2021) 18 International Journal of Advertising 534

Keen M and Lockwood B, 'The Value Added Tax: Its Causes and Consequences' (2010) 92 *Journal of Development Economics*

Khamis S, Ang L and Welling R, 'Self-Branding, "Micro-Celebrity" and the Rise of Social Media Influencers' (2017) 8 Celebrity Studies 191

Kofler G and others, 'Taxation of the Digital Economy: A Pragmatic Approach to Short-Term Measures' (2017) 71 Bulletin for International Taxation 221

Kogels H, 'The Advocate General and the Court of Justice: A Tandem Relationship' in J Englisch (ed), *VAT in an EU and International Perspective: Essays in Honour of Han Kogels* (IBFD 2011)

Lamensch M, 'Are "Fiscal Neutrality" and "Prevention of Tax Avoidance" Reconcilable?' (2015) 24 *EC Tax Review*

Levin A, 'Influencers and Endorsements: How Social Media Marketing Reshapes Traditional Advertising Principles' (2020) 32 Loyola Consumer Law Review 227

Merkx M, 'Establishment, Permanent Establishment and the Right to Deduct Input VAT' (2013) 22 EC Tax Review 138

Olbert M and Spengel C, 'International Taxation in the Digital Economy: Challenge Accepted?' (2017) 9 World Tax Journal 3

Papis-Almansa M, 'The Notion of Fixed Establishment in VAT after Welmory and Odvolací finanční ředitelství' (2015) 24 EC Tax Review 155

Petruzzi R and Koukoulioti V, 'The European Commission Proposal on Corporate Taxation and Significant Digital Presence' (2018) 46 Intertax 498

Pistone P and Nogueira JF, 'The OECD Public Consultation Document "Addressing the Tax Challenges of the Digitalisation of the Economy"' (2019) 59 European Taxation 43

Pistone P, 'Abuse of Law in the Context of Indirect Taxation: From (before) Emsland-Stärke to Halifax (and beyond)' in R de la Feria and S Vogenauer (eds), *Prohibition of Abuse of Law: A New General Principle of EU Law?* (Hart Publishing 2011)

Rendahl P, 'Neutrality and Legal Certainty' in R de la Feria (ed), *VAT Exemptions: Consequences and Design Alternatives* (Wolters Kluwer 2013)

Rixen T, 'From Double Tax Avoidance to Tax Competition: Explaining the Institutional Trajectory of International Tax Governance' (2011) 18 Review of International Political Economy 197

Swinkels J, 'Abuse of European Union Law: Practices and Principles' (2013) 20 Maastricht Journal of European and Comparative Law 330

Terra B, 'The Place of Supply in European VAT' (2005) 14 EC Tax Review 60

Tridimas T, 'The Role of the Advocate General in the Development of Community Law: Some Reflections' (1997) 34 Common Market Law Review 1349

van Doesum AJ and van Norden GJ, 'The Right to Deduct Input VAT on Supplies Used for Transactions Falling Outside the Scope of the VAT Directive' (2012) 21 EC Tax Review 308

Wattel PJ and Marres O, 'Characterization of Fictitious Income under OECD-Patterned Tax Treaties' (2003) 57 Bulletin for International Taxation 3

Wattel PJ, 'Fiscal Neutrality from an EU Perspective' in M Lang and others (eds), *Tax Compliance Costs for Companies in an Enlarged European Community* (Kluwer Law International 2008)

Weerth C, 'Customs Valuation and Transfer Pricing: Is It Possible to Harmonize Customs and Tax Rules?' (2011) 5 World Customs Journal 49

Witte P, 'The Customs Value of Goods: Commentary on the Customs Valuation Agreement and the EC Customs Valuation Provisions' in M Lux (ed), *The Customs Code: A Commentary* (Kluwer Law International 2010

Xu Y and Walpole M, 'The Holy Grail of International Consistency in VAT Administration' in Y Xu (ed), *VAT in the Digital Era* (Oxford University Press 2023).

Xu Y, 'A Multilateral Option for VAT in International Trade?' (2022) 71 *International and Comparative Law Quarterly* 857.

www.ingramcontent.com/pod-product-compliance
Lightning Source LLC
LaVergne TN
LVHW010713061126
851857LV00014B/1164